COURAGE BEYOND THE GAME

ALSO BY JIM DENT

Monster of the Midway

The Undefeated

The Junction Boys

You're Out and You're Ugly, Too!
(with Durwood Merrill)

King of the Cowboys

Twelve Mighty Orphans

Resurrection

COURAGE BEYOND THE GAME

The Freddie
Steinmark Story

Jim Dent

THOMAS DUNNE BOOKS ❧ *St. Martin's Press New York*

THOMAS DUNNE BOOKS.
An imprint of St. Martin's Press.

COURAGE BEYOND THE GAME. Copyright © 2011 by Jim Dent. Foreword copyright © 2011 by
Mack Brown. All rights reserved. Printed in the United States of America. For information,
address St. Martin's Press, 175 Fifth Avenue, New York, N.Y. 10010.

www.thomasdunnebooks.com
www.stmartins.com

Book design by Rich Arnold

Library of Congress Cataloging-in-Publication Data

Dent, Jim.
    Courage beyond the game : the Freddie Steinmark story / Jim Dent.—1st ed.
       p. cm.
    Includes bibliographical references and index.
    ISBN 978-0-312-65285-2
    1. Steinmark, Freddie.   2. Football players—United States—Biography.
3. Cancer—Patients—United States—Biography.   I. Title.
    GV939.S74D46 2011
    796.332092—dc22
    [B]

                                                              2011009348

First Edition: August 2011

10   9   8   7   6   5   4   3   2   1

For Blackie Sherrod, Frank Luksa, Larry Tarleton, and Will Jarrett
My Damon Runyon, Ring Lardner, and my two favorite bosses

Thanks, guys, for raising me in the newspaper business
so I could get the hell out and write books.

CONTENTS

FOREWORD

We have an important tradition here at the University of Texas. It involves Freddie Steinmark and I'd like to tell you about it.

My memory of Freddie began on a cold and drizzly day in 1969 as I was getting ready to watch a football game on television. The weather just seemed to hang in the foothills of the Cumberland Mountains, and it wasn't the kind of afternoon you wanted to be outside. But the truth was, we had better things to do that first Saturday in December. At the time, I was a high school football player in Cookeville, Tennessee, ready to embark on my own college career.

Through a twist of fate, ABC Television had moved the Texas-Arkansas game to the end of the season. They called it the "Game of the Century" because it was the 100th anniversary of college football. And so, along with every other college football fan in America, we gathered around the TV to watch. We couldn't wait for the game to begin.

This was the first time that I would ever set eyes on the little Longhorn safety named Freddie Steinmark. I never met him, but I feel like I knew him. His story is part of the fiber of Texas football, and it is good that Jim Dent has chosen to tell Freddie's story in this book.

I still remember being mesmerized by the "Big Shootout" that day. The plays being made by James Street and Randy Peschel will always be etched in my mind. As I remember seeing Freddie play in that game, I think about what a great inspiration he was to become.

When Sally and I came to Texas in the fall of 1997, one of the things we wanted to do was to connect with the history and tradition of Longhorn football. We wanted to get to know the lettermen, and to learn their stories. Most of all, we wanted to build on a friendship we had formed with Darrell Royal.

And all it took to understand how much Fred Steinmark had meant to Texas was to look at the glisten in Coach's eyes when he told the story. So as we completed the remodeling of our football building, we looked at the path we wanted our players to take as they left the dressing room on the way to Joe Jamail Field in Darrell K Royal-Texas Memorial Stadium.

First, we wanted the players to understand the pride and tradition of those who had come before. We arranged the plaques of all of the All-Americans and academic All-Americans in the hallway leading to the field. At the end, we placed a set of longhorns. We asked the players to touch those 'horns as a reflection of the pride of those whose pictures were on the wall—those who had honored The University, and the game.

Having learned that the concrete tower that held the video board was part of a scoreboard named for Freddie Steinmark, we decided to incorporate his memory into our trip to the field. We told our players the story of his bravery—how he played in that game against Arkansas with a leg that had been attacked by osteogenic sarcoma, a deadly form of bone cancer. They learned that he lost his leg to cancer less than a week after that game, and three weeks later walked into the Cotton Bowl on crutches to see his teammates play Notre Dame.

Most of all, they learned that he battled the disease for a year and a half. He fought with grace, class, and most of all, courage. In recognition of that courage, to this day we have the players touch a picture of Freddie with the Longhorns salute before they go down the ramp to the field. Armed with the pride of the All-Americans, and in honor of the courage of Freddie, we ask them to go out and play as hard as they can.

We had a smaller picture made of Freddie, and we take it on the road with us. It was with us at the Rose Bowl when we won the

National Championship after the 2005 season, and it has been at every game we have played away from Austin.

They say "The Eyes of Texas are Upon You," and I will never forget Coach Royal's eyes when he first talked to me about Freddie. In his short time at Texas, the young man became a hero, not necessarily for what he did (although he was a fine player), but for who he was.

That is why we salute pride and honor and courage. It's a pretty strong formula for football, and for life.

—Mack Brown, Head Coach, University of Texas

COURAGE BEYOND THE GAME

Chapter 1

FIRST KISS

On a day like no other, she saw him running over a grassy hillside with the snowcapped Rocky Mountains in the background. Linda Wheeler was sitting on the passenger side of a baby blue Jeep. She had never seen anyone as alive as Freddie Steinmark. Here was the boy with the big, sparkling eyes and the smile that chased away her blues. The mere sight of him left her breathless.

Months earlier, in the fall of 1963, he had stormed into her life in the hallway of Manning Junior High. The eighth-grade girls, hoping to ogle Freddie that first day of school, had gathered near the front entrance, anticipating his arrival. They chattered excitedly about a heartthrob more celestial than Elvis Presley.

"I hear that Freddie Steinmark is around here someplace," one of the girls loudly whispered.

"I've got my eyes wide open," another gushed. "I might just kiss Freddie Steinmark straight on the lips when I see him."

Linda could not have cared less at the time. Nothing on that first day of school in this strange place was going to make her happy. Against her will, her family had moved twelve miles from near downtown Denver to Wheat Ridge, a place a little too countrified for a girl from the city. This outpost seemed as distant from urban Denver as Memphis was to Mozambique. When the sun set over the Rockies, everyone headed home to watch *The Adventures of Ozzie and Harriett*, then went straight to bed, or so it seemed.

That first week of September, Linda was walking into an alien world she could not comprehend. Even more troubling was the realization that this strange journey into nowhere was just beginning. In two years, she would enter Wheat Ridge High School, where the cheerleaders wore overalls and the team was called the Farmers. At football games, one of the male students actually dressed like a hayseed rode around on a mule named Daisy. The drill team square-danced at halftime. Any day, Linda expected to see goats grazing on the football field.

Linda did not need to remind herself why the Wheelers had moved to the end of the earth. Simply, her mother was seeking a controlled environment where she could raise her two youngest daughters, Linda and Shannon. Marion Wheeler did not want to endure another teenage pregnancy, as she had with her oldest daughter a year earlier. In Wheat Ridge, she knew she could keep the reins on Linda and Shannon and shoo the boys away.

Linda wore black horn-rimmed glasses and a blue dress. Before heading off to school that morning, she peered into the mirror at a girl she judged to have average looks. Boys rarely gave her the time of day. Given her mother's attitude toward the opposite sex, she wondered if she would ever get a date. A boy with the status and charm of Freddie Steinmark would never show interest in her and, if he did, she wasn't feeling all that sociable anyway.

As Freddie swaggered into the building that morning, toting a passel of books and motoring like an all-district scatback, every head turned to see the raven-haired youngster with the Pepsodent smile. Amazingly, Linda felt his big brown eyes watching her. The girls were standing in line outside homeroom, waiting for the bell to ring. Freddie smiled and winked at her. *How is this possible? Why is he not looking at the other girls?* Freddie walked a little farther down the hall, turned, and set his eyes on Linda once more. She felt light-headed. She knew the others were jealous. *Why is Mr. Wonderful stuck on the new girl? We've known him a lot longer than her.*

In Wheat Ridge, Freddie Steinmark was bigger than the Beatles. They loved to talk about "Fast Freddie" and his athletic gift. They said that before long he would be playing halfback at the University of Colorado, then it would be off to the pros. A devout Catholic who attended mass almost every day, he also made straight A's. He was the hero of the football, basketball, and baseball teams. He had once played on a Denver midget league football team that won every game for eight straight seasons.

Freddie was brimming with so much energy that his vitality seemed to flow through his pores. The girls around Wheat Ridge thought he was the sweetest boy they had ever met, but the boys who competed against him in sports knew better. The kid possessed a hard edge honed by a pushy father and some pushier coaches. When Freddie walked onto the football field, or the basketball court, or the baseball diamond, look out. Winning in Freddie's world was the only way to have fun. Little wonder that Mickey Mantle was his hero and why Freddie was idolized in the same manner as "The Mick."

Linda knew virtually nothing about sports, having grown up with two sisters who did not know if a football was blown up or stuffed. Her father Selby MacMillan Wheeler was an M.I.T. graduate and a well-known architect in the Denver area. He was not the type of man who would sit in front of the TV, watching the weekend games and memorizing batting averages. So the idea of Freddie Steinmark being the best athlete in the school did not impress her. Still, she could not get over those eyes, that smile, and the way he carried himself.

As the days passed, Freddie seemed to be everywhere. One day, she peered up from her desk in homeroom and saw him walking toward her. He casually sat down in the desk next to hers. For the next fifteen minutes, until the bell rang, he stared at Linda without saying a word. The same routine followed the next day and the next.

Linda was beginning to wonder if Freddie was ever going to speak when Rocco Rofrano, another eighth grader, sidled up next to her in the hallway. Rocco was a handsome boy and he was one of Freddie's few non-jock friends, but they were extremely tight, going all the way back to kindergarten.

"You know, Freddie is really crazy about you," Rocco said. "He's liked you a lot since the day he saw you."

"Come on, Rocco," Linda said. " Are you being square with me? Are you sure Freddie's talking about *me*?"

"He only has eyes for you, Linda."

"So why doesn't he talk to me?"

"Because he doesn't know what to say."

"So why does he sit and stare at me?"

Rocco grinned. "Because he likes you. I mean, he likes you a *lot*."

Linda felt a mixture of excitement and frustration as she walked away from Rocco that day. Boys were a new phenomenon in her life, and she really wanted a boyfriend. She knew, however, that all eighth graders were still fighting off inhibitions. This agonizing game of silence could drag on forever.

Little did Freddie know that Linda was soon watching him— from afar. She went to the junior high football games and, at first, was completely confused by the confounded system of first downs and other assorted silliness. One thing was certain about the Manning Junior High games: Freddie Steinmark was the star who carried the ball on practically every play. He scored most of the touchdowns. He played offense and defense and never left the field. He was the reason the band played. When the games were over, the cheerleaders chased him all the way to the locker room.

As football was winding down in the late fall, and the heavy snowfalls arrived, Freddie took his game to the gymnasium, where he dominated the basketball court. To Linda, it seemed that no one at Manning Junior High cheered for anyone but Freddie Steinmark. *Does he possibly know how popular he is?*

The next day, she shook her head and sat down at her desk, waiting for Freddie to come bee-bopping into her life once more. She knew he would have nothing to say.

Out on the rolling farmland of Wheat Ridge, the winds were soft and cool in the spring as the sun began to warm the farmland stretching west. The basketball season was almost over in late March and Freddie soon would be lacing up his baseball cleats.

Linda was sitting in the Jeep, basking in the sunshine, waiting for her sister Shannon to turn the ignition key, when she spotted Freddie running toward her. She thought there must be some kind of mistake. His dark skin glistened and she was mesmerized by everything about him. She prayed he would open his mouth.

Shannon Wheeler, sitting behind the wheel, almost panicked when she saw Freddie tearing over the hill. "Oh, my God, what is he doing?" she yelped. She released the clutch and said, "Linda, let's get out of here!"

"No, no, no!" Linda yelled. "Wait!"

"Gotta go," Shannon said. "What would Mother say?"

"Stop! Dammit!"

The windows were rolled down because of the beautiful weather. Within seconds, Freddie's face was inches from Linda's. She had never seen such a happy boy. He flashed the smile she would never forget.

"Wanna go out?" he blurted. The voice seemed strange. She had never heard it.

"Well, sure, Freddie Steinmark," Linda said. "Of course I would like to go out with you. What are we gonna do?"

"How about let's go to dinner tomorrow night after the game?"

"Why not?" she said, turning slowly and smiling at Shannon.

Shannon rolled her eyes as her left foot searched for the clutch. "Can we leave now, Linda?"

"One second," she said. Then she turned to Freddie. "Where do you want to meet?"

Freddie named the restaurant. Again, their eyes met and they shook hands.

As the Jeep pulled away, Linda's eyes were locked onto Freddie's. She would think about him for the rest of the day. But how in the name of Pikes Peak was she going to explain this to her mother?

A date the following night with Freddie meant that Linda would sit in the stands by herself. Amid the adulation of the Wheat Ridge fans, Freddie led the basketball team in scoring and a victory over Arvada Junior High. When she saw him dribbling past opponents, and clicking on the open shots, the excitement shot through her arteries. Little Freddie was as smooth as smoke through a keyhole. Everyone knew who was in charge on the floor. Linda could never imagine how a boy as cool as Freddie would look her way.

By the time he showered and dressed and met Linda at the local diner, it was already 11:15. Linda's ironclad curfew was midnight, which meant she would have a half hour with her newfound Romeo.

"I can't tell you how frustrated I was that night," she remembered almost forty years later. "All day I'd looked forward to being with Freddie and we had about twenty minutes together. I had a date with the cutest boy in the school and it was over just like that."

It was not over. The next day in homeroom, Freddie sat next to her and started to talk. Linda finally began to wonder if he would ever stop. She had no idea of all the things on his mind. He already had big plans for the two of them.

Freddie called her every night at home. On the fourth date, he did something that stunned her into total silence. Standing next to the junior high gymnasium, beneath a moonlit sky, he kissed her. Then he looked into her eyes and said, "I love you, Linda." She thought she would cry.

Linda promised herself she would never forget the moment. It was her first kiss. Never had a boy expressed his love for her. Everything was happening so fast. *Am I supposed to feel this way?* If so, Wheat Ridge was starting to look pretty doggone good.

Chapter 2

LITTLE SUPERMAN

They said that Freddie Joe Steinmark was born with a football tucked under one arm and a baseball in the other hand.

Not long after his arrival on January 27, 1949, somebody dropped a real football and baseball into his crib. It was only the beginning. At the age of two, he got his first baseball uniform; a year later, he was firing the baseball like a little pro. "I was throwing it with the follow-through, the whole bit," he wrote in his autobiography, *I Play to Win*. (The book was co-written with legendary Texas sportswriter Blackie Sherrod, and published by Little, Brown in August of 1971.)

On Christmas morning at age four, he hurried down the stairs and across the living room to see what was under the tree. He was overjoyed with what Santa Claus had brought. He pulled the red football helmet down over his ears and buckled the chinstrap.

During Christmas dinner, his mother, Gloria, shoveled mashed potatoes into his mouth through the bars of the face mask. She knew that Freddie was not about to part with his newest treasure, which he wore day after day.

Some kids play with firetrucks, others with toy soldiers. By the time Freddie was old enough to walk, he was so consumed with sports that he needed his own locker room. When he was a year and a half old, his father, Fred Gene Steinmark, propped him up in a corner of the living room and placed a miniature catcher's mask over his head. Most kids that age would flinch when an object was thrown at them. Not Freddie. He never wanted to stop playing ball.

By age five, Freddie already knew what he was going to do with the rest of his life. He told his mother that someday he would sign a professional sports contract, either in football or baseball, and buy her a brand-new Cadillac. Gloria Steinmark never doubted that Freddie meant what he said.

So obsessed with sports was little Freddie that he became the mini-Mickey Mantle. Just like "The Mick," he could throw, catch, and run like the wind before the other kids could ride a tricycle. His Father, Elvin Mutt Mantle, had started planning a baseball career for his son long before he was born. At the age of six months, the kid was wearing a baseball cap knitted for him by his mother. Growing up near Miami, Oklahoma, little Mickey started playing baseball with the grown-ups before elementary school. So passionate were the Mantles about baseball that they did not quit at sunset. They turned on automobile headlights and kept playing beneath the inky sky of eastern Oklahoma.

In the early 1950s, Freddie was not unlike a lot of kids who already had their eye on the ball. America during the post-war era was rapidly developing into a sports-crazed country. Television had replaced radio as the number-one medium for sports. You could turn on the tube and actually see Mickey Mantle swinging from his heels at Yankee Stadium. The picture might have been a little snowy, but NFL quarterbacks like Otto Graham and Bobby Layne were emerging as national heroes. No longer were pro athletes regarded as dirty, toothless heathens who wreaked havoc and broke bones. The National Football League was cleaning up its act, putting on a more handsome face. They used to say NFL players were one generation removed from the coal mines, but that image was changing. Decent men were making decent money, and some even shaved before the games.

Freddie was mesmerized by the images dancing across the TV screen. He was drawn to the Yankees and the Dodgers and even the Notre Dame Fighting Irish, a bunch of good Catholics just like him. The team that he saw more than any other was the Chicago Bears, whose games were beamed into Denver almost every Sunday. Because the Broncos were not yet a pro football franchise, the NFL awarded the Bears the TV territorial rights to Denver. A sports-hungry city, Denver boasted a population of a half-million. The Bears quickly won the hearts of Denver. One of the most rabid fans wore a red helmet when he watched the games.

On Sunday, when the other kids were out in the yard playing ball, Freddie sat with the adult men and studied the games on TV. At the behest of his father, he often set his focus on one player. More than being entertained, Freddie was actually a young student of the game.

"Don't watch a game just to enjoy it," his father said a lot. "Learn something from it."

Just about everybody called Freddie's dad "Big Fred." He had grown up a self-made athlete with a single-minded purpose: Make it to the professional ranks. Born of predominantly German heritage, Fred Steinmark's family was not exactly rolling in money. His parents divorced in 1936 and he moved to the north side of Denver, where his sports dreams began to take shape. He was fortunate to be enrolled in North High School, a powerhouse in sports, which was the perfect fit for a kid trying to find his way. Steinmark was neither exceptionally big nor fast, but his coaches were enamored of his endless drive. Sports was going to be his ticket to the big time.

Fred Steinmark built himself into one of the best all-around high school athletes in Colorado. He believed that football was his best sport and he made all-state as a running back twice. He received a few college offers, but by his senior year, he was in love with a girl named Gloria Marchetti, a member of one of the biggest Italian families in Denver.

In the mid-1800s, Italians started to migrate into Denver, drawn to the claim of wealth and land ownership. Many settled in Platte Valley to farm vegetables, and others became miners and railroad workers. The largest segment moved into North Denver, known as "Little Italy," and by 1910, fourteen percent of Colorado's population was Italian.

Gloria Marchetti's father was a chef in Italy, and he came to America with six bucks in his pocket. He borrowed $200 and bought a grocery store. He parlayed the store into bars and restaurants. When Gloria was three years old, her father died. That is when Gloria's mother, Nana Marchetti, became the matriarch of the family, running the businesses with the help of her sons. Nana Marchetti had birthed seven children. In the years to come, the Marchettis would become almost too numerous to count with the addition of twenty-six grandchildren.

Fred Steinmark met Gloria Marchetti at North Denver High School. He was torn between getting married and pursuing his sports dream. If he was going to marry Gloria, he would need money. He was trying to choose between football and baseball when a Cleveland Indians scout strolled into his life. He offered a $1,100 signing bonus and Fred snapped it up. It was a good thing because not long after the wedding, they learned a son was on the way. Playing pro baseball, Steinmark could at least earn some money, then work construction with Gloria's brother in the off-season.

The pieces were falling together when Fred Steinmark, driving through the streets of Denver one day, failed to see a coal truck roaring out of control. His car was rammed head-on and he broke both legs. He also suffered severe knee-ligament damage and several cracked ribs. He spent almost two months in the hospital and his baseball career was shelved for two more years.

The comeback began in the Yankees organization at a minor league stop in Enid, Oklahoma, on the outskirts of Tulsa and a hundred miles from where Mickey Mantle had grown up. He was hitting over .300 midway into the season when the phone call came from Gloria. She was out of money and the miniscule paychecks he was sending home just didn't cut it. Besides, they had a three-year-old son named Freddie who needed some attention from his father. Big Fred grudgingly ditched his dream and went home.

For three years, Steinmark worked construction, then joined the Denver police force as an accident investigator and a member of the canine corps. Freddie noted in *I Play to Win*, "his main enterprise was grooming me for the sports career that he was denied."

Most kids in the second grade in 1956 were still learning sports on the school playground, but not Freddie Steinmark.

At the age of seven, he was loaded up into the family station wagon and driven across town to an area of Denver that hardly resembled the tree-lined neighborhood where the Steinmarks lived. This melting pot at Forty-first and Lipan was often described as being "on the wrong side of the tracks." It was also the home of the famous Rough Riders, the toughest and most successful collection of youth sports teams in the history of the state.

That day, with Freddie in tow, Gloria walked across a playing field and spotted a big man who looked tough enough to chew on nails.

"Will you do me a favor and take this boy?" Gloria Steinmark said to the man. "We want him to play with the best. We want him to be coached by the best. Why play if you're not going to be the best?"

Gloria was speaking to John "Muzzy" Vecchiarelli, a coach so successful that the Denver newspapers often covered his midget league games. These kinds of midget leagues were popping up all over America at a time when fathers wanted their sons to grow up to be better athletes than they had been. Living vicariously through your athletic son was a new phenomenon, but it was catching on fast. Grown men yelling at their kids from the sideline was as trendy as the hula hoop. Freddie soon would be receiving so much advice from men in their twenties and thirties that he wanted to cover his ears.

From the moment that Freddie set eyes on Muzzy Vecchiarelli, he could tell that this man meant business. He also realized that his mother knew him well. Gloria and Fred had gone to high school with Muzzy, another noted ex-jock. No doubt, the blueprint for Freddie's rise to fame, money, and eventual stardom began with Muzzy.

Freddie signed up to play both baseball and football for the Rough

Riders of the Young American League. The first few days inside the football program, he quickly learned just how much his life had changed. The team practiced on a rugged field covered with sand-spurs. They were driven hard by Muzzy and assistant coach Harry Rasoli. The players went by names like Pontarelli, Montoya, Garcia, and Radovich. They were recruited quite illegally from all parts of Denver. More than half the team was from outside the district. Each day, the coaches drove their personal cars around town pick-ing the boys up for practice, then delivered them home afterward. In this era, it was not unusual for a high school coach to sneak a stud athlete across the district boundary line to help win a champion-ship. Freddie, however, was playing with second, third, and fourth graders.

Sports in the mid-1950s might have been growing in leaps and bounds, but it was still unusual for a second grader to strap on the pads at that age. Freddie was a small child with fragile bones, and his helmet looked so large in relation to his body that he seemed ready to pitch forward. When most boys were focusing on marbles and tadpoles, Freddie came to face the cold, hard facts of a rugged sport. Practices were long and demanding. He was being hardened by older men who might have been better served coaching boys twice his age. Teaching kids to swim and play tennis at that age is one thing. Show-ing them how to ram a helmet at full speed into the sternum of another seven-year-old is quite another.

Freddie, however, was born to play sports. He was a born winner. Or something like that, the coaches said.

The handpicked Rough Riders rarely lost. They were taught that winning was the only way to have fun.

"If you're gonna keep score, then you play to win," Muzzy Vec-chiarelli repeatedly said. "If you're gonna play just to have fun, then don't keep score."

Vecchiarelli was Vince Lombardi before most people knew who Lombardi was. In 1956, Lombardi was still toiling in the back-ground as the offensive coordinator of the New York Giants. Three years would pass before he took over the Green Bay Packers and delivered one of his most famous lines: "Winning isn't everything, it's the only thing."

Vecchiarelli demanded that every player memorize the Rough Riders' pledge, and recite it on a moment's notice: "I will play the game hard and clean and never be a quitter. What matters most is courage. It's not a disgrace to be beaten; the greatest disgrace is to quit or turn yellow."

It was little wonder that Freddie once played an entire quarter in the midget leagues with a broken arm. He rarely left the field due to injury, regardless of the pain.

Vecchiarelli was insistent on his players being tough: "You hit them or they'll hit you. Somebody's gonna get knocked down. It might as well be them."

The coach often whacked his players on the helmet and was not above abusing the son of one of his closest friends from high school days. Freddie said that when he did not run the ball to Muzzy's liking, "he'd really crack me one."

Freddie was taught by his dad to avoid tacklers by zigzagging down the field. Freddie idolized Chicago Bears running back Willie Gallimore, a fast, high-stepping halfback who shifted gears like a Ferrari. Darting and dodging his way down the field one day, just like Gallimore, Freddie was caught from behind and tackled short of the goal. Muzzy let him have it at halftime.

"If you ever do that again, you won't be playing for me," he yelled.

"Well, my dad told me to dodge," Freddie said.

"Well, when you play for your dad, you dodge."

Freddie listened to Vecchiarelli's advice and started running in a straight line down the field. Soon he was scoring more touchdowns and making Muzzy a lot happier.

Freddie was smaller than most of the kids, but he overcame it with speed and fearlessness. He played offense and defense, returned kickoffs and punts. Anyone who watched these midget games knew that little Freddie Steinmark already possessed a big-boy toughness. This excited everyone, including the grown men, who were already hyping his future as a college player.

So how could a kid lose when he was playing for *two* midget league football teams at the same time? By the third grade, Freddie was doing just that. He signed on with another team called the Little Blues, of Wheat Ridge. He really didn't have much choice. His father was coaching the Little Blues and, besides, Freddie could not get enough football. He was either playing or practicing six days a week. Sundays would be reserved for growing his Catholic faith and watching his beloved Bears.

The Little Blues practiced on Monday and Wednesday, and played their games on Friday. The Rough Riders practiced on Tuesday and Thursday and played on Saturday. Everything had been arranged perfectly for a little jock on his way up.

Fred Steinmark loved the idea of being able to analyze and evaluate his son up close. Soon, Big Fred would be transformed from a coaching father to a pushy father/coach. He was not unlike thousands of men across America. However, he took it further than most. This is what Freddie wrote in *I Play to Win*:

My father was never gentle with me where sports were concerned. He'd yell at me and sometimes box me around. We would always have a session in our kitchen after every game and I can remember many, many times back in the second and third grades when I first started playing football when he'd fuss at me because I didn't play the way he thought I should. He was trying to make me perfect . . . I remember once after our team won a Young American League game by 40–0, he jumped all over me about some goof I had made. He would yell and sometimes we would both wind up crying . . .

There were times when I hated it—when he would sit in the kitchen and lecture at me. Or when I'd be on the field and he would yell at me from the sidelines. But I knew what I wanted to do more than anything else, and that was to play professional football or baseball. I realized that anybody driving me toward that goal was working for me, not against me.

Soon to join Freddie on the Little Blues was another ambitious little boy by the name of Roger Behler. Roger had moved into Wheat Ridge in 1950 from Michigan, and it was not long before his parents started searching for a midget football team. Much like Freddie, Roger rarely stopped thinking about sports.

That first year together, when Freddie and Roger were teammates on the Little Blues, Behler could not take his eyes off Freddie. He could not believe that a kid that young could be that fast.

"After taking just two steps, he was already at full speed," Behler recalled. "When he went around end, nobody could catch him. Plus, he already had the basic fundamentals down. His dad had been coaching him for years. Freddie had dedication and motivation and just about everything you could have. A lot of that came from his father."

The elder Steinmark ran tough, demanding practices. The boys were ages seven and eight, but he drove them until their tongues hung out. He would make them run the same play more than twenty straight times for the sake of getting it right.

"Big Fred was absolutely no-nonsense," Behler said. "We ran the single-wing offense and we practiced it over and over. We practiced for hours and hours. There were a lot of times that we walked off the practice field into total darkness."

Behler recalled Big Fred's aura.

"I was actually scared to death of Big Fred," Behler said. "He was a Denver policeman and he had a German shepherd. If Big Fred gave that dog a command, he would bite your leg off. At times, it seemed that Big Fred could have commanded himself to do the same thing. It was hard to tell the difference between Big Fred and that German shepherd."

In the same breath, Behler said, "You know, I was jealous of Freddie, in a way. I sometimes wished that I was living with a dad who was also my coach. Freddie got coached all of the time and I was a little envious of that. Of course, that doesn't mean that I didn't love my parents."

The first two years with the Little Blues, Freddie and Behler played on a team of third and fourth graders. Upon graduating to the Big Blues, a team of fifth and sixth graders, they went undefeated that first season and qualified for the championship game against the hated Lakewood Tigers. It was rare when a team from Wheat Ridge beat a team from Lakewood, another small town situated directly to the south.

"They always made a big deal that Wheat Ridge could never beat Lakewood," Behler said. "The high school team could never get it done. We didn't know if we could do it, either."

The battle between Lakewood and the Little Blues was called the Carnation Bowl because Wheat Ridge was considered the carnation capital of Colorado. With three hundred days of sunshine a year, the carnations grew boundlessly at the greenhouses across Jefferson County.

Lakewood and the Little Blues met in November of 1960 at the Reed Street Stadium on the campus of Wheat Ridge Junior High. Hundreds filed into the stadium to see if the Little Blues could break the "Lakewood Jinx." You could always be sure that a crowd would gather whenever a star like Freddie was on the field. It helped that he came from one of the biggest families in the Denver area. Of all the Marchetti grandchildren, Freddie was the hope of an entire clan.

Steinmark scored four touchdowns that day, and Behler added another as the Big Blues led most of the game. Lakewood, however, rallied in the fourth quarter to win 42–35 in one of the most exciting Carnation Bowls that anyone could remember. In spite of the loss, the legend of Little Freddie Steinmark continued to grow. No one could believe he was only eleven years old.

Big Fred was not the only one in the Steinmark home firing up the athletic drive inside Freddie. Gloria did not lecture Freddie the same way as her husband, but she rarely stopped reminding him that he had to stay dedicated. Gloria loved the promise that Freddie made about buying her a new Cadillac.

Gloria was only five feet tall and knew her genes were not going to produce a big man. Only through the ultimate effort would Freddie make the big time.

"Freddie, you're always going to be the smallest one on the field," she would say. "That's why you've always got to try harder than everyone else."

Gloria also wanted a well-rounded son. She was a devout Catholic and determined to mold Freddie in the faith.

"Don't ever let sports or studies or any activity make you forget about Him," she told her son. "God is the most important person in your life."

Freddie was a little machine motoring around Wheat Ridge, going to football practice, then to the gymnasium, then to the baseball diamond. When the day ended, he went straight home and studied. The prospect of being the first Steinmark/Marchetti to receive a college diploma, along with playing sports at a major university, was introduced to him by the time he reached the first grade. That is why he studied long hours every night, and it was little wonder he made straight A's.

By the eighth grade, Freddie was living his life with blinders on. Uncle Joe Marchetti once remarked that someday he would have to start thinking about females. Freddie scoffed at the notion. "Uncle Joe, I don't have time for girls." Freddie was actually pretending. Uncle Joe did not know about Linda. So he proferred a bet.

"I bet that by the time you get to high school, you'll be going steady with some girl," he said.

Freddie chuckled.

"Uncle Joe, I guess I'd better pass on that bet."

Chapter 3

YOUNG LOVE

By the time Linda Wheeler reached high school, the horn-rimmed glasses were history and she was going blond. Freddie Steinmark was the reason.

Linda and Freddie were like the king and queen of Wheat Ridge High School, and the nosey kids played the role of paparazzi without the cameras. It was almost impossible to carry on a romance with everyone staring. News traveled across the town of Wheat Ridge at the speed of a Pontiac GTO, aka "The Goat"—a sports car developed in the mid-1960s with a rumbling V-8, 389-cubic-inch motor.

Freddie's heart went boom whenever Linda entered the room. They felt the gravitational pull of each other's body. So how were they planning to conceal their necking from Marion Wheeler? One day, Freddie came up with an imaginative idea that stirred a nervous anxiety inside Linda.

During lunchtime, the kids marched up and down the hallways at Wheat Ridge in massive herds, their Weejuns and Saddle Oxfords raising a racket. A stairwell connected the first floor to the second floor, where most of the classrooms were located. Beneath the stairwell was a Coke machine situated next to a small, dark corner. In the deep shadows of this little hideaway, the lovebirds slipped away. Freddie put his arms around Linda and planted a long kiss on her ready lips.

"It was something that I looked forward to every day," Linda recalled. "It was very exciting."

The relationship between Freddie and Linda seemed as pure and natural as Colorado snowfall. They were so happy together. The unhappiest girl at Manning Junior High two years earlier could not believe her luck. Little did anyone know, though, that trouble was brewing inside the Wheeler home.

Linda's mother, Marion, did not approve of Freddie. She let her daughter hear it every day.

"He is just not right for you," her mother said. "We are not the same kind of people. You need to find somebody else besides Freddie."

When it came to money, the Wheelers and the Steinmarks lived in different worlds. The Wheelers owned a spacious brick home on the hillside of a suburb known as Applewood. The place boasted a three-car garage that most folks had never seen the likes of. At the time, you could find two-car garages and carports all over the Denver area. But a three-car garage?

Selby Wheeler was a highly paid architect during a period when Wheat Ridge was basically a rural farming community. The monied urbanites were just starting to trickle into the little town, where most of the men still wore overalls. Selby Wheeler, in spite of once being a poor boy from West Texas, seemed like a rich city slicker among the Red Man crowd.

The Steinmarks lived two miles away in a small duplex near the high school. There were four kids, including two daughters, Gigi and Paula Kay, and a younger boy named Sammy. The duplex measured no more than 700 feet and looked even smaller from the street. When the entire family of six was at home, the place seemed ready to burst at the brick mortar.

"When everyone was in the living room, you could barely turn around without bumping into somebody," Linda said. "It was that small."

"Big Fred" Steinmark struggled to keep his family afloat on a Denver policeman's salary. He took every moonlighting job that came along, and they were mostly of the five-dollars-an-hour variety. He worked security at basketball games and wrestling matches all over Denver and Jefferson County, where Wheat Ridge was located.

Linda was not aware that Freddie had once been sent to California to live with Fred's mother. At the time, money was tight and the Steinmarks were unable to pay rent. They moved from their home on the east side of Wheat Ridge and lived rent-free in Nana Marchetti's basement on the north side of Denver.

So financially strapped was Fred Steinmark that he almost filed for bankruptcy. He had gotten behind on the bills during a stretch when he was playing pro baseball. He then entered the Denver police department at the low end of the wage scale.

Big Fred thought about moving the entire family to Richmond, California to live with his mother. Instead, he sent Freddie away for a brief time in the seventh grade. He did not want his son to miss any sports during the school year. When Big Fred straightened out his finances, he drove to California to pick up his son.

Upon returning to Denver, Freddie was unfazed that his family existed on the lower rung of the Wheat Ridge financial ladder. They soon moved into the duplex on the west side of town near the high school.

By age sixteen, Freddie started to borrow the family car so he could take Linda out on dates. He always made a big entrance at the Wheelers' house. Parking the car on the curb, he would do cartwheels across the lawn, all the way to the front door. So charmed was Linda that she met him with a big hug. They would hug again and kiss some more. Then Linda would turn to see the scowl on Marion Wheeler's face.

"Freddie did everything he could do to make my mother happy," Linda said. "He knew she didn't like him, but he kept trying. My mother just wasn't going to change and that is very, very sad."

Marion Wheeler was not impressed that Freddie was a sports hero, or that he excelled at everything he tried. It did not matter that Freddie, with his warm brown eyes and a shock of hair sweeping across his forehead, was one of the best-looking boys in town. When she looked at Freddie, she saw a poor kid from an ethnic background. She was astounded to learn that Freddie was called "the spic" by some people around Wheat Ridge. "Spic" is an ethnic slur for someone of Hispanic background. During the spring and summer months, Freddie's skin turned deep brown and some people thought he was a Mexican-American. The truth was that he came from an Italian/German heritage. Looking in the mirror each morning, Freddie never thought he looked like a Mexican-American. Linda's mother, though, could not stomach the idea of her daughter dating a boy called "the spic."

"I could not believe that people could be cruel enough to call him that name," Linda said. "Here was one of the nicest boys you would ever meet in your whole life and they're calling him that."

Freddie felt comfortable in his own skin. He had an easygoing nature so it did not matter what other people were saying. If the Steinmarks could not keep up with the Wheelers, so what? It was irrelevant that his parents had never bought him a GTO, or a Camaro, or some other fast sports cars. He was proud of his strong Catholic faith. He thanked the Lord for his wonderful family and great friends, and for Linda, whom he loved dearly. Of course, everyone knew that.

Blair Work, the varsity head football coach at Wheat Ridge, did not start sophomores. So it was an achievement that Steinmark and Roger Behler even made the varsity. It also meant they would be playing football practically around the clock.

On the varsity, Steinmark and Behler were backups in the defensive secondary. With the junior varsity and tenth-grade teams, they started and went both ways. This meant they would be suiting up for games Friday night, Saturday afternoon, and Monday night—a weekend triple-header. It was reminiscent of Freddie's elementary school days, when he played for two teams and suited up six days a week.

"Freddie was the best athlete and teammate I was ever associated with," Behler said. "He would play with injuries and a broken leg and all kinds of things. He was just the most intelligent football player that I've ever been around."

The mettle of both boys would be tested practically every day. When the juniors and seniors finished practice, they showered and headed home for a big dinner. Steinmark and Behler kept on their wet uniforms and went to another practice.

Behler said, "By Friday, we would say to each other, 'I don't think I can make one more practice. I just don't know if I can go on.' I was so dog-ass tired by the end of that football season that I didn't know if I could go on. But we never complained to the coaches or anyone else. That was just part of our deal."

In spite of their fatigue, they both recorded remarkable games against the hated Lakewood tenth graders. Midway through the third quarter, the game seemed out of reach for the young Farmers as they trailed 24–10. In the defensive huddle, Behler and Steinmark cooked up a plan they thought would help them mount a comeback. Instead of simply covering the receivers, they would jump the routes with hopes of intercepting the pass. On the next play, Steinmark darted in front of the tight end, picked off the ball, and returned it 49 yards for a touchdown. All of a sudden, the Farmers trailed by only a touchdown.

Growing up in Wheat Ridge, the whole town knew of Freddie's athletic exploits. They mostly talked about the big yards he produced on the offensive side. No one could catch Freddie carrying the footall in the open field, and this was especially true on punt and kickoff returns.

What the opposing coaches knew about the youngster was that he also played defense as well as anyone they encountered. He seemed to know where the quarterback was going with the ball before it was snapped. He gained this edge by keeping his eyes inside the offensive huddle between plays. Freddie was always looking for any tip of the hand. That way, he could break in front of the receiver before the ball was thrown and steal it like a thief in the night.

After Lakewood returned the kickoff, Steinmark stepped into the defensive huddle and addressed the other ten players: "Guys, I want you to watch my back. I'm going for the pick again. If the receiver beats me, I need somebody to pick him up. We can't afford to give up another touchdown."

The receiver Steinmark was covering faked a post route, and

broke to the sideline. Instead of shadowing the receiver, Steinmark broke three yards in front of him, hoping the ball was coming in his direction. As he turned his head, the ball stuck in his chest and Steinmark was gone again—this time 37 yards for a touchdown. The game was tied at 24.

Playing more conservatively on defense, Wheat Ridge shut out Lakewood in the fourth quarter. Steinmark returned a punt 67 yards and Behler scored a 5-yard touchdown on an end sweep and the Wheat Ridge sophomores registered a rare victory over a Lakewood team by the score of 35–24. It had been ten years since the Farmers varsity team had managed a win over the Tigers.

Steinmark and Behler played so much football during their sophomore year that it seemed odd when they were not wearing uniforms. By the end of the season, Behler was not sure he could go much farther. Thanks to the long football grind, he contracted a case of infectious mononucleosis that landed him in the hospital for five days. He was so weak that he would miss the first two months of the basketball season.

Meanwhile, Steinmark continued to motor through basketball and baseball and could not wait to start his varsity football career in the fall of 1965. The fans felt the same way.

As a junior, Steinmark was quickly elevated into the starting lineup as a halfback on offense and a safety on defense. Because Behler could not beat out Steinmark at halfback, he was moved to quarterback. Behler had some experience at the position and liked the move, even though he would be relegated to second string.

The arrival in Wheat Ridge of a big fullback named Bobby Mitchell sparked plenty of "Beat Lakewood" talk. The coffee shops were buzzing about the six-foot, 180-pound muscle man who ran the football with a fire in his belly. The kids around Wheat Ridge considered Mitchell a mystery. It was unusual when anyone moved into Hicksville from California. Most of the kids in Wheat Ridge were born there.

Mitchell had spent the previous year in southern California, near Los Angeles, and went to Los Altos High School. Folks around Wheat Ridge came to know Mitchell his first year in the small town when he stepped into the shotput ring and casually unleashed a practice throw of more than sixty feet. It would have broken the state record in a sanctioned track meet. A few weeks later, he strolled onto the football practice field and looked like a man among boys. None of the players on the Wheat Ridge team lifted weights, so Mitchell seemed like Popeye with long legs.

"I liked Wheat Ridge right off the bat," Mitchell said. "It was semirural, a big farming community with horses and ranches, too. Actually, coming from Los Altos, it was very appealing to me. People were well-grounded and it was a good down-to-earth environment. It was a pretty area, right up against the Rockies."

Back in California, Mitchell had started as a sophomore on the Los Altos Conquistadors and led the team in rushing. After the fourth game against Northfield, his teammates voted him "Player of the Week." His older brother, Mark, also starred on the team, so there was hope that the younger Mitchell would someday blossom into an all-state prospect. It was a sad day when Bob Mitchell Sr. decided to pack up his family and move to Colorado. Mark insisted on sticking around for the final semester of his senior year to graduate from Los Altos. His decision gave rise to an idea among the Los Altos coaches.

"My coach in California asked my family to let me stay so I could compete in sports," Mitchell said. "They wanted me pretty bad, I guess. This coach said I could live at his house. But I was too young and my parents weren't going for it."

In September of 1965, Mitchell was excited to be lining up at fullback in the full-house T-formation next to a scatback named Freddie Steinmark. Mitchell looked around and saw talent that reminded him of Los Altos. He told himself that there was no reason this team could not beat Lakewood and win a district championship for the first time since 1945.

"I hadn't seen much of Freddie in spring when I moved into

Wheat Ridge because he played baseball and I didn't," Mitchell said. "But the first time I saw Freddie, I knew he could run. He could flat-out play."

During two-a-day practices, though, Mitchell was a little surprised to see Freddie's dad at virtually every practice. Mitchell's dad would have never considered coming out to watch the Farmers prepare for the season.

"I didn't see other fathers showing up at every practice," Mitchell said. "Sometimes, Big Fred was actually there to *coach* Freddie."

The opening game of the 1965 season against Lincoln High, Mitchell opened the scoring with a 29-yard burst around the right end. Fans soon learned that Mitchell was a long strider who could eat up the field quickly. Steinmark was more of a "fancy stepper." With his speed, he was capable of breaking the long gainer on any play. Before Mitchell's opening TD, Steinmark had zigzagged 74 yards for a touchdown on a punt return, but the play was called back because of a clip. In the second quarter, Behler returned a punt 82 yards for a touchdown, giving the Farmers a 13–0 lead en route to a 19–6 victory.

Mitchell proved that he was human in the second game against Pueblo Central when he fumbled at the 16-yard line. The turnover was converted into six points, but on the next series, he atoned with a 64-yard touchdown run. The PAT kick gave Wheat Ridge a 7–6 lead that stood up for the rest of the game.

Against Littleton the following week, Mitchell blocked a punt that was recovered in the end zone for a touchdown. Later in the second quarter, he returned an interception to the Littleton 34-yard line that set up another six-pointer. From the right halfback position, Behler threw a 25-yard touchdown pass to Doug Campbell and, with the 20–7 victory, Wheat Ridge was rolling at 3-0.

Steinmark had left the game late in the second half after feeling a pop in the lower part of his left leg. He thought everything would be fine until he returned to practice the next week and discovered he could barely walk. When the leg swelled to twice its normal size, Gloria Steinmark took him to the hospital. The X-rays did not reveal

any broken bones and Freddie was back in the lineup Saturday afternoon against Lakewood in the biggest game of the season.

Unbeaten Wheat Ridge was ranked fourth in the *Denver Post*
state-wide poll and Lakewood, 1–2, and stood at number eight. On
paper, the matchup favored the Farmers. The talk around town was
that this would be the year.

It turned bad, though, in the first half when a limping Steinmark
was chasing an equally gimpy Lakewood running back down the
right sideline. As he made the tackle at midfield, Freddie felt his leg
pop again. He fell awkwardly and could barely walk. He watched the
second half from the bench as the Farmers lost again to Lakewood,
28–14. This time, X-rays revealed a broken fibula. Freddie had played
almost three full quarters with a broken leg. Freddie's season was
pronounced officially over.

"When Freddie had to spend the last part of the season on the
sideline, it just killed Big Fred," Mitchell said. "You could see him
pacing up and down, up and down. I started getting more of the
carries after that and the college scouts were watching me. That put
a lot more pressure on Big Fred. He knew that if Freddie was going
to get a scholarship to a big school, he was going to need a big senior
season."

After the Lakewood loss, and the Steinmark injury, the Farmers
lost all momentum. They fell the following week to Arvada. Meanwhile, Lakewood won six straight Jefferson County games. The Tigers again took the district crown by two games over Wheat Ridge,
where the fans were frustrated, not so much with the 8-2 record, but
with yet another missed opportunity. Blair Work had compiled a
16-4 record the past two seasons, but he was still fired after the final
game. He could thank the Lakewood Tigers.

Chapter 4

MULLETS

In late spring of 1966, a bowlegged, freckle-faced, wise-cracking coach by the name of John "Red" Coats swaggered into town, sporting an attitude that would have people talking. Little wonder he was smiling. To his eye, the Wheat Ridge Farmers held great promise. To Freddie Steinmark, Coats looked like the right man for the job. At least he possessed the intensity missing from the previous coaching staff.

Coats had spent the last three seasons organizing a start-up football program at Arapahoe High in Littleton on the southeast side of Denver, recording three straight winning seasons without a single senior on the team. Impressive to the fans of Wheat Ridge was Coats's successful run as a high school coach in Texas before moving to Colorado. By nature, Coloradoans disliked Texans; it was something about their incessant bragging. Still, fans everywhere appreciated the brand of high school football played in the Lone Star State.

"Red Coats was funny and smart and everybody respected the hell out of him," Bobby Mitchell recalled. "He was a tough coach, a very tough coach, but he was fair."

It did not take the players long to know Red Coats. During that first team meeting, he grinned and said, "Hell, man, let me tell you how I operate." Even when he was addressing the entire team, Coats said, "Hell, man."

Setting his intense eyes on the players, Coats said, "First, I don't give a damn what your parents think. I don't give a damn what the fans think. Hell, man, I don't give a damn what the school administration thinks. I run the football team. I am the coach. I make all the calls around here. Do you understand?"

The players nodded in unison, but no one smiled. With a furrowed brow, Coats continued: "Let me tell you about my philosophy of life. I think that basketball's for sissies. Football is a hitting sport and therefore a game for men. Most of all, I don't want any superstars on my team. I will not tolerate superstars. Hell, man, I don't want to see any showboating."

Coats hailed from the Paul "Bear" Bryant school of coaching. In the mid-1950s, during a time when Coats was a young high school coach in West Texas, Bryant had turned around a languid Texas A&M program. Coats vividly recalled Bryant's methods at Texas A&M. Bryant did not care what the parents, the fans, or the college administration thought of his harsh tactics. In the summer of 1954, with the southern and western parts of Texas suffering from a historic drought, Bryant bused his team 300 miles from campus to a small town called Junction. The players practiced six hours a day with no water breaks in temperatures that often exceeded a hundred degrees. Players began to flee from Junction on the third day of the Hell Camp. Many did not even bother to inform the coach. They fled in the middle of the moonlit night, jerky silhouettes scrambling across the rough practice field en route to a cold drink of water and a world without pain. Bryant watched them through the screen of his Quonset hut, raising a whiskey glass and laughing.

Many of the players hitch-hiked home, or lit out for the Junction bus station, where an eighteen-year-old employee named Rob Roy Spiller opened the front door at seven A.M. Some mornings, Spiller counted as many as twenty players waiting on the sidewalk.

"Where do y'all want to go this morning?" he would say.

"We don't care," was the inevitable answer. "Just get us on the first bus out."

That season, with a skeleton squad of about twenty-five players, the Aggies finished with a 1–9 record, and it would be Bryant's only losing season in thirty-eight years of coaching. Before he left College Station after the 1957 season, though, he had turned the Aggies into a national power. If not for a tie against Houston in '56, or a loss to Rice in '57, he might have claimed at least one national title at Texas A&M.

Coats, like Bryant, firmly believed that football was not a game for the weak of heart. His players would be transformed into men long before their time. He had been introduced to the rugged game during the 1930s Depression while growing up in the small, oil-driven, blue collar West Texas town of Odessa. Coach Joe T. Coleman taught a hard-nosed brand of football that won him many fans and loyalists, one of them a redheaded kid named "Red."

Following high school, Coats was recruited to play center at Texas Tech in 1941 before going off to World War II. Upon his return, he completed his degree at TCU and served as a graduate assistant at his alma mater in 1947–48.

Coats was the head coach at Odessa Junior College from 1949–51, then he moved to El Paso's Ysleta High School in '52. Before his final season at Ysleta in 1962, he took a trip that would change his coaching life for all time. He traveled more than a thousand miles to Delafield, Wisconsin, for the final two weeks of the Dallas Cowboys training camp. This was an era long before the Cowboys were known as "America's Team," a time when the team's bank account could have fit inside a tackle box. When Coats checked into his dorm room at the military school, he discovered bats flying up and down the darkened hallways. There were no screens on the windows and his room was filled with mosquitoes.

Out on the practice field, though, Coats found something magical. Tom Landry's offense was so far ahead of its time that some NFL insiders thought the coach was slightly nuts. Landry was coaching the new "pro-set offense" with multiple formations and men in motion. Coats intently watched every minute of every practice and was invited by the coaches to view game film from the previous season. He wrote down everything he learned and took it back to Texas.

In May of 1966, Coats was ready to launch his new offense on the rolling farmland west of Denver. All he needed was the right quarterback to make it work.

"I remember that Red walked up to me that spring and said, 'Son, I'm going to be counting on you next season,'" Roger Behler said. "I didn't know what the hell he was talking about. But I didn't tell him that."

When Coats stepped up to the chalkboard that first day of spring practice and started drawing X's and O's, the players could not believe it. Yes, the boys had been watching the NFL on television the last few years, and realized that the Dallas Cowboys operated a complex offense. Coats's ideas, though, seemed to be beamed in from another planet. The players were accustomed to the grind-it-out T-formation taught by their former head coach. Blair Works's offense was about as imaginative as cow tipping. The playbook contained about five plays, and it was mostly Mitchell up the middle, Freddie Steinmark around end, and senior quarterback Dave Zinanti throwing quick passes to tight end Doug Campbell. Occasionally, Zinanti would lateral the ball to Behler for the halfback pass. The Farmers averaged about 10 passes and 50 running plays a game.

Behler had been playing organized tackle football since the third grade and had never seen anything like the Dallas Cowboys offense.

"I grew up wanting to be a football player," Behler said. "It was the one thing I'd always wanted to be. I enjoyed playing football every minute of every day. But when Red showed up, everything was a lot more fun. All of a sudden we get this man with a sarcastic tone and he really knew what he was talking about."

Coats's timing with the new offense was an act of brilliance. Steinmark was one of the fastest halfbacks in the state and capable of breaking a long run on any play. Steinmark and Mitchell were stellar pass receivers coming out of the backfield. Because Steinmark had missed most of the previous season with a broken leg, Coats had little film to study on him. However, the first few days of spring practice told him more than he needed to know.

One day, Steinmark was fielding a punt during a full-scale scrimmage when he darted to the right sideline, cut back across the field, accelerated between three tacklers, and dashed into the end zone without ever breaking a sweat.

"I've been coaching high school football for fifteen years," Coats told assistant coach Jack Jost, "and I've never seen anything like that Freddie Steinmark kid. If he were a little bigger, I could turn him into the number-one recruit in the entire state."

Coats's playbook burgeoned by the day. This was a conservative era in high school football when most coaches were more concerned with fumbles and interceptions than baffling the opposing defense with fancy formations. Coats was cutting edge on all levels.

For the first time in the history of Wheat Ridge football, players were required to lift weights Monday through Friday nights throughout the summer. By the time they showed up for the two-a-day practices, Bobby Mitchell was not the only player showing off new muscle.

"We quickly learned that Red would push the envelope on just about everything," Behler said.

As he prepared to address the team before the start of August two-a-days, Coats held great hope for this team. He knew that Steinmark and Mitchell might be the best running duo in all of Colorado, and Behler possessed an accurate passing arm. The offensive line, led by Dave Dirks, Kent Cluck, and Stan Politano, was small but quick. This unit was a perfect fit for the Landry offense.

As he stood before the players that day, Coats was smiling on the inside. All the players could see, though, were his angry eyes.

"Hell, man, I hear you boys are nothing but a bunch of danged mullets," he began. "The talk around town is that you've got no championship blood in you. Wheat Ridge has never won a state title. For God's sake, man, Wheat Ridge hasn't won district since 1945. Nobody around here's lived long enough to remember that. Hell, man, we can't even beat those little ol' sissies from Lakewood and they're our next door neighbor. I gotta wonder if you mullets got any pride. Boys, this shit's gotta change."

Coats had been using the "mullet" reference most of his coaching life and had first heard it from Joe T. Coleman back at Odessa High. A mullet is basically a worthless bottom-feeding fish.

Before long, the players were starting to enjoy Coats's homespun humor and his drawl, which was as thick as West Texas dust. The words, slathered with molasses, rumbled from the back of his throat. Instead of "hell," he said "hail." He said "come 'er, hoss," and "that dog won't hunt." The players soon realized that being called "mullets" was not all that bad. In fact, the coach grinned like an old mule when he said it.

"I think that Red was the funniest person that I'd ever met," Behler said. "There was just no one like him."

The first week of practice, Coats asked for volunteers to move all of his furniture and the family belongings from his house in Littleton to Wheat Ridge.

"You really don't have to help move me," Coats told the boys. "That is, unless you don't want to play football for Wheat Ridge High School this season."

The next day, a caravan of pickup trucks driven by Wheat Ridge players and loaded with Coats's possessions made the trek from Littleton up to Wheat Ridge.

Settling into his new little town, Coats was like a wheat shocker in tall grass. He would have looked comfortable wearing overalls with a pinch of Red Man between his teeth. He could talk the language of the farmers plowing up the west end of Wheat Ridge. He was as country as George Jones and Merle Haggard singing a duet. He might have left Odessa, but Odessa had never left him. Make no mistake, though, this man did not leave Texas to lollygag in the Colorado sunshine. He did not cotton to mediocrity. His eyes were as sharp and as focused as the hawks floating on the high wind.

More than anything, Coats wanted Wheat Ridge to seize Colorado high school football by the throat.

"Red really wasn't into making friends," guard Stan Politano said. "He had come to Wheat Ridge to make us winners and nothing was going to stand in his way. He got into it with the parents, assistant coaches, and the players. Some people thought he was arrogant. You were never on the fence with this guy. You either loved him or you hated him. And he just didn't care what people thought about him. His football team was not going to be run by committee."

Coats felt certain the Farmers would win the state title that first season and dominate the statistics. He knew that if one of his players led the state in scoring, the sportswriters from the *Denver Post* and the *Rocky Mountain News* would wear out the presses writing about it. So he had a tough choice to make between Steinmark and Mitchell. Only one of his running backs would be toting the football close to the goal; the other might be jealous.

In spite of the special talents of both players, the decision was actually easy. Mitchell was the bigger, stronger back, the type you wanted to pound between the tackles and into the end zone.

Coats planned to attack the scoring title from every angle. At the coach's insistence, Mitchell would kick extra points and field goals in 1966, in spite of the fact that he had never been groomed for the task and secretely hated it.

As the Farmers prepared for the opening game against Abraham Lincoln High, the offense was becoming a precision unit. Behler continued to improve with each passing day. Coats proved to be the right coach for the times, and the players were catching on quickly to the Landry schemes.

A left-hander, Behler threw soft, arcing passes with Sandy Koufax accuracy. His spirals hit the receivers between the numbers and, in spite of spinning counterclockwise, the balls were easy to catch. Behler was not the classic drop-back passer like Don Meredith of the Cowboys—he preferred to roll out and was at his best throwing on the run. So valuable was Behler to the offense that Coats would not let him play defense for fear of injury.

One of Coats's favorite players was Politano, a 5' 7", 165-pound right guard who played with passion and grit. He was not unlike a lot of smaller players playing the line around Colorado during that era. Wearing thick goggles beneath his helmet, Politano did not look ferocious, but he played with a fire that Coats admired.

The excitement was palpable as the season approached. The four-teen seniors were angry about always finishing second to Lakewood. To ratchet up the team spirit, Politano came up with an idea to sell T-shirts that read, WHEAT RIDGE FOOTBALL—1966. They were the standard gray, and as it turned out, Politano also possessed an eye for making a profit. The shirts were produced for a dollar apiece, and sold for five bucks. The seniors demanded that all the juniors and sophomores buy at least one. Several hundred were sold around town with part of the proceeds going to a seniors-only dinner at the Mount Vernon Country Club in the foothills of Golden. The supper club served a huge all-you-can-eat smorgasbord.

"We did the T-shirts to build team unity and it worked," Politano said. "The seniors also enjoyed a pretty good dinner. I think that we ate everything in the restaurant and they were glad when we were gone."

After the dinner, Stan's mother, Betty Politano, came up with another idea for a big feed. She loved the kitchen and, over the years, had served home-cooked meals to most of the kids around Wheat Ridge at least once.

"If you beat Lincoln in the first game, I'll cook a spaghetti dinner for the whole team," she said.

As the players dressed for the Lincoln game, the seniors made the rounds in the dressing room that night, making sure that everyone was wearing the gray T-shirts under their shoulder pads. Every-one was confident in the new offense. Behler was handling the quarter-back position better every day, but no one could have predicted what he would do against Lincoln. By halftime, the Lincoln High players would have sworn that Behler had been taking snaps all of his life. He completed 10 of 12 passes and the Farmers offense suddenly knew no bounds.

"I didn't feel like a rookie that first game," Behler said. "I felt comfortable in there with Red's offense. I absolutely loved throwing the football. I was ready to go."

By the end of the game, he had completed 16 of 24 passes for 212 yards with 4 touchdowns—three passing and one rushing. Behler could have beaten Lincoln by himself. The 52–25 victory told the preseason pollsters from the *Denver Post* that they were right in ranking Wheat Ridge number three in the state.

A sidebar to the opening victory was the competition between the two backs. Steinmark returned a kickoff for an 85-yard touchdown, and Mitchell responded with one from 87 yards.

Coats met the press at midfield after the game and said, "Yes, I was very pleased with everything, including Freddie and Bobby Mitchell. I was especially impressed with Roger Behler. There wasn't much more that you could ask for. That kid can play."

That Sunday evening, Tony and Betty Politano stood at the living room window of their small home on the east side of Wheat Ridge and watched the street out front being transformed into the biggest parking lot west of Denver. Betty figured that some of the boys would want to try her spaghetti, *but not the whole team.*

"I just hope that we've got enough spaghetti," she told her husband.

"I've never known you to run out," he replied.

Remembering that evening, Stan Politano said, "Everybody on the team came. All of the coaches, including Red, came. They all brought their wives. We had a small one-story house. Fortunately, we had a furnished basement."

Even more fortunate, the Politanos were the proud owners of *two* kitchens, one in the basement and the other in the main part of the house. Spaghetti, meatballs, and sausages were served to everyone. The feast was on.

For the better part of that weekend, Tony Politano had prepared the meat for the meatballs. He raised rabbits and pigeons in the backyard. On Saturday, he gutted the rabbits, then hung them out to dry on the clothesline. Little did the diners know that the meatballs were mostly rabbit meat.

"My dad put everything in the meat sauce," Stan said. " He even included the peppers that he grew in the backyard."

Tony Politano was not a bashful man and reminded Stan of Coats.

Growing up on the north side of Denver in the section of town known as Little Italy, Tony was forced to quit school in the seventh grade when he went to work for the American Beauty Macaroni Company. Years later, when he married Betty, he started the Politano Fruit Company.

The Politanos moved to Wheat Ridge because, like a lot of families, they were trying to avoid problems inherent with the city.

"My older brother liked to fight," Stan said. "And my dad just figured that we would be better off in a country environment."

As his wife prepared the spaghetti dinner that night, Tony Politano Sr. walked around the house offering the boys a taste of his jalapeño peppers. Stan walked behind his dad, telling his friends, "Don't eat that pepper. Don't even *look* at that pepper. It'll burn your mouth off."

Tony Politano did convince a couple of the coaches to try his peppers. They were so hot that the teary-eyed diners did not return for seconds.

At the end of the night, the players and coaches were so happy with the dinner that they thanked all of the Politanos and promised to come back.

"You boys keep winning," Betty said, "and we'll keep providing the spaghetti dinners every Sunday night."

Next on the schedule was Pueblo Central, the defending AAA state champs, and a team that Wheat Ridge had defeated 7–6 the previous season. Since 1921, Pueblo Central had won seven state titles playing in Colorado's biggest classification.

In the first half, with Steinmark and Mitchell gaining most of the yards, the Farmers twice moved the ball inside the 10-yard line. Mitchell scored touchdowns on runs of seven and one yards and the Farmers grabbed a 13–7 lead.

During a timeout in the third quarter, Behler came to the sideline to hear the next play. Coats grinned at his quarterback. "Well, Roger, what do you think we should run next?" he said.

"Coach Coats," Behler said, "I thought I was coming over here to hear that from you." They both laughed.

Coats called a passing play with halfback Steve Tierney breaking straight up the field, then cutting over the middle. The ball was lofted perfectly into his hands near the goal. The touchdown covered 38 yards and provided the knockout punch in a 19–7 victory. Every sportswriter in the state knew that Wheat Ridge football was chasing a state title.

As the players filed into the Politano home that Sunday evening, Coats was spotted walking up the sidewalk with something quite heavy and burdensome in his right hand. It was the team's film projector. Ever the opportunist, Coats was going to expand the team celebration by watching the game film of the Pueblo Central game.

When Coats turned out the lights and the projector began to whir, Betty and Tony Politano expected the coach to lavish praise on his players. They were wrong. It was little wonder that the players were so quiet, and why some wore pained expressions.

After the first couple of plays, Coats, standing at the front of the room, wheeled and pointed at his players.

"You mullets think you're really good because you beat a bunch of mullets from Pueblo Central," he said. "Well, let me tell you a few things. I saw a lot of missed blocks and a lot of missed tackles out there Friday night. Hell, man, that's not championship football. That's the same damn brand of football that Wheat Ridge has been playing all these years."

As the black-and-white images danced across the basement wall, Coats's eyes were focused on number 64 in the blue uniform. Politano knew that he had missed a couple of blocks and was ready for his whipping.

"Politano, where are you?" Coats said, peering through the darkness. "What the hell do you think you're doing? What's wrong with you, son?"

Politano wished to be somewhere else, even though he was sitting in his own basement.

Forty years later, he was able to laugh about it.

"Red didn't mind ripping me right there in front of my parents," Politano said. "He was just that way. He was hell-bent on turning us into winners."

A few players later, Steinmark weaved his way through seven broken tackles on a 43-yard punt return that set up the final touchdown of the game.

"Attaway to go, Freddie," Coats yelled. "Boys, now that's how you play football. That Freddie, he's no mullet."

Everyone in the room finally relaxed, realizing that Freddie had put an end to the scolding.

With a bye the following week, Coats was able to expand the offensive even more, which gave Behler more freedom. Kids all over Wheat Ridge recognized that Behler was one of the smartest students they had ever met. He was vying for valedictorian honors with Dave Dirks. Mitchell noticed that Behler went through an entire semester of calculus without ever using the eraser on his pencil.

"Roger was one of the most intelligent guys I'd ever been around in high school," Mitchell said. "It was a good thing because we were running a new offense that was pretty complicated."

Fourteen days between games left the Farmers a little rusty. They failed to score a point in the first quarter against the Alameda Pirates, but soon the touchdowns were coming in bunches. Wheat Ridge marched 76 yards down the field early in the second quarter, and Steinmark got his first shot at a short touchdown run. The Alameda defense was looking for Mitchell on the 3-yard plunge, but it was Steinmark bursting off tackle through a hole provided by Dirks.

Minutes later, Behler threw a quick outside hitch to Bower Yousse, and the speedy receiver cut up the sideline and did not stop running for 68 yards, all the way to the end zone. Minutes later, Steinmark stepped in front of a pass at the Alameda 36-yard and returned it to the fourteen. Mitchell was soon bulling his way into the end zone from the 3-yard line for yet another six-pointer.

In the second half, Behler rolled left from the 5-yard line and surged into the end zone untouched. Then on the first play of the fourth quarter, he threw a soft 11-yard toss to Mitchell in the right corner of the end zone and the Farmers closed out a 33–0 victory. The Pirates never came close to scoring.

In the days leading to the biggest game of their lives, Wheat Ridge showed its obsession with Lakewood. There were banners and parades and cars speeding up and down the streets with kids yelling, "Beat Lakewood!" Store windows along the main drag were soaped with signs that read, "Kill The Tigers!" and "Let's Finally Do It!"

On Monday, Steinmark noticed a bruise on the back of his hand. He could not remember when the injury occurred. His adrenaline the previous game must have masked the pain. Soon, it began to throb and swell, and Freddie started to worry. He decided to show it to Mitchell.

"Dang, Freddie," Mitchell said. "That hand looks like it's broken. You better get a doctor to look at that."

No way, Steinmark thought. He remembered the last time he was X-rayed at a doctor's office, and it cost him more than half of the previous season.

Instead of having one of the student trainers tape the hand, he did it himself. He placed some gauze on the back and then wrapped the hand with adhesive tape. Coats became curious about the injury during practice that afternoon and wondered if he would be able to handle the ball with the same confidence.

"Ah, Coach, it's just a little scrape on the back of my hand," he said. "It'll go away in a couple of days."

All week, a nervous tension hung over the town.

"We were intimidated by Lakewood," Behler said. "Really and truly they had about the same number of kids in their school as we did. But they always beat us in football. Always. Tom Hancock was a helluva coach and he built the Tigers into a great program."

Hancock was among the first coaches in Colorado to develop a year-round weight-training program. The Tigers were generally bigger and stronger and could stand up to the most talented players from the bigger schools of the Denver prep league.

At a pep rally inside the Wheat Ridge gymnasium the afternoon of the Big Game, the kids were going crazy when Mitchell stepped to the microphone. One of four team captains that included Dirks, Politano, and Steinmark, it was Mitchell's turn to deliver the pre-game pep talk.

The speech was going smoothly until Mitchell blurted, "We're going to beat the *hell* out of Lakewood!" In the fall of 1966, *hell* was still a pretty strong word for a place like Wheat Ridge.

Suddenly, the gymnasium went silent. Steinmark was sitting on the front row, just behind Mitchell, and he smiled like a kid eating ice cream. *"What did you say, Bob?"* His voice could be heard from one end of the gym to the other.

Mitchell turned, peered at his buddy, and placed both hands on his hips. His eyes were locked onto Freddie's. Then the two started to chuckle. Before long, everyone in the entire gym was laughing with them.

Jefferson County Stadium, built to hold 9,000 fans, would host the big game. By kickoff, fans were standing in the aisles and clogging space along the sidelines. They were sardined into the corners of the end zone. The estimated attendance was more like 12,000, and the place was rocking.

Lakewood was 38-1-1 in district play since the Jefferson County League was launched four years earlier. The lone loss had come against the Farmers in '62. Still, Wheat Ridge did not win the district that year.

Until this night, Hancock was considered the greatest coach in the history of Jefferson County football. His defensive game plan that night was to flex the defensive secondary to shut down the pass. So on the first possession of the game, the Farmers ran the ball.

Steinmark and Mitchell began to chew up the yardage—Mitchell powering inside and Steinmark gaining big chunks on the sweep.

Wheat Ridge rolled 76 yards down the field, all the way to the 2-yard line. To no one's surprise, Mitchell carried the ball on the next play and barreled into the end zone. He proceeded to miss the extra point kick and the Farmers led 6–0.

In the second quarter, Wheat Ridge moved the ball 67 yards in eight plays. Behler's 1-yard sneak provided the score and Mitchell's kick made it 13–0.

Minutes before halftime, the Lakewood offense came to life for a drive of 56 yards with Chuck Greaser scoring on a 1-yard run. The PAT kick made it 13–7.

Early in the third quarter, the Tigers set out on a long, time-consuming drive that finally started to silence the Wheat Ridge fans. Moving the ball 76 yards, halfback Lynn White took the pitch around left end from the 5-yard line and scored a touchdown. It was 13–13. The game would be determined in the fourth quarter, just as everyone expected.

With twelve minutes to play, Coats rolled the dice in a situation that was nerve-racking to the hometown fans. From the Wheat Ridge 22-yard line, on fourth-and-one, he called for the quarterback sneak. When Behler stepped to the line, the noise seemed to rise up all the way to the Kansas border. Behler drove his body between center Kent Cluck and guard Stan Politano and made the first down by inches.

The Farmers ran two more plays for a grand total of two yards, and faced a third-and-eight. Coats called time-out and Behler trotted to the sideline.

The quarterback expected Coats to call a pass, but also knew the Lakewood defense would be set to stop it. "Give the damn ball to Freddie," Coats said, then walked away. Behler smiled as he trotted back onto the field.

The play was "42-trap," one of the simplest calls in the playbook. Politano would drive the nose tackle to the left as Dirks pushed the middle linebacker to the right. As Behler stepped under center, he reminded himself to spin quickly for the fake pitch to Mitchell. He needed to move fast to make the connection with Freddie, blasting straight up the middle.

"Freddie was so fast that I was worried I might miss the handoff," Behler recalled.

Steinmark hit the hole like a rifle shot and sprinted twenty yards straight upfield. Then he planted his right foot and swerved to the left sideline. *Denver Post* high school editor Irv Moss once wrote, "Steinmark changes directions like a fly in flight." Upon reaching the left sideline, he buzzed all the way back across the field to the right sideline. Along the way, Freddie thought of his former midget league coach, Muzzy Vecchiarelli. It was Vecchiarelli who demanded he carry the ball on a straight line. *Sorry, Muzzy.*

Reaching the Lakewood 30-yard line, Steinmark straightened his course and lit out for the end zone. No one was going to catch him. By the time he scored, the little seatback had run about 150 yards. The night seemed to explode as he crossed the goal. The band played and the Wheat Ridge students finally exhaled. The cheerleaders hugged and cried. The place was soon quiet, though, as Mitchell's extra point sailed wide. The Farmers led by only six points.

Ten minutes to play, and the game was far from over. The fans on the Wheat Ridge side were beginning to think the whole affair had been scripted for another heartbreak. Drive the length of the field, kick the extra point, and Lakewood would be on its way to another district title and one more shot at the state championship.

They had forgotten something. Fans of Steinmark rarely thought past his offensive skills. In the open field, he ran like a deer, as he had done on the 77-yard touchdown jaunt just minutes earlier. They would soon learn, though, to give Steinmark credit for his terrific defensive skills.

As Lakewood tried to mount a comeback, the Tigers' largest obstacle was the single-minded, balls-out determination of Steinmark. Play after play, he made tackle after tackle. Knowing that Lakewood, with so much time on the clock, was going to run the ball, Steinmark lined up closer and closer to the line of scrimmage. He drove his shoulders and helmet into the Lakewood ball carriers. Their groans could be heard all the way to the grandstand. His weight hovering around 150 pounds, Steinmark still hit like a sledgehammer. He was a combination of Emile Griffith and Curtis Cokes, the welterweight boxing champs who dominated the classification in the mid-1960s. Rarely did a running back get past Steinmark, and, most of the time, he was stopped cold.

Late in the game, when Lakewood was forced to pass, Steinmark assumed his usual spot as the deep safety, knocking down two passes. Hancock reached deep into his playbook, but could find nothing to overcome Steinmark. When the Tigers ran a double-reverse, Steinmark held his ground, knowing that a halfback pass might be coming. Sure enough, the ball carrier planted his right foot and heaved a desperation pass that wobbled high and far into the Colorado night. Steinmark snared the interception at the White Ridge 20-yard line as Lakewood's final hopes were extinguished.

As Hancock nervously paced the sideline that night, he said to all within earshot, "There's not a danged thing we can do with Steinmark. Not a danged thing. That kid's the best high school football player I've ever seen."

At the end of the game, the Wheat Ridge players hoisted Steinmark onto their shoulders and carried him around the field. They stopped on the Wheat Ridge side and listened to the band play the school song. Freddie spotted Linda in the crowd and was not surprised to see tears flowing down her pink cheeks. They waved at each other, and Freddie mouthed the words, "I'll see you at the dance."

Across the field, Hancock met the Denver sportswriters for a quick press conference. He held a clipboard with an array of handwritten statistics. He kept mumbling, "eighteen unassisted tackles. That guy had eighteen unassisted tackles."

The coach cleared his throat and addressed the reporters: "According to the statistics we kept on the sideline, Freddie Steinmark made 18 unassisted tackles tonight. That's got to be some kind of record. I'm sure that everyone's going to remember his 77-yard touchdown run that beat us. But I think he really beat us on the defensive side of the ball. That young man is one of the most remarkable high school football players I've ever seen."

The Wheat Ridge players finally put Freddie down. Together,

they sprinted across the field to the dressing room. Not a single Farmers fan had left the stadium and they raised a racket that no one would ever forget.

Huffing and puffing, the Farmers gathered in the locker room and banged each other atop their helmets and shoulder pads. They celebrated for more than ten minutes until everyone finally sat down. Roger Behler drank in the moment and looked around the room at his teammates. He put his arm around Freddie's shoulders.

"Okay, guys," he said. "We finally beat Lakewood. Now what the hell are we going to do?"

Coats walked into the locker room and bear-hugged Steinmark. Then he kissed him on top of his head.

"Everybody sit down and relax for a minute," the coach said. "I've got a proposal for you guys."

After a pause, Coats continued, "Our season's not over. Yeah, we finally beat Lakewood, but we've got a long way to go. There's still much to accomplish. If you remember, we set our goals pretty dang high this year."

Coats took a deep breath and the room fell silent.

"Here's what I think we should do," he said, his eyes bugging out. "I think we should go out and win ourselves a Colorado state championship!"

Everyone jumped to their feet as the shouting returned.

"Win State! Win State!" they hollered.

This time, they really believed it.

Chapter 5

THE EDGE OF HISTORY

*"As far as drive and determination and discipline, there was
no one like Freddie Steinmark."* —ROGER BEHLER

Following the historic win over Lakewood, the Wheat Ridge Farmers shredded the final five opponents by the combined score of
173–13. One day, Roger Behler sat at his locker and shook his head,
thinking about the season that changed everything.

"I just couldn't believe it," Behler recalled. "Through the years,
we just hadn't been that good in football. We never had the big
colleges coming to recruit our players. Now everyone was beginning
to think we were great."

The *Denver Post* sportswriters voted Wheat Ridge number two in
the state behind undefeated George Washington High. The Lakewood Jinx was no longer on their minds. The victory over the Tigers
meant a hit of confidence like no other and, with every victory, Red
Coats pushed the mullets to greater heights.

The 9-0 Farmers were the talk of Colorado. It was almost like
the Vince Lombardi Packers had set up camp in Wheat Ridge with
names like Starr, Dowler, Hornung, Taylor, McGee, Gregg, Kramer,
Nitschke, Adderley, and Wood. At the time, the Cowboys and Packers were the favorites to meet in the NFL championship game at the
end of the season.

In spite of the resounding wins, Coats was not letting up on his
team, and the film sessions following the spaghetti dinners in the
Politano basement could be downright cruel. Some of the players
slumped in their chairs, hoping that Coats would not notice them,
but he somehow managed to find all of their mistakes, regardless of
how big or small.

One night, Politano watched a running play and saw himself pulling around right end with Dave Dirks to his side. They were supposed to provide a human shield for Steinmark, carrying the ball on the power sweep. Instead of blocking, though, Politano and Dirks continued to run and run, bypassing defenders, seemingly racing each other down the field, looking pretty stupid.

"Well, lookie there," Coats bellowed, his voice dripping with sarcasm. "If it's not the Gold Dust Twins them ownselves. I guess that Politano and Dirks didn't feel like blocking anybody on that play. Huh, mullets?"

In that era of sports, any reference to the "Gold Dust Twins" was considered high praise. The most celebrated Gold Dust Twins were Fred Lynn and Jim Rice, rookies who led the Boston Red Sox to the American League Pennant in 1975. In the case of Politano and Dirks, the coach was being bitterly sarcastic. Players normally received the tag when they played well in tandem. Dirks and Politano were more like the "Bone Head Twins."

"You could be sure that Dave and I never let that happen again on the playing field," Politano said. "Red had a way of making sure that you didn't repeat mistakes."

There was much excitement around the school as the Farmers continued to be the number-two ranked team in the state. Students at Wheat Ridge, though, were accustomed to the Farmers choking. So many times since the school had opened its doors in the 1940s they had experienced an onrushing optimism, only to see their team falter in the Big Game and fall to second place in the district. Not since 1945 had the Farmers reached the state playoffs on any level. In 1966, though, the hallways at Wheat Ridge were pulsating with new hope.

"Win state! Win state!" the students chanted as they walked the halls.

"I could not believe what I was hearing," Behler remembered. "The football players were looking at each other and saying, 'What the heck is going on around here? They actually think we can win state!'"

Freddie and Linda were still sharing their noon-hour kiss, but were more careful than ever. With Steinmark's added fame, the kids were watching them more closely.

"Freddie had always been a star around Wheat Ridge," Linda recalled. "But when the football team beat Lakewood and started heading toward state, the other kids watched him night and day."

Winning usually attracted curious new fans, and the bandwagon was filling up. The practice field behind the high school became an amusement park for the rollicking optimists. Coats worried about the crowds that were growing each day and some of the giddiness he had witnessed. *I don't give a damn what the fans think.*

A few weeks earlier he had asked Fred Steinmark to stop attending practices for fear that he was distracting Freddie. The overly ambitious father was known to loudly scold the erring son in front of the entire team. *I am the coach of this damn team.*

"Coats told Big Fred that he had to go," Bobby Mitchell said. "He just wasn't going to tolerate it anymore. We assume that he told him in private in an effort not to embarrass him. But one day, Big Fred was gone."

After chasing Fred Steinmark off the premises, Coats decided that it was time for everyone to go. The gates to the practice field were locked, even to the media. He wanted no distractions and he certainly hated the idea of attracting spies. Coats was known to add new plays every day.

The practice field was located at the bottom of a hill from the high school and the players trekked down two flights of stairs to reach it. One afternoon, Coats spotted two men at the top of the ridge. One held a pair of binoculars that were trained on his team.

Freddie wrote in *I Play to Win*, "He [Red] sent a student manager up the hill to chase the two guys off. One was my father."

Mitchell remembered, "We watched Big Fred walk up the stairs and over the hill and he was gone. Later on, though, we always suspected that he was watching from afar."

At times during the season, Mitchell said he could detect an unhappiness within the normally happy-go-lucky kid, who was beginning to experience mood swings.

"There were times when Freddie was upset and moody because he didn't please his dad," he said. "Everyone knew that Big Fred was hard on Freddie. But he would never say, 'My father is too hard on me.' We lived in a culture in those days where you respected your dad and you just didn't talk about things like that. If Freddie screwed up, he had about half of the clan down his throat."

Behler had known Freddie and his dad all the way back to the third grade, when they played sports in the backyard at the Steinmarks' home on Carr Street in east Wheat Ridge. He knew the Steinmark family as well as anyone.

"I can tell you that Freddie loved both his parents very much," Behler said. "Big Fred wanted the best for Freddie and Freddie always understood that. Big Fred was much more involved in the sports teams than my dad or any one of the other dads. That just meant that he cared about Freddie."

Behler remembered the happy atmosphere at the Steinmark home when they were kids and could laugh and play all day. Big Fred went right along with it.

"The Steinmarks' place was always a blast," he said. "We always played ball or tag or hide-and-go-seek. Big Fred was usually out there with us and he was always a lot of fun. I didn't notice any tension between Big Fred and Freddie during those times."

The Steinmarks loved to have fun, but their favorite pastime was joining the Marchetti family at Freddie's games and pulling for the number-one player of the clan. It was not unusual for the Steinmark-Marchetti congregation to fill half a section of Jefferson County Stadium. With more than a hundred in attendance, they were easy to spot.

Freddie was grabbing plenty of the headlines in the *Denver Post* and *Rocky Mountain News* and the other newspapers of the area. Still, he was not finding the end zone nearly as often as Mitchell. This became a source of frustration for the Steinmark-Marchetti clan. Mitchell had become the odds-on favorite to win the Colorado scoring title and Steinmark's statistics were suffering because of it.

Back in the days when Freddie was playing midget football, and the Rough Riders were winning every game for eight straight seasons, the games were still fun. Parents like "Big Fred" Steinmark were often vocal to the point of causing the others to cringe. Still, the games maintained an amateur feel because, after all, kids will be kids.

By the time Freddie reached his senior season, he could feel the tension mounting with every game. He knew that his father desperately wanted him to play big-time college football, and that his policeman's salary was not enough to pay tuition, room, and board for a walk-on player.

To heighten the tension around the football team, expectations for Wheat Ridge football were growing each day. That the Farmers had never reached the state playoffs was enough to send the long-suffering townsfolk into deep worry. The arrival of Coats, along with the spectacular play of Steinmark, Mitchell, and Behler, had made the dream of a state title seem suddenly within reach.

As Wheat Ridge began to demolish opponents, the first string would usually be pulled from the game at halftime, or early in the third quarter. Disturbing to Freddie's family was that Coats would reinsert Mitchell into the game after the second or third stringers had moved the ball inside the 5-yard line. Coats was persistent about Mitchell winning the state scoring title.

If Coats was playing favorites, though, you could not have convinced Mitchell of it. The head coach set a 10:30 curfew. Some of the Wheat Ridge players enjoyed a night life and cold beer was often part of the ritual. Overall, though, the boys stayed in line and dearly wanted to please their coach. They also knew that if they broke the rules, one of the captains—Steinmark, Mitchell, Politano, or Dave Dirks—was required to call the coach. In fact, Coats demanded that the captains do occasional "house checks" to make sure everyone was home on time.

One night, Mitchell was pushing curfew and rushing to get home when he hurriedly stuck the key into the car's ignition. The motor never turned over. Forced to walk home, he arrived after eleven o'clock. He sensed that someone on the team was watching him.

The next day after practice, Mitchell could feel Coats's hard eyes tracking him. The coach gathered the team around him for the normal post-practice pep talk, then said, "Bobby Mitchell, I hear you were out late last night. Do you want to tell us about it?"

Mitchell could barely find the words. He stammered and said, "Well, Coach, my car broke down. I couldn't get a ride so I had to walk. So, yessir, I did miss curfew."

"Hell, man," Coats said, "you're a team captain and you're breaking team rules. I want you to walk down to the goal-line, get down in your stance, and when I blow the whistle, I want you to run. I want you to run hard. And I don't want you to stop running until I tell you to."

Mitchell ran from one end of the field to the other and back again. Back and forth he went. Standing on the sideline, the players could hear him breathing like a spent racehorse.

"I ran and ran and then I started puking and falling down," he said. "It really hurt because my teammates were watching. I'll tell you this: I still loved Red Coats. That man made us all some danged good football players. He loved us, too."

By scoring 13 points against Bear Creek in the last game of the regular season finale, Mitchell assured himself of the Colorado high school scoring title. For the season, he tallied 137 points, five more than Mike Mangino of Trinidad. He averaged 15.2 per game. Steinmark scored a total of 83 points.

In rushing, Mitchell also led the state with a 7.5 average per attempt. He likely would have taken the overall yardage crown, but his 74 carries were more than thirty less than the state's leader.

Remarkably, Wheat Ridge scored 306 points for the season while allowing only 54. Most of the newspaper hype all season on the Farmers had centered on the offense, but the defense completed the regular season ranked fifth of the sixty-four Colorado AAA teams in fewest points allowed.

Offensively, the Farmers were fourth in the state in total offense and would face the Ranum Raiders, Colorado's yardage leader, in the first round of the state playoffs.

On November 19, more than six thousand fans came to Jefferson County Stadium to see the Farmers host the Ranum Raiders in the first round of the playoffs. Ranum High School was located in Westminster, about twelve miles north of Wheat Ridge, and, like the Farmers, the Raiders had never won a state championship. Wheat Ridge would need two playoff victories to reach the state finals.

Indeed, the Wheat Ridge defense was ready for Ranum and forced the Raiders to punt after running only three plays. As the season had progressed, Coats had bowed to Behler's wishes about playing more on defense and special teams. The coach realized his prized quarterback was tough enough to handle the extra work without getting hurt.

Behler and Steinmark were the double safeties on the punt return when the ball spiraled more than 50 yards into the arms of the Wheat Ridge quarterback. Behler cut over the middle and attracted most of the Ranum coverage team players. Then he deftly lateraled on the reverse to Steinmark, who angled to the right sideline and sprinted 83 yards along the stripe untouched for the opening touchdown of the game.

The Ranum offense would run three more plays and punt again, this time in the direction of Behler. It was clear that they were trying to kick away from Steinmark. Behler fielded the ball at the Wheat Ridge 30, headed to his left, faked the lateral to Steinmark, and sprinted 61 yards to the end zone. The Wheat Ridge offense had not run a play, but led the Raiders 13–0 after three minutes en route to a 33–7 victory.

During that week, a crew at Jefferson County Stadium went to work adding 500 bleacher seats to the end zone, increasing capacity to

10,000. For the first time since the Lakewood game, Coats seemed worried about an oncoming opponent. The Wasson High Thunderbirds of Colorado Springs, seventy miles south of Denver, were also undefeated at 11-0, having played one team more than Wheat Ridge. Like the Farmers, the T-Birds liked to throw the football.

"Wasson has by far the best team that we've faced all season," Coats told the *Denver Post*.

Since the opening game against Lincoln High, the Farmers had allowed opponents only four points per game. Still, Coats seemed antsy when coaching defensive drills leading up to the Wasson game.

"This is the one game that you mullets might just screw up," he said. "Let me tell you something: Wasson is not a bunch of sissies like some of these teams we've been playing."

A snowstorm blew into Wheat Ridge the day before the state semifinal game, and with it came the high winds. Thanks to the weather, the advanced sellout at Jefferson County Stadium shrunk to a crowd of about 6,000 fans. Warming up before the game, Mitchell realized it would be virtually impossible to kick extra points or field goals. Every time he swung his leg during pregame the ball was pushed far wide of the goalposts.

"I didn't want to be kicking in the first place and now we had this wind that was just moving the ball in all directions," he said. "It was ridiculous."

Behler was one of the best quarterbacks in the state, but the passing game was not going to work on this day. Forever flexible, Coats basically abandoned the Dallas Cowboys pro set and turned to the run option. Behler, Mitchell, and Steinmark were about to show the entire state of Colorado how to move the football on the ground.

Coats was beside himself when the Farmers turned the ball over four times in the first half. Instead of building a big lead, the score was tied 7–7 at halftime, thanks to an 8-yard run by Behler.

Coats knew that the opening drive of the third quarter would set the tone for the rest of the game. Taking possession at the Wheat Ridge 20-yard line, the Farmers finally put it all together. Behler carried on 7 of the 12 plays and gained 54 of the 80 yards. He handed off to Steinmark off right tackle for the 2-yard touchdown and the Farmers took a 13–7 lead. The try for the extra point provided one of the most embarrassing moments of Mitchell's kicking career.

"The wind was blowing so hard in my face that I knew there was no way I was going to make it," Mitchell said. "But I couldn't believe my eyes when I kicked it. The doggone wind was blowing so hard that it blew the ball back over my head."

The Wheat Ridge running game took over at that point en route to a 19–7 victory.

That day, Steinmark had impressed the college scouts in the pressbox by rushing 21 times for 106 yards, second only to Behler's 129. Still, his weight was bothersome for the high school recruiters who would be handing out the scholarships. Steinmark had slipped below 150 pounds for the first time in the long season, and his uniform hung loosely on him. His pants seemed baggy. Lining up next to the 200-pound Mitchell, Freddie looked like a junior high kid.

Air Force coach Ben Martin had watched the game from high above the stadium, and Steinmark saw him walking across the field afterward. He prayed that Martin had come to see him. Instead, he never said a word to him and walked straight up to Mitchell.

The next day, Steinmark told Linda, "Air Force likes to recruit little guys because pilots need to be small. If I can't go to Air Force, where can I go?"

Wheat Ridge's victory over Wasson was convincing, but not nearly as impressive as George Washington's 46–0 romp over La Junta in the other AAA semifinal game. Two unbeaten teams were headed for the state championship at Bears Stadium, and it was apropos that the George Washington Patriots of Denver, and the Wheat Ridge Farmers of Jefferson County, were ranked as the number one and two teams in the state.

Before there was a Mile High Stadium in Denver, the place was called Bears Stadium in deference to the Denver Bears, the AAA minor-league baseball team that was a source of pride for the people of the Rocky Mountain region. The stadium was built on the site of a former landfill in 1948. The 17,000-seat grandstand stretched from the left-field foul pole to the right-field foul pole. In 1960, capacity was increased to 34,000 as the Broncos of the fledgling AFL moved in.

In the opinion of *Post* high school writer Irv Moss, the overall talent of the Farmers would be worth a six-point edge over Washington High. The weather all week had been unusually warm for early December as the winds abated. The morning of the championship game, though, yet another front rolled in from the Rockies and the fans were dressed in winter clothes, gloves, and hats as they poured through the turnstiles at Bears Stadium just past noon.

Adjusting to the cold, Coats again forsook the passing game for the running of Steinmark, Behler, and Mitchell.

As the Farmers dressed in the home locker room that belonged to the Broncos, Coats approached Behler and said, "About the only passing we'll do today is on the sprint-out. We're gonna run it just like we did against Wasson. Whatever you do, don't forget Freddie."

Once again, Behler wanted to say, *How in the world could I forget Freddie?*

This time, Coats was in a gambling mood late in the first quarter when the Farmers faced a fourth-and-one at their own 29-yard line. Failure at that juncture would have left the Patriots less than 30 yards to travel for the opening touchdown of the game. Coats, however, knew that center Kent Cluck would blow open a hole large enough for Behler to wiggle through, and he did for the first down.

Running the option, Behler called upon himself for three straight running plays of 14, 6, and 27 yards. When the Farmers reached the 18-yard line, Behler remembered the words from Coats about the sprint-out pass. He would roll right, giving Steinmark the option of either running a short sideline route to the right, or taking off for the end zone. As they broke the huddle, Behler scanned the Washington defense. He knew that Steinmark would be bolting straight to the end zone.

"Two things I had to consider," he recalled. "The first was Freddie's speed. The second was the wind in my face. I threw the ball as far as I could and Freddie still had to slow down to catch it."

The reception was made at the goal and Steinmark glided into the end zone. Kicking into a whipping wind, Mitchell's extra point kick sailed wide of the right goalpost. The Farmers led 6–0.

All day, the Patriots would refuse to punt the ball to either Behler or Steinmark. This conservative plan cost them considerable field position. A punt angled for the sideline covered only 18 yards before it rolled out of bounds at the Wheat Ridge 48. Behler's intentions were clear as he worked the right side of the line with Mitchell and the left flank with Steinmark, calling 10 straight running plays that moved the ball to the Washington 2-yard line. On fourth down, Mitchell carried three tacklers into the end zone and proceeded to miss yet another extra point into the wind as the Farmers led 12–0.

On the ensuing kickoff, Washington halfback Rick Fisher began to seize control of the game. First, he returned the kickoff to the 41-yard line. He then carried the ball six straight times and scored a touchdown on a 16-yard run around right end. Wheat Ridge still led 12–7, but the momentum of the game was turning.

Early in the fourth quarter, it looked like the Patriots were coming all the way back when substitute quarterback Wink Wehner completed a pass to Dean Burchfield, who was so far behind the Wheat Ridge secondary that no one was going to catch him. Burchfield caught the ball at the 11-yard line and was running alone at the 2-yard line when he inexplicably lost control of the ball. It rolled into the end zone. Instead of diving on the loose football for a touchdown, Burchfield reached down to pick it up and promptly kicked it past the end line.

"I was over on the sideline and I was dying inside," Behler said. "I just knew this guy was going to score a touchdown that might beat us. Then all of a sudden, the ball is all over the ground and the coaches are yelling, 'Offense, get out on the field! Get out on the field!' "

Because the ball was kicked out of the end zone, it was ruled a touchback. Wheat Ridge got the ball at the 20-yard line, but could not move through the air or on the ground.

As the clock ticked down in the final five minutes, Washington quarterback Bruce Eggers was pass crazy. A quiet nervousness spread through the Wheat Ridge grandstand. So many times had the Farmers been close to a championship, only to be heartbroken in the end.

Eggers moved the ball to the Wheat Ridge 30 with slightly more than three minutes to play. He uncorked a high floater. The Patriots receiver was in position to make the catch until Steinmark came slashing across the field and intercepted. A sigh of relief swept through the Wheat Ridge side.

In the final minute of the game, Egger's passing moved the Patriots into Wheat Ridge territory again, but Steinmark intercepted the Washington quarterback at the 21-yard line. Not only had Steinmark scored the winning touchdown against Lakewood, he had saved the day in the state championship game.

The celebration was finally on. The players hoisted Coats onto their shoulders, and, instead of carrying him to the locker room, they carted their coach around the playing field for all to see. After a few minutes of joyriding, Coats began to yell, "Put me down, you mullets! Put me down!"

The celebration inside their locker room lasted almost an hour. Coats did most of the yelling. "I told you mullets you could win a state title! I told you."

As the team bus passed through North Denver en route to the Wheat Ridge campus, a crazy man came running out of a barbershop and into the middle of the street. He was still wearing the barber's white smock and there was shaving cream on his face.

"I just won five bucks on you guys! I just won five bucks on you guys!" he yelled.

It seemed the entire state of Colorado was celebrating. Wheat Ridge had finally won it all.

————

What else would Coats expect at the party celebrating the state championship? His players presented him with a bucket of fish—a dozen mullets over ice.

In presenting the smelly prize to Coats, Behler took the microphone.

"From one mullet to another mullet, this is your reward for finally making us champions. No way we could have ever done it without you, you mullet."

As Coats grinned from ear to ear, a tear rolled down his cheek.

"This bucket of mullets is dedicated to the best bunch of mullets I ever coached," Coats said. "But I gotta say something also about Freddie Steinmark. Without him, I don't think we would have even made it to the dang playoffs. Way to go, mullet."

Steinmark smiled, then hugged his coach. Even if he never participated in one play of college football, his high school career had been the greatest ride of his life.

Chapter 6

SO HAPPY TOGETHER

"Find something you are willing to die for, then live for it."
—1967 CLASS MOTTO AT WHEAT RIDGE HIGH

Linda and Freddie's favorite parking spot was on the edge of the woods about a block behind the Wheelers' home. Marion Wheeler's conniption could have been heard all the way to Denver if she had known what was occurring inside the Steinmarks' blue Mustang behind the fogged-up windows.

One night, Linda noticed that Freddie's mind was not on the task at hand. "What's wrong, Freddie?" she asked.

The young man sighed. "Linda, there's not a single major college that's going to give me a scholarship. They all think I'm a jockey."

It was all quite perplexing. Weeks earlier, Steinmark had won the *Denver Post*'s Golden Helmet Award as the best scholar-athlete in the state. The Colorado Hall of Fame had named him the state's Athlete of the Year. In spite of Mitchell getting the mother lode of the carries, Steinmark still finished fourth in the state with 699 rushing yards. His seven interceptions were the most in Colorado preps. Any college scout could have taken one look at Freddie and seen that his potential was without limits. Freddie could have outrun anyone in the state in full pads.

Surely the kind of recogntion that Steinmark was receiving should have earned him a place on the A-list for high school recruits at places like Nebraska, Colorado, Kansas, and even Notre Dame, his favorite university and the center of the American universe for his Catholic faith. Instead, his recent visit to Colorado started and ended with a thud when coach Eddie Crowder took one look at Freddie and said, "You're just too little."

The real slap in the face was that the Colorado campus was thirty miles from Wheat Ridge. Furthermore, Bobby Mitchell had already been offered scholarships in football and track, and several other Denver-area players were ready to sign with the Buffalos.

Steinmark's weight continued to plummet, thanks to his hectic schedule on the basketball court, further diminishing his chances for a scholarship. The Wheat Ridge hoops team had recently finished second in the district race with a 12-2 record. Steinmark would spend the rest of the spring and the summer playing baseball and there was no telling how much he might weigh when the 1967 football season rolled around.

Steinmark's best offer to date was from Dartmouth College, an Ivy League school in New Hampshire that certainly fit his academic profile. But how was Freddie going to pursue a career in pro sports with the promise of buying his mother a new Cadillac after spending four years at a small-time, second-rate athletic institution like Dartmouth? The only pro football player produced by Dartmouth over the last ten years was Jake Crouthamel, who played all of two games in 1960 for the Boston Patriots of the fledgling AFL. Most of the noteworthy NFL players from Dartmouth played all the way back in the 1920s.

Freddie was depressed by the lack of attention from the big-time colleges. Little did he know that Linda was feeling the same way. Linda figured that if Freddie received a football scholarship at Colorado she could convince Selby Wheeler to send her to Boulder. Hanover, New Hampshire, was out of the question.

Freddie visited Dartmouth and came home with a favorable opinion. Gloria Steinmark said she would be proud to have an Ivy Leaguer in the family. Freddie knew that Dartmouth would provide a diploma worth a gold mine and an engineering degree that could launch his career into one of the largest East Coast companies. Pro football or baseball, however, would be out of reach. After much debate around the Steinmark home, Freddie decided to make the decision on his own. He turned thumbs-down on Hanover and Linda breathed a sigh of relief.

Not long after that decision, Coats called Freddie into his office to talk about his college future.

"Freddie, I think you need to focus on playing safety in college," Coats said. "These recruiters just don't see you as a running back because, quite frankly, son, you just don't have the size. I don't see you growing three inches and gaining thirty pounds by the fall."

This was a bitter pill to swallow. Steinmark had fashioned himself as a star in the making. He was an all-state selection in both football and baseball. His rushing average from the 1966 season was more than 7 yards per carry, and he had returned 3 punts and kickoffs for touchdowns. The college scouts hardly considered him a "burner," but few players around the country were as quick as Steinmark. He possessed an athletic package that could fit with practically any program.

Steinmark wrote letters to Notre Dame, Duke, Purdue, Wyoming, Oklahoma, and Alabama. Notre Dame sent back a form letter and a short questionnaire. To Steinmark, this was like a rejection notice. Not so, remembers retired coach Ara Parseghian.

"If we got a letter from a kid saying that he wanted to play at Notre Dame, we always went through several steps," Parseghian recalled forty years later. "It meant we would ask his high school coach for the films and we would follow up."

Parseghian, who read every letter, said he could not remember a communication from Steinmark.

"But that was 1966," he said. "That was forty-four years. I don't know if my memory is that good."

Steinmark soon found that practically no one was interested. Alabama asked to see his films and Purdue invited him to West Lafayette for a visit. That was it. Not even the University of Wyoming, some 150 miles way in Laramie, seemed to care.

Over the next six weeks, Coats diligently worked the phones on behalf of Mitchell and Steinmark. He was getting nowhere on behalf of the latter. It seemed that every major college coach in the country wanted Mitchell and was ready to dismiss Steinmark without even looking at films. Coats called his former Odessa buddy, Hayden Fry, who was coaching at SMU, but did not even get a returned call regarding Steinmark.

Coats's ace in the hole was University of Texas defensive coordinator Mike Campbell. They had become fast friends during Coats's ten seasons at El Paso's Ysleta High, when Campbell flew a private plane all the way across Texas on several occasions to visit the coach and his top prospects.

Flying was nothing new to Campbell. His career began with the Air Force during World War II when he was based in Sicily. Campbell's lifelong passion had been to pilot airplanes and the outbreak of the war at least provided that opportunity. He flew twenty-five of the most dangerous bombing missions against the Romanian refineries. Several times, he barely made it back to the base alive, and saw more than half of the Allied planes shot down. Upon returning home, he put the bloody experience behind him and rarely talked about it.

For a couple of years, Campbell had lost track of Coats until the latter placed a call to Austin in the spring of 1967. Coats was quick to tout his two players. Coats knew Mitchell would be an easy sell to the Texas program because of his size and strength, and the fact that he had led the state in scoring during a state championship year. Campbell quickly put together a flight plan.

"Well, hell, Red, I'll be up there in the next couple of days," Campbell said. "We don't recruit many boys outside of Texas because we just don't have to. But I'll tell Darrell [Royal] that you wouldn't pull my leg."

Campbell flew with secondary coach Fred Akers to the Denver airport. That first night in Wheat Ridge, Campbell took Mitchell to dinner and was impressed with every physical aspect about him. Still, Campbell wondered why Mitchell spent most of the evening cutting up his girlfriend's steak and cooing in her ear.

The next day, Coats, Campbell, and Akers sat down to review some game film from the championship season. The Texas coaches instantly liked what they saw of Mitchell. At the same time, neither Campbell nor Akers could take their eyes off the boy wearing number 43. They watched Steinmark run circles around tacklers, then hit with the force of a big, fast linebacker.

"That boy Freddie will knock their butts off," Campbell said. "Where'd he learn to play football like that?"

"Freddie was a complete player before I got here," Coats said. "But nobody except the little schools want him because he's too small. Even Eddie Crowder up in Boulder doesn't want him."

"What the hell does Eddie Crowder know?" Campbell said with a laugh. "When was the last time he won a national championship?"

"Never," Coats said.

After watching the game film for most of the afternoon, Campbell told Coats, "Red, I want Mitchell and Steinmark to visit our campus. Mitchell is a shoo-in. But Freddie's got a chance with Darrell. He likes little-bitty boys. One of our best players a few years ago was Jimmy Saxton and he was no bigger than a popcorn fart."

Coats grinned. "Mike, you've made my day. You tell Darrell that Freddie's got a heart bigger than Dallas. He'll come to play every down."

Before leaving town, Campbell and Akers stopped by the Steinmark family's house to get a look at Freddie. When the youngster came to the door, they thought he was the younger brother, Sammy.

"I was actually stunned the first time that I saw him," Akers said. "He was even smaller than we thought. Fortunately, we liked what we saw on the game films."

The radio airwaves during this era were filled with songs by the Beatles, the Rolling Stones, Elvis Presley, the Beach Boys, and Herman's Hermits. Freddie and Linda always turned up the volume when they heard a song by The Turtles, a California band with an interesting sound and a nice beat.

When they heard their song, Freddie would pull the car to the side of the road, where they hugged and kissed. The name of the song was "Happy Together."

They sang the chorus over and over: *"I can't see me loving nobody but you, for all my life. When you're with me, baby, the skies'll be blue, for all my life."*

The couple was so in love that they were already talking about marriage—except when they were around Marion Campbell. They opened a checking account together and deposited their lunch money with hopes their nest egg would build into a down payment on a home.

Deciding where they were going to college was a different matter. Freddie threw Linda a curveball one day when he told her he was traveling down to Austin for a visit at the University of Texas.

"This opportunity just came out of the blue," he said. "Red's got a friend down there who coaches the defense and he watched some film of me. Bobby and I are flying down there to take a look at the place. I never imagined in my wildest dreams some place called the University of Texas might want me."

Linda was speechless. If Freddie bolted for Texas they might not see each other for four years. She needed to come up with a plan.

On the day Freddie was to fly to Austin, Linda drove him to Stapleton Airport. They said a tearful farewell at the gate and she watched the American Airlines jet taxi and sprint to the end of the runway before bursting into the blue sky. She stood there and wondered if it was over between them.

Sliding behind the wheel of her Jeep, she pushed the key into the ignition. Their song was already playing on the radio.

Linda drove for a block, pulled the car to the curb, and bawled like a baby. This was a moment she had not prepared for, and never had she felt so all alone.

The trip to Austin was an emotional one for Freddie, too. He tried to imagine how he would feel if Darrell Royal took one look at him and said, "Son, I'm really sorry. You're too doggone small." How would Freddie feel if Mitchell got a scholarship and Royal sent him back to Wheat Ridge empty-handed?

The last few days, Steinmark had been devouring all of the food he could get his hands on. Before leaving the Steinmark house, he stuck one of the game programs in his luggage because it listed him at 165 pounds, about fifteen pounds more than he actually weighed. Then he dug into the back of his closet and pulled a pair of cowboy boots on his feet. He rarely wore the boots, but knew the high heels would make him appear taller.

Three hours after landing in Austin, Steinmark and Mitchell were sitting across the long, oaken desk from Royal. Freddie could feel his heart thumping. He knew that Mitchell was a cinch. This might be his last chance. Royal was his only salvation.

Sitting across the desk, reading from some notes, Royal looked up and said to Freddie, "I watched some of your game film and you've got great speed. Son, you're a real hitter. I think I'm going to want you to play defense and return punts. What do you think of that?"

Steinmark tried to speak, but the words would not come out. The coach did not know what to think.

"Maybe you want to give it some time to decide," Royal said. "But . . ."

"Oh, no, Coach, I want to play football at the University of Texas," Steinmark blurted. "Coach, there's just no doubt about that." His face was now radiating. He took a deep breath and said, "But Coach, don't you think I'm too small? Everybody thinks I'm too small."

Royal took a long look at a young man he considered quite handsome.

"Son, let me tell you something very interesting," he said. "I didn't get to the University of Oklahoma until I was twenty-five years old because of the war. I was just about your size. I quarter-backed the Oklahoma Sooners to a national championship one year. On defense, I broke the school record for interceptions. I punted and did practically everything. I know you can do it because I did it. I don't care how big you are. Freddie, I'm very impressed with the way you play the game of football."

Freddie said, "Jesus, Coach, I can't believe what I'm hearing. You want me to play football at the University of *Texas*?"

"You're doggone right I do," Royal said with a grin. "You're going to fit right well here in Austin."

Freddie wanted to say, *Coach you will never regret this. I will start every game for you at the University of Texas. We will win the national championship.* Instead, he decided to save that prediction for a later date.

Royal turned to Mitchell and said, "Well, I guess you'll be coming to Texas with Freddie."

Mitchell smiled. "Coach, I'd walk all the way to Austin."

Back in Wheat Ridge, Linda was preparing her speech for Selby Wheeler, reading the morning newspaper. Here was an intelligent man with an open mind. She hoped he could accept the idea of her going to the University of Texas. For God's sake, he was *from* Texas.

She sat down next to him on the couch, and said, "Daddy, as you know, I've been looking at a lot of different colleges and my grades are very good. There are a couple of women's private universities that have accepted me. Stephens is one of them and it's going to cost you a lot of money."

Her father nodded. Linda knew she was making some progress.

For years, Linda had planned a college major of Spanish studies. She had checked the World Book Encyclopedias to learn that Texas was the number-two bilingual state in the country behind California. The University of Texas' Spanish program was second to none.

"Daddy, I've decided on the University of Texas because of Spanish studies. It's going to save you a lot of money. It's the—"

"Linda," he said, "do you want to go to Texas because of Freddie?"

"Daddy, it's the—"

"Linda, is this all about Freddie?"

"Yes, it is," she said, her anxiety rising.

"Then it's okay with me," he said. "You'll be going to Texas."

Linda jumped to her feet and blurted, "I can't believe what I'm hearing."

"It's true," her father said. "Now we've got to figure out a way to break this news to your mother."

She could not wait to call Freddie.

Chapter 7

TEAM MANAGER

By the time the Texas Yearlings freshman team reported for practice in September of 1967, the varsity had been butting heads for more than two weeks. They were preparing for a season that held great promise. Little wonder that thousands of Longhorns fans were riding around the state in long Fleetwood Cadillacs and banged-up pickup trucks sporting bumper stickers that read, YEAR OF THE HORNS.

Like most of the varsity players, Mike Campbell IV was curious about the freshman class that had been widely hyped and ranked number one in the Southwest Conference. One of the most highly recruited players in America was Steve Worster, who had committed to LSU, then changed his mind at the last minute and switched to Texas. Among the high school All-Americans were linebacker Scott Henderson from Dallas, wide receiver Charles "Cotton" Speyrer of Port Arthur, tackle Greg Ploetz of Sherman, and the best defensive linemen of all, Bill Atessis of Houston Jones High School.

One hot afternoon, Campbell, the son of Texas defensive coordinator Mike Campbell III, was walking back to the dorm after practice when he decided to take a seat in the makeshift stands next to the freshman field. He was also curious about this blue-chip class. The freshman practice field was situated about a hundred yards from where the varsity Longhorns worked out each day. Campbell wanted to find out just how talented these players were. He also wanted to take stock of the prospects that might try to take his job the next year.

Campbell was observing the defensive backs when he spotted a youngster who looked like he had sneaked onto the premises from a local junior high. That day, the freshmen were working out in shorts and T-shirts, without helmets, and Campbell could see all of their faces.

"This kid looked like he was fifteen years old and he was just tiny," Campbell recalled. "I said to myself that he had to be one of the equipment managers. He sure as hell didn't look like a football player."

A few days later, Campbell walked past the freshmen field again as the players were practicing in full uniforms. Once more, he sat down in the bleachers and watched a full-scale scrimmage. The little guy took off his helmet to fix his chinstrap and Campbell got a glimpse of his face.

"My God, I couldn't believe my eyes," Campbell said. "This was the same kid I thought was one of the team managers. But he was out there knocking heads with the best of them. In fact, he was knocking everybody silly. The kid could flat play. I was amazed. Turns out, it was Freddie Steinmark."

Those early weeks in Austin, Steinmark was a novelty among the Longhorn behemoths who were muscled up and filled with enmity. Some of the players boasted reputations as drinkers, hell-raisers, and fighters and not many men around Austin were willing to cross them. Darrell Royal loved to recruit players straight off the oil derricks, the ranches, and the stockyards. Some looked like grown men by the time they got to Austin. Royal's favorite of all time was the 235-pound human wrecking ball known as Tommy Nobis, the linebacker with the size-19 neck. Nobis became a two-way starter as a sophomore in 1963 and, two years later, won the Maxwell Award as the best college football player in America. Royal once said of Nobis, "Players keep getting bigger, smarter, strong and faster, and Tommy is one of the latest. Aside from the super ability, he's one of those trained pigs you love. He'll laugh and jump right in the slop for you."

Next from the assembly line of tough hombres was Diron Talbert, who arrived in Austin in 1964 and immediately terrorized opponents and teammates alike. Diron (1964–66) was the third brother to play football at Texas following Charlie (1957–59) and Don (1959–61).

The Talbert presence could be felt in Austin for nine straight years, both on and off the field. The brothers were hard drinkers and tougher players. Sometimes the drinking led to fighting in saloons around Austin. A sign posted on the front door of a bar along Twelfth street once read, NO SHIRTS, NO SHOES, NO TALBERTS.

Compared to the Talberts, Steinmark looked like an altar boy trying to find his way to the Catholic Student Center. More than 125 freshmen were suited up for the first few weeks of practice and the odds of an unknown player like Steinmark making his way seemed incredibly long.

"We had a very impressive group of freshmen," said Henderson, who would become close friends with Steinmark. "We were supposed to be the freshmen class that turned Texas football around. We had some big players and some hitters. But I want to tell you that Freddie thrived in that atmosphere right from the very start."

The sporting press dubbed the 1967 freshmen class the "Worster Bunch" for the big, blue-chip fullback. Worster was earmarked for greatness from the moment he stepped onto campus. The son of an oil roughneck, Worster hailed from one of the toughest towns in Texas, a brawling outpost situated deep in the heart of the refineries next to the Neches River and the Cow Bayou. Bridge City is a stone's throw from the Louisiana border and about twenty miles from Lake Charles. Folks in that part of Cajun Country considered Bridge City to be part of Louisiana, so it was assumed that Worster would accept the brand-new Camaro offered by LSU and drive it all the way to Baton Rouge.

That was before he visited Austin and shook hands with Darrell Royal, the man with the stern eyes.

"I know that you've been offered things at other schools that are trying to sign you," Royal began. "But I can assure you that you're not getting a dime from Texas. We don't cheat like the other bastards. So if you've got some pride, sign with the University of Texas."

That sales pitch would have failed with most testosterone-driven eighteen-year-olds possessing an eye for women and a cold Schlitz. It succeeded, however, with Worster, who signed on the dotted line and never looked back. He did this in spite of the fact that Texas had not won a Southwest Conference championship since 1963.

The Texas blue chippers had come from all over the state and none had ever heard of Freddie Steinmark or Bobby Mitchell. Steinmark and Mitchell were the first out-of-state players recruited at the University of Texas in the 1960s.

Two days before they were to report to Austin for the start of football drills, Mitchell had pulled up to the curb in front of the Steinmark duplex in a smoke-belching blue 1952 Ford ready for the junkyard.

"Hey, Freddie," Mitchell yelled. "How you like my new ride? I'll pick you up in the morning and we'll drive down to Austin together."

Steinmark's smile melted.

"No offense, Bobby, but I think I'm catching an airplane," he said. "No way I'm riding in that old clunker. Shoot, Bobby, you're gonna get stuck out in the wilds of Texas and you'll never make it to Austin. I want to be there before practice starts."

Mitchell's old Ford might have been the ugliest piece of work on the Colorado highways, but it offered independence. It inspired daydreams of warm evenings cruising the Austin streets with pretty young blondes. In a matter of days, Mitchell would have his coming-out party. Without wheels, the newest Big Man On Campus at U.T. would be just another dumb freshman from the sticks.

Mitchell knew that nothing was going to stop him once he got to Austin. He could not wait for the boys down at Texas to see him thundering around end like Green Bay's Jimmy Taylor, hell-bent for the end zone.

"I knew that I was about to set the world on fire," he recalled. "I thought I was going to be *the* running back of the century at the University of Texas."

The two-laner out of Denver shot southeast through the dusty Panhandle town of Dalhart en route to Amarillo. Mitchell noticed that the telephone poles lining the highways were badly bent by the battering north winds. In Amarillo, Mitchell forgot to fill the car up with fuel, and soon his eyes were searching the flat prairie for any sign of a gas station. He saw neither the Texaco star nor the Esso Tiger. Freddie's words rang in his ears. *Shoot, Bobby, you'll get stuck in the wilds of Texas and* . . .

"Every time I stopped for gas, I also had to put water in the radiator," Mitchell recalled. "After Amarillo, I was running out of both pretty fast. I was out in the middle of nowhere. I just knew that I was going to break down, just like Freddie said."

Mitchell angled toward Wichita Falls and prayed. Finally, in the tiny town of Memphis (Texas), he came upon a one-pump station that saved him. He promised himself that for the rest of the trip he would keep one eye on the fuel gauge.

The long, lonely highway, along with the vast emptiness of West Texas, provided Mitchell with plenty of time to think about where he was going. His dreams were as big as the Texas sky. Playing football at the University of Texas had been the boy's goal since 1963, when he lived briefly in Dallas and the Longhorns won the national championship. His father was an insurance salesman and a man who rarely allowed grass to grow beneath his feet. He soon moved the family to southern California, then turned around a year later and took Bobby and his mother to Colorado.

"Texas had been on my mind for four years, ever since we left there," Mitchell said. "I never wanted to leave, really. Getting back to Texas was my main goal in life. I loved everything about it. I was ready to get out of the cold of Colorado. Coming off the success that Freddie and I'd had in high school, I just knew everything was going to work out in Texas."

While Mitchell was chugging toward Austin, Steinmark arrived on campus four hours ahead of the scheduled reporting time. He toted his bags down the first floor hallway of Moore-Hill Hall and read the placard on the door. "Mitchell-Steinmark." He was surprised. Somehow he did not figure that the boys from Colorado would be roommates. Little did he know that freshman coach Bill Ellington tried to pair roommates according to their common interests. This was an attempt to combat homesickness. In the case of Steinmark-Mitchell, Ellington's thinking was that two out-of-staters from the same high school would have already formed a bond. He did not know they were as different as the topography of the Rocky Mountains and the flat sands along the Pecos River in West Texas.

In truth, Steinmark and Mitchell were not the best of friends. Sure, they liked each other and got along well. They represented the leading rushing tandem in Colorado the previous season. After the football season, though, Steinmark and Mitchell traveled in opposite directions—Steinmark to the basketball gymnasium and Mitchell to the shotput ring. In the late spring and summer, Steinmark played shortstop while Mitchell spent most of his time laboring in the weight room, preparing for the next football season.

By the time that Mitchell arrived in Wheat Ridge his sophomore year, Steinmark was already an established sports star. In spite of his instant success on the track-and-field team, Mitchell hardly lived in the public eye. Even though he broke the state record with a shot-put heave of 62' 8", most of the kids ignored the achievement.

Steinmark and Mitchell stood at the opposite ends of the spectrum in social life. Steinmark was the squeaky clean Catholic kid who went to church five times a week, while Mitchell stayed out late many nights cultivating a taste for cold beer. Mitchell ran with one of the fastest crowds in Wheat Ridge, Steinmark with the slowest.

At times, it seemed they could not keep their girlfriends straight. A quick glance at the 1967 yearbook conveyed the feeling that Bobby and Linda Wheeler might have been dating. They were voted "Prom Royalty" and the full-page picture of the couple gave the impression they were meant for each other. Near the front of the yearbook was the photograph of Freddie and Candy Kesner as "Homecoming Royalty."

Not surprising, Steinmark and Mitchell held different plans for their high school honeys. A couple of weeks before taking off, Mitchell broke up with his girlfriend, telling her that the long-distance relationship would never work. No way was Freddie leaving his girlfriend in

Colorado. Linda Wheeler would be flying into Austin in about two weeks to enroll at U.T. They were planning to be married after graduation.

A half hour after arriving at Moore Hill Hall, Steinmark's clothes were neatly hung in the closet and he was moving at a fast pace toward Memorial Stadium. Walking up San Jacinto Street, he spotted a low, black cloud and heard the growl of the 1952 blue Ford. Mitchell had finally hit town. His friend rolled down the window and said, "Who're you rooming with, Freddie boy?"

"You, Mitch," he said. "And you'd better clean up your act."

Mitchell laughed. "Whoa. Does this mean I have to start going to church?"

"Every day," Steinmark said, smiling.

Upon walking into the freshman locker room that first day and scanning the roster, Steinmark could not believe what he was seeing. He was listed number one at the safety position even before he put on the pads. It seemed hard to believe that the player virtually every college had shunned was starting on one of the most coveted freshman teams in the history of U.T.

Standing next to Steinmark that day, Mitchell was scanning the offensive roster when his heart sank into his shoes. Hoping to find his name on the halfback list, he read from top to bottom. Nothing. Then he checked the depth chart for the fullbacks. He was number five. *How is this possible? I led the state of Colorado in scoring, led my team to a state championship. Don't they know who I am?*

Mitchell wanted to get behind the wheel of the old Ford and drive all the way back to Colorado.

It was not surprising that Worster was already ranked by the coaching staff as the preseason number-one fullback. But Mitchell saw names ahead of him that made no sense, players like Billy Dale, Jay Cormier, and Terry Collins. Because Collins stood only 5'6" and weighed 170 pounds, he would become known as the "little teapot."

"Anyone who knew anything about football knew that I was a

better running back than any of those guys except Worster," Mitchell recalled. "I just was. But because I was the Colorado out-of-state boy, and they were from Texas, they got their chance instead of me."

Mitchell learned that Collins hailed from San Angelo High School, and that his head coach, Emory Bellard, had been hired by Darrell Royal months earlier to coach the Texas offense.

"Most of the guys ahead of me on the depth chart were from West Texas and had a personal relationship with Bellard," Mitchell said. "The Texas coaches knew virtually nothing about me. Mike Campbell had come to Denver to take me to dinner one time. He watched some film of me for just one afternoon. Meanwhile, he was watching the Texas guys play their high school games every Friday night."

In that era, the biggest Texas sporting event of the summer was the high school all-star game in July that was rotated annually between Dallas, Houston, and San Antonio. Royal and staff were front and center at the 1967 game to watch more than twenty of their players already signed by Texas.

Meanwhile, Steinmark and Mitchell were playing in the Colorado High School All-Star game, leading the North squad to a 41–7 victory over the South. Not a single Texas coach showed up for the game. Instead, Royal and his staff were on their way to Hershey, Pennsylvania, for the annual Big 33 game between the high school all-stars from Texas and Pennsylvania. The Big 33 game pitted the top players from Texas and Pennsylvania for four years beginning in 1964. The Texas team was coached by legendary quarterback Bobby Layne, who played at Texas in the late 1940s. Eleven of his thirty-three players were future Longhorns.

The 1967 Texas team defeated the Pennsylvania all-stars by the score 45–14. Royal and his coaches came away with a greater familiarity with the players who would suit up for Texas. Needless to say, Mitchell was not prominently on their minds as two-a-days began in early September.

"It was preordained before I got to Texas that I wasn't going to get a chance to play my freshman year," Mitchell said. "That's all there was to it. I really believe that the Texas coaches had already made some promises to the kids from Texas about how much playing time they would get. They never made those promises to me."

Unlike the forgotten Mitchell, Steinmark was the golden boy from the moment he walked onto campus. Royal was not kidding when he told Steinmark that his size would not determine his playing time. This was especially gratifying for a youngster who tipped the scales at 154 pounds that first day on campus. Not since Jimmy Saxton made the Shorthorns roster in 1958 at 145 pounds had any Texas freshman been smaller than Steinmark.

All Steinmark had to do was study Saxton's history to catch a glimpse of his future. Saxton was voted a first-team All-American running back in 1961 and finished third in the Heisman Trophy balloting to Ernie Davis of Syracuse. It could be said that Steinmark had some small shoes to fill.

The ironic twist to the story is that Mitchell, not Steinmark, had initially drawn the interest of the Texas coaches. More than likely, Texas would have overlooked Steinmark if Campbell had not traveled to Colorado to recruit Mitchell. That first day of practice, however, their roles were reversed. Soon, the buzz around the entire football complex was about the Steinmark kid.

"I was just amazed at the little guy," said Bill Atessis, a freshman in 1967. "You knew right off the bat that the kid could run. But what surprised us even more is that he could hit. He wouldn't back down from anybody. *Anybody.* He hit Steve Worster as hard as anyone on our defense."

Unlike most defensive players, Steinmark did not need to bend his knees and dip his shoulder to deliver a solid blow. He slammed into the ball carrier at full speed and brought him down on the spot most of the time. It was much like the tackling form that Cliff Harris made famous with the Dallas Cowboys. The biggest difference was that Steinmark was forty pounds lighter than Harris.

In 1967, Bill Ellington was the head coach of the freshman team.

In most cases, though, Royal and Campbell were making the personnel decisions and they made it clear to Ellington that they wanted Steinmark to start every freshman game.

On the fourth day of freshman workouts, a curious Campbell walked down from the varsity field to observe the new recruits. He stood behind the defensive unit and signaled Ellington to join him.

"What about Steinmark?" he said.

"Nothing to worry about, Coach," Ellington said. "He hits like a ton and he's not afraid of anything."

Just as Ellington made that assessment, Steinmark cut in front of wide receiver Charles "Cotton" Speyrer and intercepted a pass, returning it up the sideline for a touchdown.

"That's his second interception of the day," Ellington said. "This kid must be a geometry major. He sure knows the shortest angles to the football. It's like he's got a sixth sense."

While most of the freshman players were amazed at Steinmark's football maturity, Mitchell had seen it all before.

"Nothing surprised me about Freddie," Mitchell said. "I'd seen it many times. Still, I think the Texas coaches were amazed that he rose up like he did that first few days of freshman practices. He knew where to be at all times and he could hit you. Freddie was just flat-out good."

The best recruiting class anyone could remember at U.T. reeled off four straight victories with ease. Steinmark recorded two interceptions and led the conference freshmen in punt returns. The fifth and final game would be played against Texas A&M in San Antonio and, once more, the matchup looked like a blowout. A couple of days before the game, Ellington stood before the team and asked, "How many of you guys have not been in a game this season and feel like you deserve to play?"

Mitchell had not played one down. In fact, his only participation on game days was standing behind the goal posts during warm-ups and catching kicks. How could a player offered more than twenty major scholarships be suddenly reduced to a fifth stringer shagging pregame field goals?

When Ellington asked who wanted to play, several of the scrubs raised their hands, but not Mitchell.

"I was just too prideful," he said. "I didn't want to play if that's all there was. Normally a guy who was feeling sorry for himself would have raised his hand and jumped at the opportunity. I just didn't care. I wasn't going to raise my hand so I could go out there and play for two or three minutes."

With Mitchell on the sideline, the Texas freshman handled Texas A&M by the score of 45–0. Steinmark registered his third and fourth interceptions of the season and returned a punt 76 yards for a touchdown. His future could not have seemed brighter.

Mitchell, on the other hand, felt left out. One night as they were studying in the dorm room, Steinmark could tell that his friend was down.

"Just hang in there and one of these days you'll get your break," Steinmark told him. "You know that you're a great football player and now you've got to show the coaches. We've got a long way to go before our football careers are over."

"Thanks, Freddie boy," Mitchell said. "I am going to keep that in mind."

Never had Mitchell felt so out of place. Weeks earlier, he had been informed that freshmen were not allowed to have cars, so he drove the old Ford down to a local used car lot and sold it for $150. At the moment, he had no girlfriend and no wheels to find one. Freddie had a steady girlfriend and a starting job. Mitchell knew nothing but heartache.

During his freshman year, Mitchell could look around the Texas campus and see some of the most beautiful women anywhere. Without a car, he could not make his move. The suntanned blondes wanted nothing to do with him. That fall, Mitchell spent a lot of time ogling photos of one of the most stunningly beautiful women on the U.T. campus. In the dorm room of backup quarterback Greg Lott, Farrah Fawcett's modeling photos were plastered all over the walls.

Fawcett was from Corpus Christi and enrolled at Texas in the fall of 1965. She pledged the Delta Delta Delta sorority and met

Lott during the fall semester of her freshman year. They began a relationship the following spring when they met again at a fraternity party.

"She had on a black crop top and leopard-skin pedal pushers that looked like they had been painted on," Lott recalled. "And she could dance. I danced with her and fell in love with her. I fell absolutely blind in love with her."

During her sophomore year, Fawcett was chosen as one of the "Ten Most Beautiful Coeds" from the university. A Hollywood publicist saw the photos, placed a phone call to her, and over the course of a year, convinced her to move to Hollywood. By 1969, she was doing commercials for Wella Balsam shampoo and Noxzema shaving cream. In her most famous TV spot, she rubbed shaving cream all over the face of New York Jets quarterback Joe Namath. In 1976, the famous poster of her wearing a one-piece bathing suit sold 12 million copies. It was the same year she began playing the "golden girl," Jill Munroe, in one of the most famous TV shows of the 1970s, *Charlie's Angels*.

Of course, Mitchell already knew all about Farrah Fawcett. He also knew he would never find a girl like her.

Chapter 8

THE KING IS ALMOST DEAD

"The sun don't shine on the same ol' dog's rear end every day."
—DARRELL K. ROYAL

Darrell Royal could not remember the last time he felt the sun shine on any part of his body. In December of 1967, the Longhorns were coming off a third straight disappointing season. Losing to Texas A&M 10–7 in the final game was the biggest embarrassment of the decade. The Aggies were so proud of the victory that they left the scoreboard lit for the next nine months.

So disappointed was Royal with yet another 6-4 record that he announced he would not accept a bowl invitation of any kind. The coach rolled up his sleeves and went to work on the 1968 season. He knew that successes of the past would not be duplicated until he embraced the relentless work ethic of his early years at Texas.

Four years removed from a national championship season, the crickets were chirping. The newspaper columnists were writing that if Texas did not win the Southwest Conference championship in 1968, Royal could go back to Oklahoma and stay there.

Royal wanted to blame it on the stupid YEAR OF THE HORNS bumper sticker unveiled four months earlier in September. Texas lost the first two games to USC and Texas Tech, and soon there was another bumper sticker going around town: JUST WAIT TILL '68.

Darrell Royal knew he was in trouble when the phone call came from Governor John Connally after the 1967 season, inviting him and his wife, Edith, to a weekend retreat in the Hill Country near Wimberley.

"When we had a bad season, John would call just to see how I was doing," Royal remembered. "He usually didn't call when we were winning big. But he was always there for me when things went bad. He was ready to give me a pep talk. I needed one."

Never before in his coaching career had Royal felt this low. The 1967 season represented his third straight four-loss effort. It seemed incomprehensible that a man who had saved the program in 1957, then won a national championship in 1963, could be standing in judgment. No longer were the Longhorns one of the elitist bullies of college football.

For the first time in many years, the press was questioning Royal's use of talent, the wealthy alums were tired of spending big bucks on a mediocre program, and the fans were saying the players were "half-assing it."

Were the fans spoiled? Yes, when you consider what the Longhorns accomplished during a 4½-year stretch. From the first game of the 1961 season to the fifth game of 1965, the Longhorns compiled a sterling record of 44-3-1. During that stretch, they were in the Associated Press Top Ten all forty-eight weeks. They were ranked number one nineteen times. If not for a 6–0 loss to TCU in 1962, and a 14–13 defeat by Arkansas in 1964, Texas would have won two more national titles. The loss to Arkansas was especially heartbreaking in that Texas failed to convert a two-point conversion pass in the final minute.

The bottom fell out for the Longhorns after the fifth game of 1965. Ironically, it was a last-minute 27–24 loss to Arkansas that sent Texas into a tailspin. From that defeat to the final game of 1967, the Longhorns stumbled to a record of 15-12-1. Hardly the stuff of national champions.

Royal accepted much of the blame for the Longhorns' swoon. Everyone, including him, had gotten lazy.

"Every weekend, it seemed that I was gone on the road for some banquet or something," he remembered. "I missed a lot of recruiting. Saturday is when the high school seniors are coming to the campus for their visits. They showed up and I was nowhere to be found. Other coaches around the SWC were saying to them, 'Well, you met me. But did you meet Darrell Royal when you were down in Austin?' No, they hadn't."

Royal reorganized the scouting strategy and made sure that Mike Campbell had plenty of fuel in his airplane. For the first time in several years, the Texas recruiters rolled up their sleeves and reached beyond the state borders to grab Steinmark and Mitchell out of Colorado. In 1968, they were going to start a new dynasty with the "Worster Bunch."

Backed into a corner, Royal knew there was only one way out. He decided to rebuild his team's toughness from the inside out. There would be a reemphasis on conditioning and fundamentals, a balls-out effort to toughen both the mind and body. After the first few days of spring drills in 1968, some thought he was borrowing liberally from the blueprint designed by Paul "Bear" Bryant at Texas A&M in 1954. That year, the team traveled to Junction for preseason camp and seventy-three players quit the team in ten days. It was the most brutal training camp in the history of college football. Still, it would become the springboard to a Southwest Conference championship two years later when the Aggies finished 9-0-1.

As spring practice began at Texas in April of 1968, Royal was hoping for the same result. He called the coaches together for what he considered the most important staff meeting in his eleven seasons at U.T.

"I want you to work their butts off," he told them. "Don't ever let up. I'm not telling you to cuss them. I'm not telling you to demean them. I'm telling you to work them until they are dead-ass tired. Work them until they grasp the gravity of the situation. There will be no more quitting in the fourth quarter."

The night before the start of spring drills, Bobby Mitchell lay on his twin bed inside the cramped dormitory room that he shared with Freddie Steinmark. He stared at the ceiling for hours and said nothing. The silence was stifling. Steinmark was more accustomed to a chatty Mitchell. He could tell his roommate was depressed. His energy level was so low that he often went days without shaving. His hair was much longer than it had been during their days in Wheat Ridge.

Unable to bear the uneasy silence, Steinmark said, "You know, Bobby, you need to stop thinking about quitting. Going back to Colorado isn't going to solve a dang thing. You'll just have to start over somewhere else, and that's not going to be easy, either."

Mitchell rubbed the whiskers on his chin and contemplated the words. It seemed that nothing was ever going to cheer him up. Six months earlier, he had arrived at the University of Texas with a truckload of piss and vinegar. At the time, nothing was going to stop a determined young man from his appointed glory. Alas, in the midst of his second semester, he was not sure if the game had not passed him by.

"You know, Freddie boy," Mitchell said, his head down, "I didn't participate in one doggone play during my freshman season. If I can't play on the freshman team, I sure as hell can't play on the varsity."

Mitchell looked up to see the familiar warm smile. It had been stated many times that Freddie Steinmark was wise beyond his years. His maturity was unmatched among the college crowd. He could decipher a problematic situation and deliver the proper solution in no time. He knew more about life than most adults twice his age. Freddie rarely spoke long or loudly, but people were always drawn to him. There was an air of destiny about him.

"Bobby, you're a great football player," Steinmark said. "I've known that from the day I met you. Shoot, you ran the football in high school like you owned it. Every time we needed a tough yard, you got it. I still don't understand why the coaches won't give you a chance."

"I'm not so sure they're not going to kick me off the team," Mitchell said. "I've got to go to a meeting tomorrow morning with Coach Royal. What could that all be about?"

Mitchell knew that being called into Royal's office could be as pleasant as cutting off your big toe.

As he walked to the stadium the next morning, nightmarish thoughts flooded his mind. He visualized himself sitting down in front of the old oaken desk and hearing these words:

Bobby, I'm sorry, but we're going to have to take your scholarship back. Son, you just haven't performed. We brought you in here with high hopes, and quite frankly, boy, you've played like a pissant.

Mitchell peered at a man who sat ramrod straight in his chair with every hair in place. There was never any question about who was in charge at the University of Texas. Some of the players called him "Daddy D," but never to his face. His office was as neat and orderly as the First Baptist Church. A knot formed in Mitchell's stomach as he waited for Royal to speak.

Royal cleared his throat and read silently from a long typewritten sheet. The man had done his homework. Mitchell had heard about Royal's passion for thoroughness, his zeal for analyzing everything all the way down to lint.

Mitchell was braced for the worst. So it was quite a surprise when Royal looked up from his scouting report and smiled.

"Bobby, I know you're frustrated you never got to carry the ball on the freshman team," Royal said. "These things happen. Every year, we slap together a starting lineup for the freshmen, and the next thing we know the season's over. Freshmen play only five games. That's why we can't evaluate every player until the last game has been played."

Mitchell wondered what Royal had found to evaluate. Did he actually study him as he stood on the sideline, killing grass?

"Bobby," Royal said, "we've got too many running backs around here. Seems we recruited every kid that toted the leather from here to Denver. Yeah, I know that you were one of the best backs in Colorado. But you're never going to beat out Steve Worster."

Mitchell wanted to say, "Then why don't you move me to halfback, Coach? Halfback is my natural position, you know."

Royal's eyes were now locked onto Mitchell's. Here came the bad news, he thought.

"Bobby, you're a big, strong, country boy," Royal said. "You lift weights. You might be the strongest player on our team. That's why we're moving you into the offensive line—to guard."

Mitchell felt the world going dim around him. How much more bad news could he take? Enough was enough. No longer would Bobby Mitchell carry the ball and make the headlines. No longer would the pretty girls wait for him outside of the locker room. He would never lead the Southwest Conference in scoring. Folks back in Wheat Ridge would forget his name. Mitchell's only comfort was that offensive line coach Willie Zapalac was sitting next to him. Zapalac, in spite of his gruff manner, imbued a country charm that could be disarming. Most of the players liked him.

"Willie here thinks you will make a great guard," Royal said. "I know this hurts, but this is a decision we're making for the good of the team. Actually, I think you might like playing in the line. Anyway, ol' ugly's better than ol' nothin'."

Zapalac placed a meaty hand on Mitchell's shoulder and smiled.

"Son, I can't tell you how happy I am that you are moving into the line," he said. "If you will just listen to me, everything's going to be just fine."

Days later, Mitchell was listening to Freddie again. His friend had been going on and on for the last fifteen minutes. Mitchell appreciated Steinmark's high energy and his stubborn belief that everything was going to work out. His pep talk, though, was growing more and more tiresome.

"Freddie, you just don't understand," Mitchell blurted. "You've got it made in the shade. You started the whole season on the freshmen defense. You're the Golden Boy. Me, I just went from last string on the freshman team to the offensive line on the varsity. I hate this."

So many things bothered Mitchell that he had trouble keeping track.

"Freddie," he continued, "I don't even have a girlfriend and I've been on campus for six months. You're the luckiest guy in the world because you've got Linda. Every time I see you and Linda walking across the campus, I want to cry."

In less than one year, Freddie and Linda had become the talk of the entire campus. All of the male students knew of Steinmark's exploits on the freshman team and heard the rumors that he was about to become one of the few sophomores to ever start for Royal on the varsity. Linda Wheeler, meanwhile, had negotiated her way through the sorority system, pledging one of the most well-known women's groups on campus, Delta Delta Delta, aka Tri Delt.

Mitchell wondered if he would ever meet his perfect match. As each day passed, the idea of transferring to another college dominated his thoughts.

"I've got nothing here at Texas," Mitchell told Steinmark. "I mean nothing."

Steinmark smiled again. "Maybe you just need to reset your goals, Mitch. Think about what you *can* become."

Mitchell dropped his head and said, "Okay, Freddie, tell me what your goals are."

"I want to start every game in my entire career at the University of Texas," he said. "It'd be cool to make the all-conference team. But what I'd really like to do is win a national championship."

Mitchell realized he was no longer living the same dream as Freddie Steinmark.

His teammates could not get over the wallop that Steinmark packed on the practice field. Many times, the player he pulverized wobbled to his feet with a look of disorientation. Meanwhile, the little safety trotted merrily back to the huddle sporting that big, toothy smile.

"I remember seeing him for the first time and wondering who the heck this little guy was," remembered starting center Forrest Wiegand. "First of all, I thought it was odd that he came all the way to the University of Texas from some place outside of Denver. It was so rare when a kid came from out of state. On top of that, he was so small. But I'll tell you that it sure was fun watching him play. Man, that little guy could hit."

Because of his dark features, quarterback James Street often referred to Steinmark as the "border bootblack" and the "Mexican shoeshine boy." Steinmark knew these were terms of endearment and nothing to be insulted about. Street made up nicknames for just about everybody on the team, and most were nothing to write home about. Bob McKay was called "Big 'Un" and Randy Peschel went by "Pasquale."

Street's words meant no harm and did not carry the same enmity as "little spic" back in Colorado.

"Freddie knew that there was nothing derogatory about it," Street said. "It was just part of the bonding. It was like saying, 'the four of us are going out there and we're going to bust some ass.' It was like telling everybody, 'I can say anything about you, and you can say anything about me.'"

Thirty minutes before his first practice with the varsity that spring of 1968, Steinmark took a walk to the front of the locker room, where the chalkboards were set up. He knew that he would find a depth chart with all of the players listed from first to last string. There were at least fifteen players at his position. So Steinmark was neither disappointed nor overjoyed to learn he would begin practice as the number-four safety.

As he walked out of the locker room and headed toward the practice field, he said to himself, "I can handle fourth string for now. But it won't take me long."

With 300 players in uniform, there was barely enough room to move around when calisthenics began that day. A stranger walking past the practice field that day might have thought that three college teams were holding practice. With no recruiting limits in that era, Royal seemed determined to sign every high school senior in the state. He knew that 80 percent of them would never make it. Still, he was keeping some of the semi-stars from suiting up for SMU (Southern Methodist University) or Baylor or Texas A&M and possibly scoring the winning touchdown to beat Texas. Royal was keeping a few strong-armed quarterbacks from thriving in Hayden Fry's wide-open passing offense at SMU, and a few good running backs from toting the leather for Gene Stallings at Texas A&M.

Five months and counting until the start of the 1968 season, it was time to start the weeding-out process. No one understood this dreaded exercise better than tackle Bob McKay. "If you didn't like the way things were going at the University of Texas, the coaches didn't give a shit. You were more than welcome to haul ass. The coaches weren't going to try to talk you out of it unless you were a star. The stars weren't leaving because they had starting jobs and a future."

Other Southwest Conference teams would suit up no more than a hundred players for the April workouts that lasted twenty-one days. They did not have the Longhorns' recruiting megabucks, so they settled on signing about twenty-five players a year.

At the end of warm-ups that day, Royal gathered the herd of players around him and told them to take a knee.

"Gentlemen," he began, "this year's spring practices are going to be different. You all know that we haven't been to the Cotton Bowl the past four years and there are reasons for that. It's time we get a new attitude around here. We're going to work you harder than you have ever worked before. So get ready. I hope you're all in shape. This is going to be the toughest spring practice you've ever been through. So buckle 'em up and let's get after it."

The popping and the head-butting had already begun before he reached the top of his tower. Normally Texas practices began with a grace period of calisthenics and light noncontact drills, but not this time. Players moved straight into brutal hitting drills known as "the nutcracker" and "eye-openers." Royal was not concerned with injuries and he knew he had at least ten backup players at every position. Besides, his quarterback of the future, James Street, was pitching for the Longhorns baseball team and safe for now.

It took Willie Zapalac about fifteen minutes to realize that the Texas practice field inspired a familiar feeling. Back in the summer of 1954, he was one of the young turks on Bear Bryant's coaching staff in Junction.

Zapalac approached Royal later that day and said, "You know, Coach, this all reminds me of something from my past. Are we in Junction?"

"Not yet, Willie," Royal said with a wink. "But we're on our way."

Unlike Bryant, Royal did give his players water breaks. Still, the spring drills were pure hell. Linebacker Scott Henderson watched it all from the sideline. In the final game of his freshman season, Henderson had torn two knee ligaments. Leaning on crutches, he watched dozens of players either limping from the field or being carried off on stretchers. So many players were being carted to the hospital that trainer Frank Medina could not keep an accurate count.

"It was brutal and hot and Coach Royal had the guys scrimmaging every day," Henderson said. "They were going at it. Four or five guys were quitting after every practice. I was really glad I was not out there."

Players were hanging up their uniforms left and right, and not all of them were scrubs. One of the first to go was Tommy Orr, who was expected to challenge for a starting position at right tackle. Jack Freeman, who had come from the vaunted Odessa Permian program and was one tough hombre, quit after the third day. Star end Deryl Comer was so drained one day after practice that he could not pick himself off the ground. He quit the next day, telling Royal "I've played football all of my life and I'm just danged tired of it."

Later that day, Royal told Coach Mike Campbell, "I'm just sick about Comer quitting. I wish I could have done something about it."

The next day, Comer did an about-face and returned to the team. Still, he had to run extra wind sprints after practice as punishment for leaving.

One of the few rewards for surviving each day was going to dinner at the training table inside Moore-Hill Hall. There were always ample helpings of steak, chicken, pork chops, mashed potatoes, and vegetables, along with heaping desserts.

"Eating in the dorm was one of the greatest things about being a Longhorn player," Mitchell recalled. "Nobody ever missed a meal."

Bob McKay almost missed lunch following the second day of practice. The 240-pound tackle with the lumberjack appetite showered and dressed at the stadium and started the long walk to the dorm. His legs soon gave out. He was crossing the bridge over Waller Creek when he sat down and dangled his legs over the ledge. Several players encouraged him to keep going, but McKay gave up.

"I just can't make it, guys," he said. "I'm exhausted. I'm never going to make it back to the dorm."

It took three teammates to hoist him to his feet and he finally managed to wobble on rubbery legs the final hundred yards. It was not the last time a Texas player barely made it home.

"Late in spring practice I tore the rotator cuff in my shoulder," McKay remembered. "I swear to God that I was the happiest man in the world when I got to the hospital."

During the final week of practice, Street left the baseball diamond and made his way over to the football field to witness the torture. He spent most of his time wincing at the bloodletting. He overheard Royal say, "The circle's getting tighter. We're losing a lot of players, but the ones who are staying want to play ball."

Mike Campbell IV said that some players were afraid to approach Royal and tell him they were quitting. Instead, they stopped going to class for the purpose of flunking out. They would gladly pack their bags at the end of the semester and take the next bus home, never to return.

One player reveled in the madness. Day after day, as the players quit or fell out, Steinmark became stronger. He rarely left the field.

"He never got tired," Fred Akers said. "I don't care what you did to him, he was always fresh and he was always smiling and patting somebody on the butt and encouraging them. I don't care if it was hot or what, two-a-days were nothing to him. He could last all day every day and that's one of the biggest reasons we believed in him. Freddie's motor never stopped."

Watching from the tower, Royal realized each day that Steinmark was the ultimate team player who grasped everything about the defense. There was little wasted motion in his pass coverage. He knew all of the angles and took the shortest path to the receiver. It was little wonder that he was intercepting so many passes.

As spring practice moved into the dog days, it seemed the duo from Colorado was growing stronger by the day. Mitchell was shaving each morning and knocking down defensive linemen in the afternoon. He was hearing encouraging words never before uttered to him at Texas.

"The coaches were actually encouraging me and that was a first," he said. "They were actually spending time with me and pointing out things. I could tell that Coach Zapalac liked what I was doing. I actually felt pretty good about things."

Mitchell, like Steinmark, moved all the way to second team, playing behind Danny Abbott at the left guard. He might actually see playing time in the fall. The pep talk delivered by Steinmark had worked.

America in 1968 was searching for individual freedoms and new radical forms of expression. The drug culture in Austin could be measured against anything going down in Berkley. The Vietnam protests raged around the clock, and middle-aged men who had fought in other wars could not fathom what they were witnessing.

Royal hated the very idea of individualism. He had grown up dirt poor without a mother in the Dust Bowl of Hollis, Oklahoma, and survived a rough childhood that most kids could not have endured. He joined the military, came home, and started a football career at the University of Oklahoma. He married Edith, his childhood sweetheart, and they soon started a family. Everything that Royal accomplished had been by the book. He did not subscribe to the philosophy of singer-songwriter Bob Dylan that "the times they are a-changin'." Royal saw the world through the same lense each day. As the country moved into the tie-dyed, drug-tripping days of the late sixties, Royal got a haircut once a week.

There would be no revolution on his watch. Joe Willie Namath, with his long, flowing hair and double-scotch-on-the-rocks lifestyle, would have never worked in Austin. Namath played on his own stage. There was no room in Royal's world for singular achievement.

Nearly a third of the Texas team had quit during the brutal spring, when the Longhorns had spent more time in torturous hitting drills and running gassers than actually practicing football. In most cases, Royal didn't care that the quitters had hauled ass. If the Longhorns were to pull out of this tailspin, team concepts would rule.

In Steinmark, Royal saw a player who subscribed to everything he believed in. Steinmark was a throwback to the 1950s, a decade that coaches loved because players held higher values. As Forrest Wiegand would say forty years later, "Freddie was not arrogant and there was no bullshit about him. That's why Coach Royal loved the boy."

So it was not surprising that in a span of twenty-one days that spring of 1968, Steinmark rose from fourth on the depth chart to second-string safety. All that stood between Steinmark and the starting lineup was Scooter Monzingo, a 6'1", 190-pound senior from Del Rio, and the number-one safety for the entire 1967 season.

Even to the casual observer, Steinmark had enjoyed a spectacular spring. One afternoon during a full-scale scrimmage, he intercepted back-to-back passes thrown by starting quarterback Bill Bradley. Royal was impressed with Steinmark's nose for the ball.

Steinmark was on Royal's mind almost every minute as spring practice officially ended. That day, the head coach walked off the field alongside defensive coordinator Mike Campbell.

"That Steinmark boy is going to play for us this season," Royal said.

"Dang right he is," Campbell responded.

Chapter 9

A PROMISE KEPT

In September 1968, Freddie Steinmark stood on the brink of an accomplishment that no one ever dreamed possible. The Texas coaches were trying to decide if they could trust this 155-pound peach-fuzz kid to lead the secondary. So determined was Steinmark to make the starting lineup for his first game on the varsity squad that he moved to Austin two weeks early to acclimate his body to the heat and humidity. He moved into the home of one of his closest friends, Bill Zapalac, the son of offensive line coach Willie Zapalac. Steinmark and Zapalac had double-dated as freshmen, thanks, in part, to Linda Wheeler pledging the same sorority as Michelle Vilcoq, Zapalac's girlfriend. Steinmark had gravitated quickly to Zapalac for all of the obvious reasons. The young man studied every night, went to church each Sunday, and said "yes sir" to anyone five years older.

Among Steinmark's closest friends on the team were Scott Henderson, Greg Ploetz, Scott Palmer, and Zapalac. It was no coincidence they were studious, religious, and as well-mannered as they come.

Zapalac, like the Campbell twins, suffered the added stress of having his dad on the coaching staff. The elder Zapalac, a disciple of Paul "Bear" Bryant, could be a wild-eyed, demanding drill sergeant on the practice field. He did not cotton to scholarship athletes not playing with pain. Because Bill Zapalac lined up at tight end, he came under the daily scrutiny of his father's overly critical eye.

Bobby Mitchell said of Willie Zapalac, "He had that real magical ability of pushing you to the limit. You never wanted to disappoint him. He was hard on all of us. But he was a hundred times harder on his own son."

Two days before the annual spring scrimmage, Bill Zapalac suffered a broken hand that was placed in a cast by team physician Dr. Joe Reneau, who told him not to return to contact drills for at least two weeks. An hour before the scrimmage that Saturday, Bill was sitting in street clothes in the locker room as the other players strapped on the pads.

"What are you doing?" his father said.

"Well, I don't think I'm supposed to go," Bill said.

"To hell with that!"

That day, Bill went beyond the call of duty, catching passes all over the field. Still, it was not the highlight of his young college career. That would come weeks later when he was moved into the defensive line, leaving his father behind. "That was the happiest day of my life," he said.

For Steinmark one of the toughest aspects of two-a-day practices in Austin was the adjustment from the cool and mild climate of Colorado to the scorching heat. That is why he and Zapalac started working out twice a day some two weeks before practices commenced. It was evident that both players were hell-bent on playing a lot in 1968.

"I'm going to take Scooter's job," Steinmark told Zapalac. "You just wait and see. I'm going to be so ready for the start of practice that the coaches will have no choice."

Zapalac smiled. "Don't get too cocky, Freddie. You know how these coaches are. They don't like anybody acting overconfident."

Steinmark's teammates were never afraid to kid around with the safety from Colorado. They knew he was tough as nails, but could also laugh when the joke was on him. That first day in Austin, Steinmark was driving Linda Wheeler's 1962 Ford Galaxy through the hills of Austin en route to a workout with Zapalac and tackle Scott Palmer.

Palmer and Zapalac followed Steinmark down hilly Highway

2222 in a pickup truck. Zapalac decided to have a little fun with his friend.

"We started ramming him from behind," Palmer said. "We did it almost all the way to the stadium. We thought he'd be mad. But when we got to the stadium, he was laughing harder than any of us."

Bobby Mitchell also left Wheat Ridge a couple of weeks before the start of fall practice. He wanted to stop in Mineral Wells, Texas, to visit his brother, Mark, who was about to be shipped to Vietnam as a helicopter pilot.

As he drove through the Texas Panhandle and headed south, Mitchell's heart was still heavy with the sadness of his first season as a Texas player. It was a year that seemed unfathomable to a young athlete who had succeeded at everything he had ever tried. At the moment, he was ready to seek the advice of an older brother whom he admired for all of the experiences he had endured the past few years.

The last time the brothers were together, Bobby was a sophomore fullback and Mark a tackle at Las Altos High School in southern California. They were two of the best players on the team. Mark led the team in tackles and Bobby finished second in scoring.

When the Mitchell family moved to Colorado and left Mark behind, no one could be sure what was going to happen to him. He was a volatile personality. He was a street fighter. Few things scared him. When the family lived in Dallas in 1963, he attended Bryan Adams High School and got swept up in the rivalry with Garland High. The football teams of both schools butted heads on Friday nights before the blood hate spilled into the streets.

"My brother was a very strong, physical guy," Bobby Mitchell said. "He was a great boxer. He broke the school record by doing 725 push-ups. He was an impressive specimen and a lot of people got out of his way."

While in Dallas, Mark Mitchell surprised his family by running away from home for several weeks. Upon his return, the letters M-A-R-K were tattooed on his knuckles. It was not long before the family packed up and moved to California, hoping it might help settle their oldest son.

In the last few years, though, he had turned his life around. That summer of 1968, Mark Mitchell was being trained at an Army helicopter school in Fort Wolters and living with his fiancée in a trailer house in Mineral Wells. Not far away were the pristine waters of Possum Kingdom Lake with its scenic countryside and tall, craggy cliffs carved out of the Palo Pinto Mountains. Mark Mitchell loved to fish and it was time to introduce his younger brother to some of his favorite honey holes.

For most of the day, it was just two brothers talking. They remembered childhood memories and openly shared their hopes, dreams, and fears. Floating across the blue, sparkling water fed by the Brazos River, they bonded again after several years apart.

Near the end of the day, Bobby steadied himself and delivered some news he had been carrying around like a bag of cement. It made his brother bristle.

"I don't know if I'm going to finish my football career at the University of Texas," Bobby said. "In fact, I've even thought about turning around tomorrow and heading back to Colorado. I think I'm quitting. The coaches just aren't treating me right."

Mark paused and set cold eyes on his brother. "You've got to be kidding," he said. "You've never once been a quitter in your life. You can't just up and leave the University of Texas. Dad will never stand for this. Have you talked to Dad?"

"Dad wouldn't care," Bobby said. "Shoot, he never went to more than two or three of my games the whole time I was in high school. I don't think he knows what football is all about, really. He doesn't know what you have to go through."

"I don't care what happened with Dad," Mark snapped. "I don't care what the coaches think. You get your butt down to Austin and show them what you got."

After catching, cleaning, and cooking a skillet full of fish, the brothers got down to the most important business of the day—arm wrestling. For the first time in his life, Bobby beat his older brother.

He had never been more proud. They drank beer far into the night and celebrated a reunion they would never forget.

The next morning, Mitchell pulled out of Mineral Wells and caught Interstate 35 south from Fort Worth to Austin. He had never felt stronger. Spending time with Mark served to rekindle his spirit and to repair his resolve. The prospect of competing for a starting job in the Texas offensive line seemed like a new beginning.

That September, everything was subject to change around the Texas football program. On the first day of practice, Steinmark moved ahead of Scooter Monzingo as the starting safety.

"We could see pretty quickly that he was going to be our guy at safety," Fred Akers said. "He was just too smart. He didn't make mistakes. None whatsoever. Some of the older guys made mistakes. But not Freddie."

Steinmark moving into the lineup made headlines across the state, but not like Royal's decision to start overhauling the offense. He asked his new offensive coordinator Emory Bellard to design a scheme that would reestablish his commitment to smash-mouth football. The Longhorns had won a national championship in 1963 by ramming the ball down the opposing team's throat, and they were going to do it again. It was time to buckle the chinstraps and to tighten those jock straps.

Royal's number one concern centered on the quarterback position. Bill Bradley had arrived in Austin in 1965 with supersized expectations and a nickname to match—"Super Bill." Before his freshman season, Bradley led the Big 33 team from Texas to a 42–13 victory over Pennsylvania. A coach on the Texas team was former Heisman Trophy winner Doak Walker, who told Bradley after the game, "Take off your jersey and let me see if you've got a big S on your chest." The Superman image was born.

At Texas, Bradley seemed quite human most of the time. He missed most of the 1966 season with a severe knee injury, and his 1967 performance was a disaster that reflected the rest of the team.

With "Super Bill" under center, the Longhorns were an I-formation team with a passing quarterback. Royal was losing a lot of sleep. He wanted to run the football and to avoid turnovers.

As the season approached, Royal kept his eye on a running quarterback by the name of James Street. Because Street loved to dole out nicknames, it was appropriate that he carried a couple around himself. He was dubbed "Rat" as a freshman when he and Bradley were racing canoes at Town Lake in Austin. Street turned over his canoe and was trying to right it when Bradley started ramming the side. Everyone knew that Street was not a strong swimmer. He did not particularly like being in the water.

"Look at that son of a bitch," Bradley yelled. "Street looks just like a drowned rat."

From that point forward, he was James "Rat" Street.

Royal wondered if Street possessed the talent, the size, or the brainpower to engineer the new offense. The first week of fall drills, the Longhorns began to experiment with a veer offense that used three running backs instead of two. It was an experiment that Bellard had conducted during his final high school season of coaching in San Angelo. It was borrowed from Fort Worth's William Monnig Junior High School coach, Charles "Spud" Cason, who, in the late 1950s, ran the T-formation with a big, slow fullback. He moved the fullback one step closer to the line, and all of a sudden he was breaking through the defense for long gains.

At first, it was called the Y-formation. Later, it would become known as the "wishbone," aka the pully bone from the chicken that was pulled apart to make a wish. As the wishbone offense began to take shape, Royal wished for its success and said a few prayers.

Royal and Bellard knew from day one that Bradley was not the quarterback for this new offense. He looked awkward and clumsy trying to execute the belly fakes and the quick pitches. Street, on the other hand, possessed the quick, nimble fingers of a blackjack dealer. He was a born gambler and everyone who played in the dormitory card games knew this.

The first decision made by a wishbone quarterback was to either hand off to the fullback or keep the ball. He would stick the ball in the fullback's belly, then check to see if the hole in front of him was opening. If the fullback had running room, Street would hand off. If not, the quarterback would slide down the line and make a decision on whether to run the ball or pitch it to the halfback.

Royal liked what he saw of Street running the offense, but was not quite ready to turn the keys over to him. So the Longhorns opened the season with "Super Bill" under center and the backs lined up in the T-Formation, not the actual wishbone. Still, Bradley would be operating the option offence.

The first opponent that season was the University of Houston, a team that Royal despised like no other. Head coach Bill Yeoman was known for playing fast and loose with NCAA recruiting rules. He kept a gray can in the second drawer of his desk from which he doled out cash to players. Yeoman was reviled for running up scores against the weaker teams, and in 1968, would rub Tulsa's flu-ridden team in the mud by the score of 100–6. In Royal's mind, Houston was an outlaw school that needed to be taught a lesson.

Thus it was brutally frustrating when the fourth ranked Longhorns tied the Cougars 20–20. They were lucky they did not lose the game as the Houstonians missed a chip-shot field goal with ten minutes to play, and failed to score after driving all the way to the Texas 1-yard line with 3:34 remaining.

Royal knew the critics would be howling. The newspapers were already cranking out rumors that 1968 might be his last in Austin.

"What we failed to recognize," remembered Mike Campbell IV, "was that Houston was one of the best teams we'd play all season. There were no flies on that team. They had a lot of good athletes and we were lucky they didn't beat us."

Indeed, the Cougars would finish the season as the number-one scoring team in the nation, averaging 42.5 points per game. The passing connection of David "Moon" Mullins to Elmo Wright led all of the major schools in yards through the air. That season, Wright invented the end-zone dance and the touchdown spike. The veer triple-option offense that Yeoman had introduced three years earlier no longer seemed like weird science.

Upon reviewing the film of the Houston tie, Royal expected to see several breakdowns. Instead, he found solace in the solid play of Steinmark, who intercepted a pass and did not allow a Houston receiver to get behind him. He separated receivers from the ball on two passes in the final Houston drive that, if completed, would have produced the winning touchdown.

In the Associated Press poll the next week, the Longhorns fell only two places to number six. In spite of the sporting press still holding the Longhorns in high regard, no one was prepared for what would happen next.

Playing Texas Tech in the second game of the season should have been a breather for the Longhorns. Everyone knew that Royal had assembled a team whose talent ranked with the top five teams in the country. Furthermore, egos were still bruised from Texas Tech's 19–13 victory in Austin the preceding season. Surely, an angry Longhorn team would demolish the Red Raiders. So it was not surprising that the Longhorns went into Lubbock as two-touchdown favorites.

The week leading to the game, Royal toyed with the idea of shifting to the wishbone and moving Worster a step closer to the line and Street to starting quarterback. He postponed the move, though, because he wanted to give Bradley one more chance to prove he was a championship level quarterback.

Admitted into the Southwest Conference in 1960, Texas Tech was nothing more than a blocking dummy for Texas early on. From 1961 through '65, Texas defeated the Red Raiders by the combined score of 181–28.

When Tech opened the 1968 season with a 10–10 tie against Cincinnati, no one expected the Red Raiders to keep the Texas game close, even though Lubbock, with the Longhorns coming to town, was a loud and rowdy place.

"That was my first time to go out there and see those Texas Tech people," Mike Campbell IV remembered. "Their fans came from the farms and oilfields and oil rigs all around West Texas. They really didn't have anything but Texas Tech football back then. They were crazy as hell and we didn't know how to deal with it. They were ringing their danged cowbells and you couldn't hear yourself think."

From the first play after the opening kickoff, the Red Raiders forward wall knocked the Texas defense off the ball. Texas Tech put up two quick touchdowns, a 21-yard pass from Joe Matulich to Roger Freeman, and a 3-yard run by Freeman. When Larry Alford returned a punt 84 yards for a touchdown in the second quarter, the noise at Jones Stadium made it almost impossible to hear the signals. Texas Tech led 21–0 at halftime. Down in the Longhorns dressing room, Royal approached Emory Bellard with the expression of a coach who had just been fired.

"It's time," Royal said. "It's time to get James in there and get the wishbone rolling."

Fans were surprised to see James Street trotting onto the field for the start of the second half. They were even more confused when the Longhorns lined up in a boxlike formation with Worster in the middle.

Street stuck the ball in Worster's gut on three straight plays and he thundered like a runaway train for 37 yards. Even in the seasons of disappointment of 1966–67, Royal learned that he could always depend on Chris Gilbert. The 5'9" halfback was a squirming speed demon who was superbly effective both inside and outside. He scored on a 9-yard run around left end, cutting the lead to 21–7, giving the Longhorns new hope.

It did not last long. Minutes later, Alford returned yet another punt 49 yards to the Texas 2-yard line and Freeman scored on the next play to make it 28–7.

Texas would lose 31–22, but it was still a historic night as the wishbone offense officially rumbled up and down the field for the first time. Worster's 2 touchdowns in the second half took away some of the sting. Still, from the expressions on the faces of Texas players and coaches after the game, you would have thought the season was already over.

The long chartered flight back to Austin was both painful and silent. Everyone knew the Longhorns boasted the best talent in the Southwest Conference. Everyone also knew that Texas was 0-1-1.

Chapter 10

DARRELL AND FREDDIE

Darrell Royal barely slept and went straight to work before dawn Sunday morning. As he strode into the coaches' office inside Memorial Stadium, his eyes were riveted on the task. He assumed a rigid posture behind his desk. His mind was focused on saving the Longhorns.

Players were normally allowed to sleep late and were not required to report until 5:30 on Sunday afternoon, when Royal addressed the entire squad and critiqued the film from the previous game. This day would be different. During the long and restless plane trip back from Lubbock, Royal had decided to make five lineup changes. There was no time to waste. By midmorning, he had dispatched one of the student managers to knock on Bill Bradley's door.

"Bill, Coach Royal said he wants to see you right away," he said. "You'd better get dressed."

Bradley knew what was in store. He did not need to ask. He awakened his roommate, Bill Hall, and said, "I'm no longer the quarterback of the Texas Longhorns. I'm on my way to Coach Royal's office to get the axe."

A half hour later, Bradley walked across the burnt orange carpet of Royal's expansive office and sat down in a chair in front of his long oaken desk. He remembered the words of Bob McKay: *When you get called to Coach Royal's office, it's never good.*

Royal had agonized for weeks over the Bradley decision, and finally it was time to pull the trigger. One of the top-recruited blue chippers in the history of the program was being demoted.

"Bill, we're gonna make some changes around here," Royal said. "We're starting with you. We're moving you out as quarterback. Now, if you want to come back, we'll find a spot for you."

Bradley looked down at the floor and realized that he didn't feel as bad as he had expected. If someone had told him a year earlier that he was going to lose his starting job, he might have imagined himself throwing up on the floor. At the moment, though, he felt a sense of relief.

"Coach, what are you planning to do with me?" Bradley said.

"Well, you're still going to be one of the captains," Royal said. "I would imagine that you'll be playing wide receiver the rest of the season."

The story was soon burning up the wire services. The reign of "Super Bill" Bradley, the most-prized recruit in America in 1965, was officially over. All the hype that had once driven his reputation seemed like nothing more than hot air. A desperate Darrell Royal, a man with a 0-1-1 record, needed a quick fix.

Within an hour, every player at Moore-Hill Hall knew of Bradley's demise. Cocaptains Chris Gilbert and Corby Robertson walked up and down the hallways, banging on doors.

"We're having a players-only meeting at five o'clock," they said. "Be there. Be there on time."

Every Texas player was seated by five o'clock sharp and the captains made sure the doors were sealed before they addressed the team. The coaches would be out of earshot. Robertson, an outstanding linebacker and the most talented player on the Texas defense, had won All-American honors the previous season. No one on the team was more respected than Robertson. He spoke first:

"Guys, I know that some of you went out drinking last night and that's pretty bad considering that we just lost a big game to Texas Tech. Some of you guys amaze me. We still have a long season ahead and there's nothing that says we can't win the Southwest Conference championship. We've got to keep up with your conditioning. That's all there is to it."

Gilbert stood and reiterated Robertson's remarks. Then Bradley walked slowly to the lectern. His eyes were bloodshot. He had not shaved. He started to cry. Rivers were forming on his cheeks and his eyes were fire-engine red. He opened his mouth, but the words were stuck in his throat. Finally, they came tumbling out.

"Rat'll get it done," he said. "I promise you guys. Rat'll get it done."

The deepening tension inside the room had finally subsided. In translation, Bradley was saying that James "Rat" Street could handle the wishbone offense and that the season was far from over.

"I might be a backup now but I'm still a captain on this team," Bradley continued. "And you know what I'd really like to do. I'd like to get to know you guys a lot better. I feel like I don't know half of you. I say let's get together over at the Flagon and Trencher after the meeting tonight and drink some beer. Let's have some fun and get to know each other."

Bradley knew the Longhorns were a fractured football team. Texas football was not a happy place. There was little or no team chemistry. Losing will do that to a team. Lines of communication barely existed between the classes. Seniors rarely talked to the juniors, the juniors ignored the sophomores, and the freshmen felt as if they did not exist.

In the spring of 1968, the University of Texas football program was in need of fresh leadership. Not since the mid-1950s had the program faced such a crossroads.

That night, every varsity and freshman player showed up at the Flagon and Trencher on the western edge of campus, just off Guadalupe. Even Steinmark was in the crowd and drank Cokes all night. The beer flowed and Scott Henderson enjoyed a few. Bradley shook hands and spoke with every teammate. Before long, players were hugging each other like long-lost friends. From the newfound camaraderie, it was hard to imagine that a winless team could get along so well.

"You would have thought it was Friday night the way everybody turned out," Mike Campbell IV remembered. "Bill Bradley loses his starting job one day and pulls the team together the next. It could not have happened any other way. Everybody was talking to each other and we were acting like a team. I don't care if it's a football team or a fraternity, you have to throw a party to pull people together. It's just like the great line from Bum Phillips: 'If one guy let's go of the rope, everybody falls.' All of a sudden, we were a team."

To Darrell Royal, the long shadow of adversity had seemed like a constant companion. The 0-1-1 record was frustrating, but he had faced larger obstacles in life.

The uphill battle began during childhood. He never knew his mother, Katy, who died of cancer when he was four months old. His two sisters died when he was young. He grew up in the Dust Bowl of Hollis, Oklahoma, during a hopeless time when the rain stopped and the sun flared down on the dying crops. As a child, the Great Depression and the Dust Bowl arrived at the same time in the southwestern corner of Oklahoma. The land was dying of thirst. Dust was so thick that it derailed trains. Residents slept with damp washcloths covering their noses and mouths to filter the dust. Entire families were literally tractored off their property by the banks that would never be able to collect on the loans.

When it was evident that the farms would never produce again, the rattletrap cars with leaky radiators and worn tires took off for the long journey to California. John Steinback's epic novel *The Grapes of Wrath* depicted Oklahomans as dirty, destitute, sullen, and dispossessed. Most did not find decent work in California. Instead, they were arrested, pistol-whipped, kicked, and left to starve. Signs at the movie theaters read, NIGGERS AND OKIES SIT IN THE BALCONY.

Little Darrell grew up quite alone. By the time he was ready to play football in the backyard, his brothers were grown and gone. He was raised by a grandmother known as Grandma Harmon. The relationship was loving, but Darrell rarely had anyone to play with.

Because the kid could not sit still, he was always running barefoot somewhere in Hollis. Most of his childhood, he had no shoes. Still, he would stand on the side of a dirt road and wait for a car to come along. One day, he was happy to see a burgundy Packard turn onto Cactus Street, kicking up dust.

As the car approached, Darrell got down in a three-point stance, ready to take off. He bolted into a full sprint, arms driving and knees pumping.

"Need a ride, Darrell?" the driver said through an open window.

"Nah, I'm racin' ya," the boy said.

"You're racin' what?"

"You."

The man laughed. "Why, Darrell, you're gonna tucker out."

"I'm gonna beat you."

A woman spotted the boy running alongside the car and said to her husband, "That poor child needs somebody to play with."

What sustained little Darrell was the hope that he would some-day play football for the Oklahoma Sooners. On Saturday afternoons in the fall, the family and neighbors would gather on the front porch of Grandma Harmon's house and listen to the Sooners' games on the radio. When the Oklahoma band played "Boomer Sooner," Darrell closed his eyes and dreamed they were playing it for him. In spite of the abject poverty, Hollis did produce a handful of OU players, who returned home during the Christmas holidays and walked the dirt roads of Hollis, wearing letter jackets with a large O sewn on the front. Darrell often followed the players around town and eaves-dropped on their conversations.

By junior high, Darrell found himself addicted to the game of football. He was the fastest kid in town. He played quarterback and halfback and could punt the ball fifty yards in a tight spiral. He dreamed of earning a football scholarship to the University of Okla-homa.

In 1939, the year of *The Wizard of Oz*, Darrell woke up one morn-ing to find his life spinning like a tornado loose on the Oklahoma hardpan. His life's journey was about to take a horrible turn. His father, Burley, was out of money. He had worked as a jailer, bookkeeper, trucker, and deputy sheriff. With no more jobs to be found, Burley decided to join the harvest gypsies on Route 66 heading to California. As the smoke-belching Whippet pulled out of Hollis that day, the fifteen-year-old boy tearfully said good-bye to his dream.

As might be expected, nothing went right in California. Fearing the locals would recognize his Southern drawl, Darrell rarely spoke. He did learn to say finger instead of "fanger," and street instead of "strait." Okies were often blocked from entering the public schools, but, through sheer willpower, Darrell found a school that would take him. When he approached the football coach about playing for the varsity, he discovered yet another roadblock. "You are too damned small to play for me," the coach said. "Grow up and maybe you can play next year."

His disappointment did not last as he soon received a letter from the varsity coach back in Hollis with the promise of a starting job on the varsity and a real job with the local Ford dealership. Of course, he would have to find a way home.

Darrell had only nineteen dollars to his name. So Burley arranged a ride for Darrell through a friend of a friend. Burley might have changed his mind if he had checked out the driver.

A few miles into the trip, Darrell noticed that the man behind the wheel had only one arm. A box below the steering wheel was filled with whiskey bottles, mostly empty. As the jalopy traversed into the mountains leading into Nevada, a blowout caused the car to swerve toward the edge of a cliff. Thanks to some timely luck, it stopped about two feet from the edge. Darrell surveyed the old man and said, "Do you want me to drive?"

"Nah," the man said. "But you can get out and fix the flat."

The more the one-arm man drank, the less attention he paid to the road. Darrell finally bailed out in Amarillo and hitchhiked the final 150 miles.

As promised, he became the starting quarterback and safety on the Hollis varsity, and before long was living his dream at the University of Oklahoma. He finished his career with 17 interceptions, led the Sooners to an undefeated national championship, and was named first team All-American. Adversity be damned. In the fall of 1968, he was ready to do it again.

The Texas players were accustomed to seeing Royal walking with his head down across the locker room, lost in thought. Out of frustration, he often kicked the toilet lever with enough force to open a geyser from the pipes. A little-known fact was that Royal suffered a germ fetish dating back to the Dust Bowl. So he always finished up in the restroom with a swift kick to the toilet lever.

Under strict orders from Royal, coaches rarely yelled at players and almost never cussed them. Still, the tension around the locker room and the practice field that October was palpable. The winless season was taking a toll on everyone.

"Like most of the players, I was scared to death of Coach Royal," tackle Bob McKay said. "I just knew that if we didn't beat Oklahoma State it was going to be hell on earth around the Texas football program."

Steinmark was always the first player to arrive before the start of practice. His locker was situated next to the door leading to the field. Dressed in full pads, he would sit on the wood bench in front of his locker, studying his chemical engineering books.

Thursday before the Oklahoma State game, Royal looked like a man marching off to war. As he approached the back door, he spotted the radiant smile of Steinmark. In the blink of an eye, his hard expression was transformed to one of sheer happiness.

"Why, Freddie Steinmark, what are you studying now?" the coach said with a bright smile.

"Just catching up on some of my classes," Freddie said. "You know, Coach, I have to stay on top of things in chemical engineering."

"Well, let me tell you that I'm proud of you, son," Royal said. "You are as focused a young man as I've ever seen in my life."

"Thanks, Coach," Steinmark said. "I can't tell you how happy I am to be playing football for the University of Texas."

Many years later, with emotion in his voice, Royal told the story of how he stopped at Steinmark's locker every day.

"No matter how down I was, that kid could always make me feel better," Royal recalled. "He had that smile and those bright eyes and he just made you feel good about things. He picked up my whole day for me. I will never forget that."

Chapter 11

NOW OR NEVER

The sporting press arrived early for the Monday practice for the purpose of writing the obituary. The once-heralded Texas program was on its deathbed. Soon, the Longhorns would join the likes of Baylor, Rice, and TCU (Texas Christian University)—the bottom-feeders of the Southwest Conference.

For the second straight season, the Longhorns had failed to register a win in their first two games. Never in the history of the seventy-two-year-old program had that ever happened. Only one other time had the Longhorns staggered winless through the first two games of *any* season, and that was 1938.

Little wonder the practice field was like a morgue. As players loosened up, the silence was soon broken upon the arrival of "Super Bill" Bradley.

All eyes were on the disgraced Texas quarterback as he jogged from Waller Creek to the edge of the practice field. Bradley stopped and unbuckled his belt. Then he trotted the length of the field with his football pants shoved down around his ankles, laughing all the way. The message was clear: *It's time to loosen up, guys. We might have been caught with our pants down, but better days are coming.*

The laughter was all-consuming. Even the grim face of Darrell Royal was punctuated by a smile. Royal blew his whistle to commence the practice, and, in a matter of minutes, the coach was witnessing a new snap, crackle, and pop. The hitting was more crisp than he could ever remember. Bradley's inspirational speech the previous night, plus a show of solidarity at the Flagon and Trencher, was already paying off. Even Bobby Mitchell had shaken the blues and moved about the practice field with a new energy, knowing that he was about to get some playing time at left guard.

The Longhorns normally spent at least the first twenty minutes in calisthenics and position drills. This day, though, Royal was anxious to see how the wishbone was running. It had been a sputtering, hit-and-miss offense with Bradley at quarterback, but James Street was the new sheriff in Austin. Everything would center on how he handled the football and dealt it to the backs. Most of all, Royal wanted to see if Street could light a fire beneath a languishing football team, and how soon.

In a rare departure from Royal protocol, the Longhorns' first team offense quickly lined up against the first defense. Normally, it was number one versus number two. With the first snap, Street turned and handed the ball to Worster, who bolted through a hole at right guard and gained steam like an eighteen-wheeler tearing downhill without brakes. Worster gained 8 yards before he was cut down at the knees by Freddie Steinmark.

Worster smiled as he got up. "You know, Freddie, you're an ornery little son of a bitch," he said. "Damned if I've ever seen a little peckerwood hit like you."

Steinmark stood up, straightened his helmet, and grinned. "Gee, thanks, Woo-Woo," he said, making light of Worster's new nickname, which he hated with a passion.

Standing behind the offensive huddle, Royal stepped back and set his eyes on the new backfield of Chris Gilbert, Ted Koy, Steve Worster, and James Street. They composed the first wishbone configuration in the history of college football. No one could blame the head coach for feeling like new money. Lining up at left halfback was Gilbert, the second-leading rusher in America behind O. J. Simpson, who would gain 1,709 yards and score 22 touchdowns en route to winning the Heisman Trophy in 1968. Like Simpson, Gilbert could cut on a dime and accelerate like a brand-new Camaro. He had gained more than 1,000 yards in two straight seasons.

USC coach John McKay did not mind bringing Gilbert's name

into any conversation involving Simpson. "I think that Gilbert is the second-best runner in the country—second to Simpson—and I mean that as a big compliment."

By creating an opening for right halfback Ted Koy, Royal managed to answer one of his own prayers. Koy was one of Texas' top-five recruits of recent seasons, and the sophomore boasted a football IQ beyond his years. Koy's father, Ernie, was a Longhorns Hall of Fame fullback dating to the early 1930s, and Ted's older brother, Ernie Jr., played halfback at Texas for three years and suited up on the national championship team in 1963 before six strong seasons in the NFL.

Worster moving to fullback in the wishbone was almost too perfect for the moment. He was a banger who carried the ball like a man boiling over with rage. He hammered both sides of the line with Herculean power, but was rarely effective on the end sweep because he possessed hands of stone. He could barely handle a pitchout, much less a pass. So the plan was to stick it in his breadbasket and let him rip.

The centerpiece of this newfangled offense was Street, who swaggered about the field between plays with the anxious feet of a gambler searching for a dice table. In Darrell Royal's ultraconservative world, it was hard to imagine a gunslinger like Street engendering so much hope so soon. After all, he had come to Texas weighing 149 pounds and most people thought his best sport was baseball.

"There was something about James that you never really saw until you put him in a football uniform," Worster recalled. "He threw the ball like a wounded duck. But when the shit hit the fan, you wanted the ball in his hands. He was like nobody I ever saw."

In the freewheeling Street, Royal saw a player whose hair and sideburns were too long. As it turned out, it was more statement than style. When a Texas A&M coach offered Street a football scholarship out of Longview High, the boy said, "Naw, I don't want to go down there and have to cut my hair."

He grew up poor on the wrong side of the tracks in Longview, fifty miles from the Louisiana border, without a father and a television. His father, Grover Street, was diagnosed as a paranoid schizo-phrenic and was often convinced that somebody was behind the next tree to get him. Without role models, James decided to invent himself.

Street was blessed with never having folding money growing up. He worked in the high school cafeteria just to be able to feed himself. He was moved from halfback to quarterback his senior year when a new coach moved in. Ty Bain told Street, "our quarterback should not be working in the damn cafeteria." James walked away from the job, and Bain handed him an envelope each Monday morning with $2.50 inside.

"That was fifty cents a day for me and my twin sister to eat on for five days," Street told author Terry Frei in *Horns, Hogs & Nixon Coming*. "I thought I was rich."

Street was forever scratching, scrambling, clawing. With a little jingle in his pocket, he could always find more. His teammates quickly learned that he was the second coming of Amarillo Slim. The Bourre and poker games went on almost around the clock in the athletic dor-mitory and Street was forever ready to deal the cards.

The rooms in Moore Hill were small, but you could still fit a card table and seven chairs between the bunks. Bill Atessis hosted most of the games. As many as fifteen players would be crammed into the room, the remaining eight waiting for a precious seat to open up.

Bill Atessis remembered, "James was just incredible because he never lost. That's how he got his nickname 'Slick.' In poker, James would take his five cards and win on that hand."

Mike Campbell IV was playing cards one night and watching one of his fellow teammates lose hand after hand. When all of his money was finally gone, the player vacated the seat and Street grabbed it like a hungry man seizing a turkey leg.

"Not a single hand had been won in the chair all night," Camp-bell said. "Then James sat down and he started winning and win-ning. Pretty soon, he had everybody's money at the table. I'd never seen anything like it."

On the practice field in the fall of 1968, Street was dealing the cards and dragging all of the chips. He ran the wishbone flawlessly. Practically every play went for a first down against Texas' number-one defense. Royal did not know whether to laugh or cry. Was the wishbone this good, or the Texas defense that bad?

Royal instantly knew why Street was the perfect veer option quarterback. Most signal-callers made up their minds on where the play was going the moment they stuck their hands under center. Street was different. He knew he had to read and react to the defense *after* he took the snap. As he patiently slid along the line of scrimmage, he waited for the defense to make its move. Only then would he hand off to Worster, or pitch the ball to Gilbert or Koy. His reflexes were so quick that he could hold off until the last second. It also helped that he had ice water in his veins.

That first day of practice leading to the Oklahoma State game, Worster rumbled for big gains up the middle. When Street pitched it to Koy or Gilbert, the halfbacks were quickly into the open field. Finally, Street faked to Worster and Koy, then toted the leather around left end. He never saw the 155-pound Mack truck that hit him. To his dismay, he looked up to see number 28 standing over him, flashing that familiar smile.

"What the hell you think you're doing, boot black?" he said to Freddie Steinmark.

"Boot black?" Steinmark said, laughing. "Well, I guess this Mexican just knocked your white ass off."

On any given day, it was not unusual to hear the Longhorn Band in the middle of the afternoon belting out songs that resounded across the campus. The band normally practiced up the hill at the stadium, or just outside the band hall. Because of the 187 instruments that included ninety-seven horns, the sound was like a locomotive rolling through the streets and over the hilly terrain. As Street continued to move the offense down the field, the cacophony seemed to be getting closer.

Darrell Royal turned his right ear to the sound. "Our band

sounds so close that you'd almost think they're coming down San Jacinto right now," he said.

Indeed, they were. In a matter of minutes, everyone on the practice field could see the drum major high-stepping toward them and the scantily dressed twirlers tossing batons high into the air. They could see the golden trombones and tubas glinting in the sunlight. They could see band director Vincent R. DiNino walking at a fast clip, straight as an arrow, toward Royal.

Royal felt a mixture of regret and joy. Regret because as athletic director he had failed to allocate money for the band to travel to Lubbock. It was a huge mistake on a day when 45,000 rowdy Red Raiders fans managed to rattle the Longhorns. It was always comforting on the road to hear the band playing "Texas Fight" or "The Eyes of Texas," even if the musicians were stuck high and deep in the cheap seats.

The band's absence in Lubbock had become such a big issue around campus that Ted Koy had addressed it in his weekly column for *The Daily Texan*. Koy was a bit of a novelty around the football team. He was a journalism major and wrote a weekly column each Wednesday for the campus newspaper. Teammates chided him for playing the role of the spy reporter around the locker room.

"If the band had been in Lubbock perhaps the score would have still been the same, but the band's absence was a definite factor in the Longhorns' performance," Koy wrote. "The sounds of silence are still a haunting memory. The Tech experience made you more aware that this business of winning is a partnership deal. Without the fans cheering and the band playing, it could be a very lonely journey."

DeNino was not happy that the band had been left out. He was a high-energy, dynamic man. He arrived in Austin in 1955, two years ahead of Royal, and was the Darrell Royal of college bands. That day, he marched straight toward the coach, who smiled and offered a handshake. The two were friends.

"Coach Royal," DeNino said loudly, "we are here to pep up your boys. As you know, we missed the Lubbock trip—"

"I know, I know, Vince," Royal said. "We're sorry that you guys didn't go. We sure could've used you. Go ahead and play us some tunes, if you will."

DeNino raised his conductor's stick as Royal turned to his players and instructed them to remove their helmets.

The director tapped his foot and shouted "One-two-three" and "Texas Fight" was soon blasting across the practice field.

Texas Fight, Texas Fight,
And it's good-bye to A&M.
Texas Fight, Texas Fight.
And we'll put over one more win.
Texas Fight, Texas Fight,
For it's Texas that we love the best.
Give 'em Hell, Give 'em Hell, Go Horns Go,
And it's good-bye to all the rest.

That afternoon, the Longhorn Band played two more songs leading to the grand finale, "The Eyes of Texas." As the band belted out the university's alma mater, an electricity passed over the practice field that felt like a crackling thunderstorm. Players could never remember goose bumps popping up during practice. As "The Eyes of Texas" concluded with "Till Gabriel Blows His Horn," the players were jazzed with a new spirit. A few were misty-eyed. After the band marched away, Royal blew his whistle and the pads were popping even louder. It was one of the best practice sessions the coach could ever remember.

When Royal and Campbell walked off the practice field side by side thirty minutes later, the head coach said, "Those boys really showed me something today."

"Those boys," Campbell said, "are finally ready to play some football."

No one expected the wishbone in its infancy to inflict such damage on the Oklahoma State Cowboys. Street opened the scoring with a 60-yard touchdown pass to Cotton Speyrer to build a 10–0 halftime lead. Fans couldn't believe what they were seeing from Street, once considered the worst passer of all the Texas quarterbacks. Street was operating the offense as if he had known it all his life.

Early in the third quarter, Royal turned Worster loose on OSU—He gained 73 yards on 10 carries in the second half alone. Worster scored on a 2-yard run and Bill Bradley proved his career was not over. He caught a 4-yard scoring pass from Street in the fourth quarter, and Mike Perrin returned an interception 26 yards for a touchdown as the Longhorns rolled 31–3.

The following Monday, coach Mike Campbell was walking across the practice field, past the offensive drills, when he spotted an idle Bradley, listed as a fifth-string wide receiver, sitting on his helmet. He grabbed Bradley by the jersey and yanked him to his feet.

"Hey, Coach Royal," Campbell yelled, "if you don't need Bill Bradley anymore, I sure could use him on defense. Whatdaya say?"

"He's all yours," Royal said.

Bradley followed Campbell to the other end of the field, where the defense was running through drills. He would never return. Some said that the Campbell-Royal conversation in front of Bradley had been rehearsed. Regardless, Bradley was the happiest player on the practice field that day. He was moving to right defensive back and it would become a life-changing experience.

Next on the schedule for Texas was the game that everyone in two states talked about for 365 days a year—Texas versus Oklahoma at the Cotton Bowl. When Bud Wilkinson's Oklahoma teams dominated the college landscape in the 1950s and early '60s, Texas-OU was often the Game of the Year in college football. Five years after Wilkinson's departure, the Sooners were finally putting the pieces back together. They were coming off a 10-1 season in 1967, with the only loss to Texas.

In 1968, the record of the two teams looked out of whack. The Sooners were 1-1 and the Longhorns stood 1-1-1. Moreover, it was a rarity on the second Saturday in October when neither team was ranked in the top twenty.

The outcome would come down to the final 2:37 with Texas trailing 20–19 and the ball at its own 15-yard line. Steinmark had halted an Oklahoma drive with his second interception of the season.

No one figured Street to be the quarterback to lead this kind of comeback. Still, he completed three wobblers of 21, 18, and 23 yards to end Deryl Comer, the tight end who had quit the team in spring practice, then returned the next day.

When Texas reached the 2-yard line with thirty-nine seconds remaining, everyone knew what was next. Worster had racked up 119 yards on 13 carries. Street handed him the ball off right guard and two Sooners rode him piggyback over the goal. Happy Feller's PAT kick made the final score 26–20 and the Longhorns were suddenly celebrating again.

Any victory over Oklahoma was sweet, and this one removed a few tons from Royal's shoulders. The Longhorns were back in the top twenty, weighing in at number seventeen. Still, Royal knew what the critics were saying: Why had his team played with such nonchalance early in the season? Why had he waited so long to ditch Super Bill? And why in the world was he going to a run-it-down-your-throat offense in this era of passing madness? As Dan Jenkins wrote in *Sports Illustrated*, "the wishbone was three yards and a cloud of protest."

On the eve of the Arkansas game in Austin, Royal sounded off to Jenkins: "I may be one of the few people around here who recognizes what has happened in our conference. Other people have gotten good, that's what. Other people have athletes in school, under conference rules, that could not play at Texas because our scholastic requirements are higher. Anyone who does not believe that, I can show them some documentation."

Coming to Austin on Saturday was the undefeated ninth-ranked team in America. The Arkansas Razorbacks averaged 35 points a game while not losing a game all season. The Hogs hated Texas, and Texas hated the Hogs even more. One Longhorns fan held up a sign outside the stadium that read, LET'S MAKE ARKANSAS THE NEXT NAGASAKI!

Causing most of the stir for Arkansas was a sophomore quarterback named Bill Montgomery, who was burning up the national passing rankings. Montgomery was a tall, lithe quarterback with a whiplike throwing motion and the accuracy of William Tell. His favorite receiver, Chuck Dicus, was one of the best young players in America.

On the morning of the Texas-Arkansas game, Mike Campbell called Steinmark into his office to discuss the Montgomery-to-Dicus predicament. Campbell already considered Steinmark someone the coach could depend on and the coach needed his help. He was also concerned with Bill Bradley making his first start at right defensive halfback.

"Freddie, quite frankly, Bradley doesn't know what the hell he's doing out there," Campbell said. "It's not all his fault. He hasn't played a whole lot of defense since he got to the University of Texas. You're going to have to help him. There's a pretty good chance he's going to let one of those Arkansas receivers behind him today. Most likely, it will be that number 20 [Dicus]. If number 20 gets past Bill, you've got to keep him from scoring. I know that's asking a lot considering all of the other things that you've got to worry about."

The first rule of pass defense in Campbell's world was never to allow a receiver behind the secondary. One of the reasons Campbell chose Steinmark as the starting safety was his ability to keep receivers in front of him.

As Freddie smiled and left Campbell's office, the coach shook his head. Running through his mind were the obvious thoughts: *Freddie Steinmark is a sophomore. He has started a grand total of five games on the varsity. He's nineteen years old. And I've just entrusted my entire pass defense to him.*

Campbell shook his head and chuckled. He knew that Steinmark could handle it.

In the opening minutes of the game, Montgomery had the Longhorns on the run. He was completing passes all over the field. The scoreboard was starting to pinball. Arkansas led 3–0. Texas tied it 3–3. Arkansas went ahead 9–3. Texas rallied for a 10–9 lead. Arkansas jumped ahead 15–10. Texas made it 18–15.

In the second quarter, the Hogs were headed for the end zone once more, this time to take the lead. Montgomery had already thrown a 6-yard touchdown strike to Dicus. In the huddle, he called the same pass route for Dicus. Only this time, somebody was reading Montgomery's mind.

Steinmark had worked overtime with his film study of Montgomery and the Arkansas offense, and was ready for what was coming. By midseason, Steinmark was totally comfortable with the Texas defense. He knew how Campbell wanted him to operate in the secondary and the need to shut down the long pass for the quick six. If the time was right, though, he was free to toss aside his deep responsibility and to angle for the interception. As Freddie dug in his cleats, he transitioned into attack mode without showing his hand. As the Arkansas quarterback dropped into the pocket, he could see Montgomery's eyes tracking his favorite receiver sprinting over the middle. Sixty thousand Texas fans were on their feet, howling for the Longhorns to shut down the Hogs. This was the biggest play of the game and everyone knew it.

Montgomery's pass was about to drill Dicus between the numbers when Steinmark stepped into the breach. The little safety knifed in front of the receiver at the 5-yard line, intercepting his third pass of the season while saving the day. He returned it 20 yards to the Texas 25-yard line. From there, the Longhorns took control of the game, marching down the field with Worster scoring on a 16-yard run for the 25–15 lead. By the midpoint of the third quarter, Texas led 39–15, thanks to a 1-yard run by Worster and a 51-yard reception by Speyrer. The game had turned on Steinmark's pick.

Arkansas's Bill Burnett would score two fourth-quarter touchdowns, but Texas still prevailed, 39–29.

After the game Royal told the press, "We figured that Bill Montgomery would get his yards today, and he did. But Freddie Steinmark was there when we needed him. He made a great play on the interception. That was the turning point of the game."

———

The next week, Texas clobbered Rice 38-14 by rolling up 440 rushing yards. The Texas defensive backs were instructed to lay 10 yards off the Rice receivers. In the second half, though, Bradley rushed to the line of scrimmage as the ball was snapped and clobbered one of the receivers, still in a three-point stance, with a forearm to the head.

Bradley's bold move managed to kill Rice's entire offensive momentum. A passing game that had been clicking early in the game suddenly went moribund.

From the sideline, coach Mike Campbell yelled, "I don't know what the hell you're doing out there, Bradley! But keep doing it."

It was not the last time that Bradley would freelance with Campbell's defense.

A week later, experts around the Southwest Conference were not convinced that the Longhorns could handle national passing/receiving leaders Chuck Hixson and Jerry LeVias of SMU. Two years earlier, the Mustangs had registered a rare victory in Austin by the score of 13–12 en route to winning the Southwest Conference championship. Coach Hayden Fry's zany passing schemes had a way of upending heavily favored teams like Texas. Fry often found himself playing with the shortest stick in the conference, thanks to the fact that SMU was a small private university with limited recruiting. It always seemed the big studs went to Austin and the small, smart guys wound up in Dallas.

In Hixson, though, Fry boasted one of the best passing quarterbacks in the country. Hixson's arm was so accurate that he could throw a football into a shopping bag at 50 yards. Watching film of the Mustangs, Steinmark knew his hands would be full with Hixson and LeVias, already a shoo-in for All-American honors. What bothered him the most, though, was a quote in the *Dallas Morning News* attributed to Fry and surely aimed at Freddie himself.

"Texas has a great defense," said the master psychologist. "But that secondary is a little green. We think we can score on Texas and score a lot."

Steinmark felt an emptiness in the pit of his stomach when he read what Fry had to say. He realized the coach was trying to rent space in his head.

On the third play of the game, Steinmark watched LeVias cut straight over the middle and recognized that speedy wide receiver might break the route into a deep post. Still, instinct told him that this was the bread-and-butter routine he had seen so many times on the film. Hixson liked to fire the quick strike to LeVias, hitting him on stride as he sprinted past the secondary and into the end zone.

Freddie quickly got the jump on LeVias and, in the blink of an eye, snared the football and took off in the other direction. He returned his fourth interception of the season 20 yards to the SMU 26-yard line and Texas suddenly owned all the momentum. It took Street only 3 plays to push the ball into the end zone, keeping on the option around right end for a touchdown that covered 3 yards. Again, Steinmark had captured lightning in a bottle and the Longhorns never looked back in a 38–7 victory.

Gaining 557 rushing yards against Baylor the next weekend, Texas breezed past the Bears 47–26. Chris Gilbert, the second leading rusher in the country behind Simpson, was virtually unstoppable with 212 yards, followed by Worster with 137, and Street at 108. It was the first time in sixteen years that three Longhorns gained more than 100 rushing yards. By the ninth game of the season against TCU, James "Happy" Feller was firmly entrenched as the Texas kicker. Royal, however, decided to keep backup Rob Layne on the traveling roster, partly in deference to his father, Bobby Layne, who was an All-American quarterback at Texas in the mid-1940s before leading Detroit to two NFL championships in the 1950s.

The elder Layne was a football legend around Texas. But there was another dimension to his personality that brought him even more notoriety. *Los Angeles Times* columnist Jim Murray once wrote, "Wherever there was a drink to be drunk, a dance to be hoofed, a song to be sung, a crap shoot to fade, a horse to bet, a card to be dealt, Bobby sat in. For Bobby, life was all fast Layne."

The wild-and-woolly life of Bobby Layne began at Highland

Park High in Dallas. The star quarterback's crap games were held in the seedy little roadside motels along Harry Hines Boulevard, where the local hookers operated. Bobby thought no one would ever bust the games until one night he was down on his knees, rolling the dice, and in walked his high school coach, Rusty Russell.

Russell was a kind and gentle genius, a man who years earlier had built a dynasty out of a tiny orphanage on the east side of Fort Worth known as the Masonic Home. In the midst of leading the Mighty Mites to a state title and three trips to the state semifinals, Russell also managed to invent the spread offense. Still, he did not cotton to crap games organized by his star quarterback. The next day, the boy was running stadium steps until he felt like dying.

In the mid-1940s, the center of the gambling universe at U.T. was located inside the dorm room of Bobby Layne. The card games often went all night, which left little time for studying. The sins of the father would be passed along to the son.

One of Rob Layne's self-appointed duties was to chaperone a trip each year for a handful of freshmen players down to the Mexican border town of Laredo, a good four-hour drive from Austin. They went straight to the "Boys Town" section, where the *prostituas* plied their trade. In the beer halls of Boys Town, the Texas players were seduced by the *chicas* in sheer black lingerie, who sat on their laps and whispered dollar amounts in their ears. Soon, the young men were led to the dark rooms behind the saloon, where some lost their virginity.

In the summer of 1968, Layne organized a trip for a large contingency of teammates to Las Vegas. It was evident from the moment he walked into the Sahara casino that the twenty-year-old Layne knew what he was doing.

"I was a sophomore when we went out to Vegas," Bill Atessis remembered. "Rob was just wild, unbridled. His dad got us set up at a show. Rob tried to tip the guy at the door a twenty and he said, 'Keep it. I think you need it more than I do.' When we started gambling, Rob just went stark crazy wild. He was always pushing the limits. He tried to be just like his dad. His dad was bigger than life. Unfortunately, he could not live up to his dad's image."

Late in the '68 season, Layne was focusing less on his place-kicking and more on the point spreads offered by local bookmakers. As a backup kicker, he was a forgotten man by Royal and staff. Layne was standing on the sideline of the TCU game in the first half as Texas ran up a 23–0 halftime lead, thanks to Steinmark stopping a TCU drive with his fifth interception of the season.

Layne was smiling at halftime. He had bet on the Longhorns as 17-point favorites. Thanks to a late influx of Texas money, the line had moved from minus 12 to minus 17, according to records from the *Gold Sheet*.

Because Bradley was now on defense, Royal did not have a viable option as a backup quarterback. The second stringer was Joe Norwood, who rarely got on the field. Norwood was a strong-armed, drop-back pocket passer who struggled with the wishbone's ball-handling demands. As the team prepared for the second half, Royal approached Norwood and said, "Joe, I'm sending you in to start the third quarter. It's okay to throw the ball. But I don't want you throwing any sideline routes. I don't want them picking off a pass and returning it for a touchdown."

Norwood smiled and nodded. Royal figured he understood the instructions.

Mixing the run and the pass, Norwood moved the Longhorns fifty yards to the TCU 30-yard line. To Royal's dismay, Norwood tried to complete a quick sideline pass and BANG!, it was intercepted by James Fondren and returned 80 yards for a TCU touchdown.

Royal was livid. He walked more than 10 yards onto the field and waited for Norwood. Before Royal could open his mouth, though, he felt Rob Layne brush past, marching straight toward Norwood. Layne yelled at the backup quarterback, "What the hell do you think you're doing, Joe? Coach Royal told you not to throw a sideline pass. Don't you listen to your coach? You know, Joe, sometimes you're a damn dimwit."

It was such an angry ass-chewing that Royal decided to let it go at that. He did not say a word to Norwood. Of course, he was not aware that Layne's diatribe was based on his financial stake in the game and that the 17-point spread was suddenly in doubt. The Long-horns did rally with touchdowns by Worster and backup fullback Bobby Callison in the second half and won by 26 points, 47–21, thus covering the spread.

That Texas would ascend to number six in both wire-service polls the week after the TCU game was virtually the equivalent of the New York Jets' climb toward the Super Bowl in 1968. The Longhorns' season had begun on notes of despair with the tie to Houston and the loss to Texas Tech. The mere act of returning to the top twenty seemed like a miracle. To think that the Longhorns had dispatched seven straight opponents by the combined score of 276–114 was to believe that the Jets could pull off one of the biggest upsets in foot-ball history in Super Bowl III by beating the Baltimore Colts.

Last on the regular season schedule was Texas A&M and the game that Texas had waited for all season. The previous Thanks-giving, Texas A&M had defeated Texas 10–7, then left the home scoreboard lit for nine months, until the start of the next season. The adjective "angry" could not describe the mood of the Texas Long-horns. As kickoff approached, they were ready to knock down the walls of Memorial Stadium.

"We were ready to kill those guys," recalled tackle Bob McKay, who was building a reputation as one of the best offensive linemen in the country. "There was nothing like the feeling that day. We were going out to take care of the Aggies."

Steam was coming out of Bill Bradley's ears as he walked to the middle of the field for the coin toss. When Texas A&M captain Billy Hobbs called heads, and the coin came up tails, the referee turned to Bradley.

"Captain Bradley, Captain Hobbs has called heads and it came up tails. What would Texas like to do? Take the ball or choose to defend one of the goals?"

Bradley blurted, "We don't give a shit!"

The referee stepped back, startled at the response. Regaining his composure, he said, "No, Captain Bradley, you have to make a choice."

"We really don't give a damn," Bradley said. Then he paused, thought about it, and said, "Ah, hell, we'll take the damn football!"

When Bradley returned to the sideline, Royal said, "Bill, what was going on out there?"

Bradley smiled. "Don't worry, Coach. We're gonna kick their asses."

The dethroned Texas quarterback was determined to have the best game of his college career. This would be his final rodeo before the bowl game. Campbell decided to make it easy for him. He knew that Bradley still did not know how to play defensive halfback nor did he comprehend most of the cover schemes. So Campbell decided to turn him loose.

"Just go out there and play centerfield," Campbell said. "Get your hands on every damn football you possibly can."

Campbell knew that A&M held little hope of moving the ball on the ground and that quarterback Ed Hargett would be winging it all day. Indeed, Hargett threw the ball 45 times and 4 passes were intercepted by Bradley, tying a Southwest Conference record. Ironically, Bradley had thrown 4 interceptions against Texas A&M the year before.

Texas scored touchdowns in the first half by Worster, Gilbert, Street, and two by Speyrer. Royal emptied the bench in the second half and the Longhorns cruised to a 35–14 victory. Finishing the SWC schedule with a 7-1 record, they earned a tie with Arkansas for the championship. By virtue of beating the Razorbacks, the Longhorns would represent the conference in the Cotton Bowl against Tennessee. There was still much to prove.

Three days before the Cotton Bowl, Bob Galt of the *Dallas Times Herald* wrote, "Freddie Steinmark is one of the most special players in college football. Every coach in America would like to have one like him. He stands about five-foot-nine and weighs less than 160 pounds. But he'll crack you like he weighs 230. He's the heart and soul of the Texas secondary."

Royal was quoted in the newspaper as saying, "We couldn't be happier with Freddie. That kid's got a tub full of guts. Not only that, he's one of the smartest players I've ever coached."

With five interceptions, Steinmark finished the season as the co-leader in the SWC with Russell Serafin of Baylor. His success was not lost on his teammates. "Pound for pound, Freddie Steinmark was the best player in the Southwest Conference," Tom Campbell said. "Freddie did more with less than anyone that I've ever met, and that's a lot of people."

One of the happiest players on the Texas team as the Cotton Bowl approached was Bobby Mitchell. After languishing on the freshman team, Mitchell was on the field for about 30 percent of the offensive snaps in 1968, and started one game. He could not wait for the 1969 season to begin.

Tennessee versus Texas was an interesting matchup on paper. The Volunteers—with stars like tailback Richmond Flowers and line-backers Steve Kiner and Jack "Hacksaw" Reynolds—were ranked eighth in the country with an 8-1-1 record. Texas, with the same record, had moved up one slot to number five in the A.P. poll after throttling A&M.

It seemed like an even match. As it turned out, the comparable statistics and the similar personnel did not factor into the outcome. Simply, Texas was on a mission and could have beaten any team in America that day, including number-one Ohio State.

Street threw touchdown passes of 78 and 79 yards to Speyrer in the first half, while Worster and Koy added two more scores for a 28–0 halftime lead. It was odd to see a coach sending wholesale sub-stitutions into the game in the second half of a big-time bowl game, but Royal did just that. In the second half, Gilbert added another touchdown of 5 yards, the final one of an illustrious career.

Texas 36, Tennessee 13 was never a contest.

An hour later, also on national TV, Ohio State (9-0) defeated USC (8-0-1) in the Rose Bowl 27–16 in spite of O. J. Simpson rush-ing for 171 yards on 28 carries.

Ohio State made an excellent case for winning the national title in both wire-service polls. Only Michigan State had come close to beating the Buckeyes, losing 25–20. Ohio State trampled archrival Michigan 50–14 in the final regular-season game. So it made sense that the Buckeyes won the national championship in a landslide vote over number-two Penn State. Texas finished third.

Down in Austin, though, the consensus was that Texas could have beaten Ohio State on any parking lot or dirt road in Columbus or Austin. Based on the results of the final nine games, Texas might have won the debate. Only undefeated Arkansas had come within 10 points of Royal's team, and the Razorbacks needed 2 late touchdowns to make it that close.

"I am very proud of the way we finished," said Corby Robertson, who played his final game against Tennessee. "What I really feel good about is that we went through a lull my first two years in Texas. Our senior year, we got the thing back. We finished third in the country. I thought we were the best team in the country, but that didn't happen. If you leave the world a better place than you first found it, that is a very nice feeling. I had no regrets."

In truth, one regret followed Robertson for decades.

"At the end of my senior year, after the bowl games, I thought about sending a telegram up to Ohio State to challenge them to a game," he said. "We would have played it in Cotula [a small town between San Antonio and Laredo in far South Texas]. I really think we could have beaten them."

Why Cotula? "Because I owned some land down there and very few people have ever heard of it."

On January 1, 1969, Darrell Royal was carried off the field by his players. His smile was visible all the way to the top row of the Cotton Bowl. The Longhorns were once again all the rage of college football. The wishbone had turned out to be a savior. Street, Worster, Koy, Henderson, Atessis, Wuensch, Steinmark, and several other great players were coming back for a season that just might be "The Year Of The Horns."

Chapter 12

BROTHERS FOREVER

Like Freddie Steinmark and most of his teammates, Bobby Mitchell was disturbed by the unruly war protests spilling onto the campus in January of 1969, just weeks after the victory over Tennesssee in the Cotton Bowl. America was four years deep into the frustration known as Vietnam and there was little sign of the war winding down. The death count the previous year had risen to 14,589.

Austin the past few years had become a magnet for the hippie culture. The radical element was turning a laid-back town into a hotbed for activism. Most of the protest marches occurred in the central part of town, not far from campus, and the students were getting more involved by the day.

Mitchell constantly thought about his brother, Mark, flying jet helicopters over Tay Ninh. On two occasions, Mark's helicopter had been shot down. Mark sent his brother pictures of him standing next to the bullet-ridden choppers.

Bobby Mitchell held mixed feelings about the war. He believed that the American government's tactics in Southeast Asia of pushing forward, then pulling back, was dead wrong. The lack of commitment to winning the war roiled his stomach. On the other hand, he could not stand to see the protestors on national newscasts spitting on the soldiers coming home.

"I had a brother on the other side of the world, getting shot at, and it didn't seem that anybody cared," Mitchell remembered. "It really tore me up inside. There were times when I didn't know what to think."

Mitchell came from a family of patriots. His father, Charles Mitchell, had fought at the Battle of the Bulge, and was briefly a prisoner of war. His mother, Marie, trained for several months during World War II as a transport pilot. This was during a time when women were performing men's jobs back in the states. She was about to be shipped to the South Pacific when the atomic bombs were dropped on Hiroshima and Nagasaki, and the Japanese surrendered.

It was not uncommon for college football players to clash with the longhairs and the pot-smokers. In general, Longhorn players could not stand the sight of the hippies. Walking across the bridge at Waller Creek, the aroma of the devil's weed was prominent each day. Waller Creek, named for the first mayor of Austin, Edwin Waller, flowed southward for six miles to join the Colorado River in the dammed area known as Town Lake. Amid the oak and juniper trees, it was a hangout for the cannabis crowd in the late 1960s. Of course, marijuana in those days could be found just about anywhere in central Austin.

"You had to be careful of which parties you walked into," Mitchell said. "A football player could not afford to get caught smoking pot, or even being around it."

In the late sixties, football players were conservative by nature, even though some were wearing their hair a little longer and questioning the system a little louder. Still, their drug of choice was a cold Budweiser. Most of the players entertained themselves with card games, or a trip to the Flagon and Trencher.

In spite of the tumultuous times, Freddie Steinmark's focus remained riveted on the Big Four—football, faith, chemical engineering, and Linda Wheeler. In many respects, Steinmark was a throwback to the age of black-and-white TV, when the most outlandish character on the tube was Eddie Haskell on *Leave It to Beaver*.

Like Darrell Royal, Steinmark got his hair cut once a week and seemed deaf to the radicals screaming f-bombs around him. The first time Freddie smelled marijuana, he thought somebody was burning rope. Scott Henderson had to set him straight.

"Freddie rarely changed," Henderson said. "If a bomb had blown up around him, he would have shrugged it off. He had his goals and he was sticking to them. Besides, he never talked about politics."

Austin was center stage for the great clashing of wills in 1969. While the protestors marched and carried signs, the campus was still ruled by the iron fist of Frank C. Erwin Jr., the chairman of the Texas Board of Regents and a man who made Barry Goldwater seem liberal. If Erwin could have locked the campus gates to the hippie culture, he would have handled the chore himself. He managed to single-handedly ban *The Rag*, a radical newspaper, from campus because it was not licensed by U.T. Like a lot of underground newspapers of the day, *The Rag* glorified the Black Panthers and turned the "Chicago Seven" into saints. It promoted the mantra of the counterculture—"Outasight, groovy, and far-fucking-out." It was distributed out of the YMCA on Guadalupe Street, where the hippies were taking root, and sold for twenty cents. Erwin considered *The Rag* a latter-day *Communist Manifesto*.

Most of Austin was still in tune with country music, and the rednecks did not dig the hippie culture. It was said in Austin that the number-one traffic violation was driving without a haircut. A deejay on country station KOKE denounced the protest marchers as "Hanoi's Little Helpers." One of the hippie hangouts near campus, the Chuck Wagon, was closed to nonstudents when it was learned that the patrons were having sex inside the restaurant. Assistant District Attorney Herman Gotcher said, "The longhair radicals use that place to fornicate their desires."

In a historical piece for *The Austin Chronicle* in 1994, Craig Hattersley wrote, "In the late sixties, you might say that Austin became a city full of hippies finding themselves, finding what worked for them. This included artists, writers, musicians—the whole range of fanciful spirits besides your ordinary-but-longhaired folks."

Austin had not yet burgeoned into America's second fastest growing city, as it would in 1971. You could still rent a small house for fifty dollars a month. Before the cultural revolution, Austin was a medium-sized town that kicked up its heels on Saturday nights with loud country music and a six-pack to go. Other days, it was a quiet place where huge, ancient trees lined the streets. Many of the avenues climbed and dropped like roller-coaster tracks. It all began to change in the mid-1960s with the coming of the Vietnam War and the arrival of the peace movement along Guadalupe Avenue.

Mitchell tried not to notice. His world was changing rapidly and he was happy at last. He was playing more and drinking it in like a man thirsting for water.

In the fall of '68, Mitchell had finally met the girl of his dreams, Honor Franklin, who had visited campus one weekend. She was a friend of backup quarterback Eddie Phillips and both were from the small town of Mesquite, outside Dallas.

Upon Honor's arrival on campus each weekend, Phillips handed her a game program and told her to pick any player. She considered running back Billy Dale and tackle Bill Atessis, whom she described as a "Greek god." She settled on Mitchell and was quite happy with her choice until he showed up for a date unshaven and his hair long and unkempt. Instead of paying attention to the beautiful brunette with the shining eyes, he decided to read the newspaper. When they were seated for dinner, Bobby chose to eat with his fingers. She instantly dubbed him "the animal." He possessed the manners of a hungover raccoon.

When Honor suggested he try his knife and fork, Bobby said, "You know, I've been eating at the training table too long. Can you help me with my manners?"

Honor smiled. "The first thing you need to do, Bobby, is put that napkin in your lap."

After the fifth date, Honor knew that Bobby was a changed man. His table etiquette was vastly improved and the newspaper was long gone.

"I think I can do this," Mitchell told her. "I think this is doable."

Honor was responsible for raising Mitchell's spirits. He no longer felt like the loneliest cowboy on campus. With the graduation of Danny Abbott, he was moving into the starting lineup, where he planned to stay for his final two seasons at Texas.

"I was just about the happiest guy on the Texas campus," he said.

"Things started off badly for me, then they got a little better when I was moved into the offensive line. Then Honor comes into my life and I was a new man."

On the evening of January 17, the phone rang and Mitchell's life changed again. It was his mother, Marie, calling from Wheat Ridge.

"Bobby, your brother Mark is dead," she said. "He died in a helicopter crash this morning. Bobby, Mark is gone."

Mark Mitchell was Bobby's dear brother. More important, he was the hero of his life. Little brothers need strong big brothers, and Mark was all that. He lifted weights and played football and fought when he had to. When Bobby needed a sermon about quitting football, Mark delivered it. The last time Bobby saw Mark, they were floating in a johnboat across Possum Kingdom Lake. That day, Bobby heard the words that would change him forever: "You cannot quit. You will not quit." The reason he was still playing football at U.T. was Mark David Mitchell, dead at the age of twenty-one.

On the morning of his death, Mark had been dispatched twice over the village of Tay Ninh to pick up wounded soldiers. He should have been finished for the day after his second trip, but Mark insisted to his commanding officer that he make one more excursion. Coming back to the base on the second go-round, Mark had taken it upon himself to scout the area for more wounded comrades. He spotted downed American soldiers hiding from the Viet Cong in the heavy brush. It would be risky to make a third flight into the wooden area that was heavily guarded by the enemy. Mark, however, was a brave pilot, and he managed to pick everyone up. As the chopper rose from the trees, though, it was rocked by heavy artillery and burst into flames, killing everyone on board.

On the night he received the news, Bobby Mitchell left Moore Hill Hall and started walking. He kept thinking and crying and wondering why it had to happen to his brother. He encountered a group of war protestors. One carried a sign that read, STOP THE BABY KILLERS. Mitchell wanted to wade into the group, fists swinging. Something held him back. A violation of team rules might lead to his suspension, he thought. It was Mark, after all, who had turned his football career around. Mark would have been plenty pissed if he got kicked off the team.

Recounting the story some forty years later, Mitchell's eyes welled with tears.

"The day that Mark died, I felt horrible, horrible," he said. "I was low, low, low. I didn't know if I could handle it or not. I really didn't."

An hour later, Mitchell walked back to his dorm room and found Steinmark studying. They talked well into the night.

"I know that you are not a spiritual person, Mitch," Steinmark said, "but that doesn't mean you can't call upon God when you need him. You're going to need all of the strength you can muster these next few days. It wouldn't hurt to talk to God."

Mitchell had watched Steinmark drop to his knees every night in front of his bed to say his prayers. He thought about the undying strength of the young man. He thought about how his friend Freddie had battled his way into the starting lineup, becoming a great player in spite of his size. Just then, Freddie turned and placed his hands on his bed. He closed his eyes.

Bobby sat and watched Freddie, then closed his. It had been a long time, but he had a prayer in his heart. *Our Father, who art in heaven, hallowed be thy name . . .*

Chapter 13

WORRY

One of the most anticipated days of summer was the arrival of a certain magazine at drugstores and dime stores that did not feature busty, seminude women in cute bunny costumes. Because football was religion in Texas, Dave Campbell's *Texas Football* served as the Bible.

Right there on the cover of the 1969 edition of *Texas Football* was the color photograph of James Street weaving through traffic against Texas A&M, shaking a leg toward the end zone. A headline on the inside further excited the Texas faithful: THE BALLOT BOX GLOWS ORANGE. Of the twenty-seven sportswriters asked to predict the champion of the 1969 Southwest Conference race, fifteen had chosen Texas and eleven sided with Arkansas. Two ballots predicted the same result as the 1968 season—a tie between the two.

In picking Texas to win it all, Blackie Sherrod, the most celebrated sportswriter in the history of the state wrote, "[James] Street is the ideal man to run one of the country's best offenses."

Naturally, the seven-page spread on Texas was laden with statistics and trends produced by the monster offense known as the wishbone. The Longhorns averaged 40 points in the final nine games in 1968, while bolting to leads of 35–0 and 28–0 against Tennessee and Texas A&M.

Beyond Freddie Steinmark, the surprise player of the 1968 season was Cotton Speyrer, the swift wide receiver who caught passes of 51, 60, 78 and 70 yards. His overall receiving statistics—26 catches of 449 yards—were a bit pedestrian, but he averaged 34.8 yards on four end-arounds. As the 1969 season approached, Speyrer was considered the second-most-dangerous receiver in the Southwest Conference behind Arkansas's Chuck Dicus. So a statement coming from Speyrer about Steinmark caused people to listen: "Steinmark is the best safety I've ever played against." After all, Speyrer had squared off against Steinmark every day in practice and knew him better than anyone.

Tight end Randy Peschel was another Texas receiver who rarely got the best of Steinmark.

"If you could beat Freddie in practice, you could beat the guy you were going up against in the next game," Peschel said. "No one was better than Freddie. He could run like a deer and he was quick. So there weren't many times in practice that I beat him."

After starting eleven games and intercepting 5 passes the previous season, Steinmark was the *Dallas Times Herald*'s preseason choice at safety for the 1969 All-Southwest Conference first-team. If the Longhorns contended for the national championship, he was a sure choice for some of the All-American teams.

Back in Wheat Ridge, Steinmark was preparing for the 1969 season, running wind sprints each night at the high school stadium and lifting weights. He also played summer baseball three times a week.

Steinmark's day job for the third straight summer was in the tire department at Rickenbaugh Chevrolet in Denver for Frank Caputo, a friend of the family. One afternoon in mid-July, he was hustling across the car lot en route to the tire department when Caputo stopped him.

"Freddie," he said. "I don't know if you realize this or not, but you're dragging that left leg. What the hell happened to you, son?"

Steinmark looked down at his left thigh, shrugged his shoulders, and said, "I'm not sure, Mr. Caputo. I think I might have wrenched my knee sliding into third base. I just don't know."

Freddie was puzzled at the pain in his left knee. He sat down and rubbed his thigh, but felt no swelling. He rolled up his pantleg, but found no bruises. He admitted to himself that the leg hurt. But he was just going to ignore it. Like every other injury of his long football career, it would soon go away.

At age twenty, going into his junior year at Texas, nothing was going to stop Steinmark, the starting safety for the most-talked-about team in America. A little pain was not going to get him down.

"Freddie liked being a star," his friend Scott Henderson said. "He was a down-to-earth guy. But he liked shining on the playing field. He liked people watching him. He was not about to give up his starting position."

Steinmark loved every minute of playing football. Halfway through the summer, he planned to step up his conditioning program and forget his darn leg.

When Freddie was not working or working out, he was spending as much time as possible with Linda Wheeler. Their relationship was growing in leaps and bounds. Linda could not have been happier with her first two years at the University of Texas. She was proud that she had stood her ground on going to U.T. with Freddie. She was glad her father had said yes and was willing to convince her doubting mother.

"I absolutely loved the University of Texas," she recalled. "I loved my sorority, my friends, my classes. It was great feeling all of the excitement Freddie was causing on the football field. Everybody on campus was talking about him. They were always picking my brain about Freddie. There were a lot of stars on the Texas football team, and Freddie was one of them."

In the summer of '69, Freddie and Linda were going to the movies and parking in the woods behind the Wheelers' house. These were the best days of their lives.

When they dated in high school, Freddie liked to pull the Mustang up to the front curb of the Wheelers' house and do somersaults across the front lawn. In July 1969, Linda was looking for Freddie through the front window of the house one evening when she saw him limping up the sidewalk. She met him at the door. "Freddie, why are you limping?"

"I didn't know I was," he replied. "Mr. Caputo said the same thing the other day. I told him that I hurt my knee sliding into third base. At least, I think I did."

Linda smiled. "Freddie, you're trying to do too much. You've always done more than anyone else. Save it for the football season. It's a long grind, you know."

The next afternoon, Freddie's workout plan was to lift weights for ninety minutes, then run twenty 100-yard dashes at top speed. He was halfway through the wind sprints when his father, Fred Sr., walked into the stadium. He watched his son for several minutes, then approached him. He was not smiling.

Heavily winded, Freddie held up his right hand and said, "I know, I know, Dad. You think I'm limping. I think I'm limping, too."

Big Fred frowned. "Son, if you know you're limping, why don't you stop? Take a little break. Rest for a few days. Try to gain some more weight." Since entering Texas as a freshmen two years earlier, Freddie's weight had risen from 150 to 160.

"I can't stop working out, Dad," Freddie said. "We're going for the national championship. It's like you and Mom always told me: I'm smaller than everybody else. I've got to work twice as hard."

Big Fred put his arm around his son's shoulders. "Come on, get in the car. I'm taking you home for a big dinner. Then you're going to take a few days off, Freddie. I don't want you limping into Austin."

The previous year, Steinmark had traveled to Austin two weeks before the start of two-a-days to acclimate himself to the scorching heat and miserable humidity. This time, he was going to Dallas to be with his best friend, Scott Henderson, the linebacker who had found his way into the starting lineup in the second quarter against Oklahoma State in 1968 and never returned to the bench. Henderson and Glen Halsell composed one of the best linebacker tandems in the SWC. Royal often called Halsell a "rolling ball of butcher knives," and acknowledged that Henderson was the second biggest hitter on the team.

Steinmark was drawn to Henderson because of his no-nonsense ways and because both were Catholic. Thanks to his low-key nature, Henderson was called the "old man" and "the professor" by his teammates.

"I really did look old, even then," Henderson recalled. "But I was a very competitive athlete. I don't care what you are like off the field. I was one of those guys who could throw the switch on the field and take care of business. One of our teammates, Billy Dale, was one of the nicest guys you would ever meet. But he could be an absolute terror on the field."

Henderson came to enjoy Steinmark's friendship because he was opinionated and never afraid to say what was on his mind. Steinmark was not one to talk endlessly. Still, when he had something to say, he said it. This trait came from his grandmother, Nana Marchetti, who lived in the Bottoms of Denver and became the matriarch of the family after the death of her husband.

"Freddie was this funny Italian guy who wore his feelings on his shirtsleeve," Henderson said. "Freddie could be very entertaining. I loved being around him and he was just a great friend."

That August, Steinmark moved into the Henderson home. The next day, they headed to the Hillcrest High School Stadium and went right to work. The duo found several high school players throwing a football around. The kids soon learned that Steinmark and Henderson were starting defensive players from the great Texas team of 1968.

"Come on, let's play some touch football," one of them said. "We want to see if you Texas guys are as good as advertised."

On the first play, the kid who Steinmark was supposed to cover blew past him and caught a long pass. Ditto for the second play. Soon, the high school boys were scoring touchdowns left and right. When Steinmark fell and struggled to get up, Henderson became concerned.

"Freddie, you don't look good," Henderson said.

"I know, Scott, everybody's telling me the same thing. I'm limping. I don't think it's that bad. Plus, this is my first day in this danged heat."

Steinmark sat down and rubbed the leg. "I really don't know what's wrong with this thing. But I'll be happy when it goes the hell away."

Henderson rarely heard Steinmark swear; even "hell" sounded radical coming out of his mouth.

"Freddie, I guess you had a pretty bad summer," Henderson said.

"Oh, I think I hurt my knee playing baseball. No big deal. But the whole thing is pretty weird. I don't know if it's a pulled muscle or some kind of tendon problem in my knee. I will say this, nothing has ever lingered on like this. But I'll be okay by the time we put on the pads."

In truth, for the first time in his life, Steinmark was not looking forward to putting on a football uniform. His leg ached and he wondered what the coaches would think if he limped around the practice field. Most of the time, Steinmark cherished the long, arduous workouts. Players who relished two-a-days were as rare as an Aggie fan flashing the "Gig 'Em" sign in downtown Austin. Steinmark reminded the coaches of Tommy Nobis, who practiced as hard as he played.

"Nobis never let up on a single play during the game or practice," defensive coordinator Mike Campbell remembered. "We'd be going through two-a-days and just roasting out there in the Texas sun. Players would be falling out left and right. And Tommy Nobis would be knocking them into the cheap seats. In many ways, Freddie was just like Nobis."

Nobis was also one of the few sophomores to start his first game under Royal.

"Freddie was such a hard, hard, hard worker, and that's why he started as a sophomore," Fred Akers said. "It wasn't enough for him to do it right. For him, he wanted to do it exceptionally right. In his way, Freddie was a very inspiring leader. He was a pepperpot. He was all the time encouraging his fellow teammates. There was never any pessimism about him. None. He was a born leader."

On the first day of preseason practice, Royal gathered the team around him in the center of the field.

"Boys, I know these summer workouts are hard on you," he began, "but they are a necessity. A hundred miles east of here, the Aggies are going through the same thing. Up in Fayetteville, Arkansas, they are practicing twice a day just like we are. They're going to be as sore as we are. Our successes or failures will depend on our willingness to work. Remember that every other team in the Southwest Conference is working as hard as us. They'll be trying to knock your nuts off this fall because we beat 'em all last year. Well, we didn't beat Texas Tech because we didn't give our best. But we're gonna beat 'em this year."

The players came together in a circle and built a huge pile of hands in the center. Together, they yelled "Texas Fight," then took off running in all directions. The two-a-days had officially begun.

That September, seven offensive starters were returning. Bobby Mitchell was finally moving into the starting lineup at left guard, next to one of the best tackles in America, Bobby Wuensch. Mike Dean was promoted to the starter at right guard next to Bob McKay. No team in America could boast of better tackles than Wuensch and McKay, surely the best in the history of U.T. football.

Everyone agreed that Mitchell and Dean were up to the new challenge. As backup guards in 1968, they gained a lot of experience, thanks to the liberal substituting done by Royal in the second half of many games. Over the past two years, Mitchell had been a leader in the weight room, piling on the muscle and increasing his weight by thirty-five pounds to 235. His transition from running back to right guard had been seamless.

In 1969, the Texas offensive line would be blocking for the best fullback in the country. The previous year, Worster had rushed for 806 yards and tied Chris Gilbert for the team touchdown lead with 13. Remarkably, he averaged 5 yards per attempt while toting the ball straight up the middle. Worster was a warrior who never complained and rarely opened his mouth in practice.

"He just goes out and causes wrecks," defensive coordinator Mike Campbell said. "Then he gets up, straightens his headgear, and goes back to the huddle."

Royal was even more impressed with his big, battling fullback. "Steve Worster plays his position as well as anyone we've ever had here outside of Tommy Nobis."

One of Campbell's side duties was leading the bed checks the night before road games. So valuable was Worster that Campbell would tell the other coaches, "Don't ever catch Worster doing anything wrong! If he gets kicked off the team, we're all *dead*."

Like Worster, Street was about to get his first full season in the wishbone. The offense could not have fallen into better hands. Street had improved with every game in 1968, even though his overall statistics of 304 rushing yards and 1,099 passing seemed ordinary. He was the engine that drove the wishbone. Not a single opposing defense could ever guess his next move.

The Texas defensive secondary was about to be rearranged with the departure of Bill Bradley. Tom Campbell was moving from rover linebacker to defensive halfback and the speedy Danny Lester would be promoted to the other corner.

No doubt, the biggest loss on defense was linebacker Corby Robertson, an All-American in 1967 and a player who showed great leadership during the '68 season that began with such chaos. It was the steady hands of captains Robertson, Gilbert, and Bradley that turned the season around. Royal worried that he would never find that kind of leadership from the 1969 bunch.

The 4-4-3 defense, adapted from Notre Dame defensive coordinator Johnny Ray, was an excellent scheme against the run. It did, however, put a lot of pressure on the three defensive backs. Ninety-five percent of the college teams in 1969 were using four defensive backs. There would be games against SMU and Arkansas when Steinmark, Campbell, and Lester would be trying to handle as many as five receivers. It would be the job of the new rover, Mike Campbell IV, to drop into coverage and help out.

In order to employ the 4-4-3, a team needed four great linebackers. Texas had no trouble supplying that need. From left to right, it would be Mike Campbell IV, Scott Henderson, Glen Halsell, and David Richardson.

The defensive line in the 4-4-3 was a novel arrangement in that the tackles lined up on the outside shoulders of the guards, and the ends were outside the tackles. In effect, the outside linebackers, Campbell and Richardson, were stand-up defensive ends.

From left to right, the starting line for the opening game against California would be Bill Atessis, Greg Ploetz, Bill Zapalac, and Leo Brooks. The coaches could not wait to turn Atessis loose for a full season at defensive end. He was the biggest player of the Royal era at 6'3" and 260 pounds, and some people thought he was still growing. He loved to eat. At the age of fourteen, he went to work for his father, James, in the kitchen of a Greek restaurant in Houston. His dad figured it was cheaper to put him to work where he could eat free.

Coeds around the Texas campus were enamored of Atessis's good looks. His fellow teammates, however, viewed him as Godzilla without the long tail. Atessis was known as a fighter on and off the field. The previous spring, during Royal's Hell Camp, he had broken two helmets running head-on with Worster.

"Bill Atessis never had to worry about getting in fights because there was nobody on that Texas campus who wanted to fight somebody that big," Mike Campbell said.

With fourteen starters and thirty-six lettermen returning, Texas was finally ready to make another serious run at the national title. This was how the preseason Associated Press Top Ten stacked up:

1. Ohio State
2. Arkansas
3. Penn State
4. Texas
5. Southern California
6. Oklahoma
7. Houston
8. Georgia
9. Ole Miss
10. Missouri

Back in June, an idea had been hatched at ABC Television headquarters in New York to move the Arkansas-Texas game from October 18 to the last weekend of the season. Network publicist Beano

Cook had convinced his boss, Roone Arledge, that the chances were excellent that Arkansas and Texas would be the number 1 and 2 teams in the country on December 6. Cook also projected that undefeated Arkansas and Penn State would play in the Cotton Bowl in the postseason national championship game. If that was not enough, Cook confidently told Arledge that Ohio State, the defending national champ, would get knocked off along the way.

To sweeten the pot, ABC promised that if Texas-Arkansas carried national championship implications, President Richard Nixon would attend. Nixon had been contacted by ABC analyst Bud Wilkinson, the former Oklahoma coach who was politically active with the Republican Party. When Wilkinson presented the proposal to Nixon, the president had said yes. After all, Nixon considered himself the number-one football fan in America.

In convincing Royal and Broyles to switch the game to December, Arledge informed the coaches that it might be called "The Game of the Century." A hundred years earlier, in 1869, Princeton and Rutgers had played the first football game ever.

Steinmark just prayed that he could make it to December. During the first few days of preseason practice, he rarely limped. As the two-a-days wore on, though, and temperatures soared into the high nineties, Akers noticed a change. Steinmark's acceleration was not the same. Passes that normally would have been intercepted were being knocked down. He was not getting across the field as quickly as he used to.

"I could see that something was wrong, but just like everybody else, I couldn't figure it out," he said. "I asked Freddie about it one day and he told me it was a charley horse." That is a colloquial term for a painful contusion of the quadriceps muscle that often results in a hematoma, resulting in several weeks of pain and disability. It can be caused by dehydration, low levels of potassium, calcium in the blood, or a blow from an opponent's knee, which is common in football. It felt like a kick from a horse, and therefore was called a "charley horse."

Top: Freddie Steinmark (43) takes the pitch from Roger Behler (14) and follows a block by Bobby Mitchell (42) during Wheat Ridge's state playoff game against Wasson High in 1966. *(Wheat Ridge Yearbook: "The Agrarian")*

Above Left: Freddie Steinmark with Candy Kesner. The two were elected as "Prom Royalty" at Wheat Ridge High in 1967. *(Wheat Ridge Yearbook: "The Agrarian")*

Above Right: Freddie Steinmark (middle of front row) laughs after Bobby Mitchell, next to microphone, boasted to the Wheat Ridge student body that the Farmers would "beat the hell out of Lakewood" in 1966. *(Wheat Ridge High School Yearbook: "The Agrarian")*

Top: Linda Wheeler and Bobby Mitchell as the Wheat Ridge Queen and King in 1966. *(Wheat Ridge Yearbook: "The Agrarian")*

Top: Bobby Mitchell carries the ball on the Wheat Ridge practice field in 1966. *(Bobby Mitchell collection)*

Middle: L to R: 1968 cocaptains Chris Gilbert, Corby Robertson, and Bill Bradley. *(University of Texas Archives)*

Left: Bobby Mitchell with girlfriend Honor Franklin at a campus party in 1968. *(Bobby Mitchell collection)*

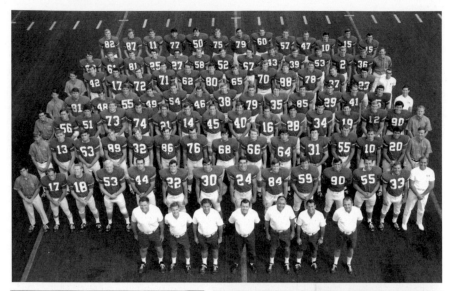

Top: The 1969 Texas national championship team. Freddie Steinmark, No. 28, is in the third row of players, sixth from the right. *(University of Texas Archives)*

Above Left: Darrell Royal on the sideline during a game in 1969. *(University of Texas Archives)*

Above Right: Freddie Steinmark, No. 28, tackles Rice quarterback Stahle Vincent in a game in 1969. *(University of Texas Archives)*

Top: L to R: Tom Campbell, Mike Campbell III, and Mike Campbell IV the day before the Cotton Bowl on January 1, 1970, against Notre Dame. *(University of Texas Archives)*

Middle: Freddie Steinmark (center in second row) celebrates 1970 Cotton Bowl victory over Notre Dame with teammates Bobby Wuensch and Bill Atessis (back row) and Scott Palmer and Scott Henderson, front row. Photo was taken less than a month after Freddie's leg was amputated. *(Scott Palmer Collection)*

Left: Coach Darrell Royal kisses Freddie Steinmark after Texas scored the winning touchdown against Notre Dame in the 1970 Cotton Bowl. *(Texas SID Department)*

Top: L to R: Freddie Steinmark, President Richard Nixon, and coach Darrell Royal at the White House in April of 1970. *(Father Fred Bomar Collection)*

Middle: L to R: Freddie Steinmark, President Richard Nixon, coach Darrell Royal, actor Fess Parker, and Father Fred Bomar in April of 1970 at the White House. That year, Parker, a graduate of the University of Texas, was president of the American Cancer Society. *(Father Fred Bomar Collection)*

Above Left: L to R: Freddie Steinmark with Father Fred Bomar at the White House in April of 1970. *(Father Fred Bomar collection)*

Above Right: Freddie Steinmark stands on the sideline of the January 1, 1970 Cotton Bowl against Notre Dame with his brother, Sammy, to his left. *(University of Texas Archives)*

Middle: Former Texas coach Darrell Royal with Bobby Mitchell at the Texas Football Reunion in 2010. *(Bobby Mitchell collection)*

Top: Texas coach Mack Brown horns Freddie Steinmark's photo as he heads down the tunnel for a home game in 2010. *(University of Texas Archives)*

Bottom: All-American cornerback Aaron Williams horns the Freddie Steinmark picture before a game during the 2010 season. Williams was the 34th selection of the Buffalo Bills in the 2011 NFL draft. *(University of Texas Archives)*

Bobby Mitchell realized his friend was hurting when he noticed him rubbing the leg while lying on his bed at the new dormitory called the Jester Center, where the football team had moved.

"Freddie, I know there's something wrong with your leg," Mitchell said. "Maybe you should go to see [trainer] Frank Medina tomorrow."

Steinmark shook his head. "Not yet, Mitch. I still think it's just a charley horse or a pulled muscle. I've had these things before and they always get better."

"Then why are you rubbing it all the time?" Mitchell said.

"I don't know what else to do."

"Look, Freddie," Mitchell said. "A charley horse shouldn't last this long. Sooner or later, the thing should loosen up. You need to go see Medina."

Players were reticent about seeing trainer Frank Medina because he normally was not happy to see them. Unless the bone was sticking through the skin, Medina did not believe in rushing into treatment. Mike Campbell said, "I don't think that Frank Medina ever healed a single player unless he did it with religion."

Steinmark wrote in *I Play to Win*, "Athletic trainers are inclined to be a little hard-boiled and skeptical. They've all had experiences with guys who might put a little overemphasis on an injury and escape weekday work."

In the 1960s, a code existed that said players worth their salt did not complain about pain. You were expected to play through the bleeding, bumps, and bruises even if they did not subside in a reasonable time. Players who were spotted in the training room for two or three straight days became outcasts. Each afternoon, Darrell Royal and his assistants walked through the training room for the purpose of counting heads and identifying the players they considered "malingerers."

Bill Atessis hobbled around on a broken ankle for several weeks before the start of the 1967 freshman season without the injury being diagnosed. Due to a team rule, he had to seek permission from

Medina to see the doctor. When Dr. Joe Reneau X-rayed the ankle, he discovered the break and put Atessis's foot in a cast, ending his season.

"When I got hurt, everybody said, 'suck it up and go play,'" Atessis said. "'Put some tape on it and go play.' That was the mentality back then. In those days, there was never an investigation into what the hell was wrong with you. Nobody really knew what was wrong with you because they weren't checking."

After the season-opening 17–0 victory over California, in which sophomore starting halfback Jim Bertelsen and Street recorded touchdown runs, Steinmark's pain was becoming more intense. It felt like a hot poker had been stuck into his left thighbone just above the knee. He was sitting next to Henderson on the Braniff Electra returning home. Over New Mexico, he told his best friend, "Scott, I really don't understand this. My leg is starting to kill me. What in the world is wrong with me?"

"Freddie, you've got to go see Medina," Henderson said. "You don't have any other choice. You've got to get some help."

Not once had Steinmark stepped foot inside the trainer's room other than to have his ankles taped. Henderson knew that confessing to an injury was going to be difficult.

"Look, Freddie, just go tell Medina that you need to sit in the whirlpool for a while. It's not that difficult."

Monday morning, Steinmark pondered his dilemma for more than an hour and took off for the training room. After waiting outside the door for several minutes and pondering the situation, he walked in and nervously approached the trainer.

"Look, Mr. Medina," he said, "I'm really not hurt that bad—"

"Then why are you here?"

"Well, you see this pain in my leg has been bugging me for over six weeks. There's no reason for me to sit out the next game. I just need to spend some time in the whirlpool."

"Look, Freddie, it's okay to go in the whirlpool," Medina said.

"Just remember that if you're in there every day, the coaches are going to wonder what's up."

The job description of Frank Medina applied to the majority of college football trainers of the time. He spent much of his time supervising the harsh conditioning drills and doling out punishment for such crimes as drinking, cutting class, and missing curfew. Medina was a fire-breathing, 4'10" full-blooded Cherokee Indian who scared the hell out of the Texas players.

Medina was given broad authority by Darrell Royal to run his operation as he saw fit. He treated injuries by any means he chose, so long as the broken player was back on the field lickety-split. Sprained ankles and separated shoulders could wait until the end of the season. Texas, like most big-time football teams, was in the business of winning games, not healing the wounded.

Players were expected to play with whatever ailed them, a concept dating to Knute Rockne in the 1920s. This was a mentality extolled by the great coach, John Heisman, for whom the Heisman Trophy was named. Heisman once told his team, "Gentlemen, it is better to have died a baby than to fumble this football."

Injuries in the late 1960s were fixed with rolls of white adhesive tape and an analgesic balm that smelled like a nuclear holocaust. Trainers of the times were expected to shove players off the training table and back onto the field. Frank Medina did his job as well as anyone. The look of disdain on his face made them feel small and actually worked as a screening process.

Medina was not unlike other trainers of the previous twenty years. Texas A&M's Smokey Harper believed that a player who could not play with at least one broken bone was not worthy of a scholarship. Harper's boss at Texas A&M, beginning in 1954, was Paul "Bear" Bryant, a man who devoutly believed that a player was never too injured to strap on the pads. As an Alabama tight end in the 1930s, he had once played an entire game with a broken leg.

So it was not surprising that Bryant's trainer would be a hard-drinking, hard-of-hearing man whose motto was quite simple: "If the pain's above the neck, take an aspirin. If the pain's below the waist, get your ass in the whirlpool. Otherwise, get your ass out of my training room." A sign in Harper's training room told the whole story: GET WELL OR GET GOING.

Tolerance for injuries was still almost negligible in college football. Coaches seemed more concerned with toughening their players than healing them. Royal had subscribed to this ideology since his playing days at the University of Oklahoma, when he came under the tutelage of Port Robertson, one of the most rugged characters in sports at the time. On June 6, 1944, Robertson had stormed the beachhead at Omaha and marched across France as the captain in charge of an artillery unit. One day, Robertson was holed up in a foxhole when the German eighty-eights successfully pinpointed their target and blasted him twenty feet into the air. Somehow, he managed to survive the fall and wound up teaching this brand of fearlessness at the University of Oklahoma.

Medina was a cross between Harper and Robertson. He was mostly known for the torturous "Medina Drills" during the off-season, when in early January, players reported to a closed-off room at the top of the stadium, where steam heaters pushed the temperatures past 120 degrees. They wore sweat suits, wrist weights, ankle weights, fifty-pound vests, and carried a thirty-pound dumbbell in each hand.

Each year, before embarking upon his version of physical conditioning, Medina gave the players the same speech:

"Some of you will make it and some of you won't. The ones who do not make it will not have the character to do so. Simply, you do not have what it takes. Now, men, I am going to work you and work you because I want to see you become men. But I also know that some of you will not make it. Some of you will quit."

The trainer wore his trademark white towel draped around his neck each day as he barked orders while pacing back and forth on a bench. With the dumbbells held above their heads, the players ran in place with knees driving higher and higher. Then they would pump the dumbbells up and down. Medina ordered them to stop and to hold the dumbbells straight out from their chests until their arms gave out. This was followed by jumping jacks, armlifts, and sit-ups. They would run in place for a half hour. Then, as they jumped back and forth over the bench, Medina counted each one. This drill continued until one of the players, soaked in sweat, collapsed from exhaustion, giving Medina yet another target for his venom.

"Get up, dammit," he would yell. "I knew you couldn't do it. I knew you would quit."

When a player fell out from total fatigue, everyone in the group was required to repeat the drill. Soon, teammates were yelling at each other for giving up. Before long, the players were ordered to do hundreds of sit-ups while still holding the dumbbells.

"You'll be doing sit-ups on that concrete floor until your butts bleed," Medina yelled. Indeed, many of them came away from the rough concrete with cuts and scrapes that would ache for weeks.

Players were required to climb a forty-foot rope all the way to the ceiling. Many times, they lost their grip on the rope, sliding all the way to the floor while suffering deep rope burns that often bled. Regardless of the pain, or the severity of the burn, Medina demanded that they climb all the way up again. Gasping inside the steam-heated room, some of the players stuck their heads into the open windows, desperate to breathe fresh air. During these times, players described Medina as being "half maniacal" with "evil eyes."

"Trainer was not the right word for what Medina did," Mike Campbell said. "A better description would be the general manager of conditioning, punishment, and pain."

One of Medina's methods for getting players back on the field quickly was to clean scrapes, gouges, and gashes with a razor.

"One time, he cut a scab right off my hand with a razor and made it bleed," Bobby Wuensch said. "He just cut the infection right out of it. Then he put a bandage on it and sent me back out to play. I didn't like it. The doggone thing hurt. But it healed faster and I didn't miss any time."

Complaining would not have mattered. Players who spent too much time talking about their injuries were either demoted or sent packing.

"Football was the survival of the fittest and that was especially the case at the University of Texas," Wuensch said. "At Texas, you were expected to perform regardless of the injuries or pain. The bottom line is that you either make it or you don't."

Before his leg started aching, Steinmark actually loved the tough Medina Drills and excelled at a level that made Medina smile.

Near the end of the sessions, Medina liked to order the players to stand shoulder to shoulder in military formation. Then he would ask Steinmark to step out.

"If all of you guys were as tough as Freddie Steinmark, we'd win the national championship every year," he would holler. "This little guy is one of the toughest players ever to pass through the University of Texas. He should be an example to all of you for what hard work can do. Just look at him. This boy is barely sweating."

One of Medina's duties was writing memos to Royal to grade each of the players' toughness. Steinmark always received the highest marks and this helped accelerate his rise to the starting lineup.

Like Steinmark, Bobby Mitchell never faltered in the Medina Drills. Because Mitchell trained year-round and worked harder in the weight room than anyone else, he was already in shape by the time the Medina Drills rolled around. He could withstand the punishment doled out by the little madman.

A year earlier, though, Mitchell had been cited for underage drinking. Royal found out and the coach informed Mitchell, Steve Worster, and a few others that he could either kick them off the team, or assign them to Medina for some extra running in the morning. Medina loved nothing better than to have his players puking before sunrise.

They began the drills by running ten yards up the field and rolling over and over and over on the ground until their stomachs emptied. Then they ran stadium steps until they puked some more.

"Let me tell you, it wasn't much fun throwing up that much at five in the morning," Mitchell recalled.

Mitchell detested the entire Medina experience, and like many of the ex-players, still loathes the Texas trainer and his chamber of horrors.

"If Hitler would've had Frank Medina, Germany would have won the war," he said. "Medina was insane. He was the henchman from hell. His job was to run everybody off that Coach Royal didn't want hanging around."

For the rest of the 1969 season, Steinmark would live in Medina's world, adhering to his rules. Being injured for the first time in his career often left Steinmark feeling confused and disoriented. He knew the coaches were watching his every step. His lifelong dream now hung in the balance. He could not fail. *He could not fail.*

Chapter 14

THE TWINS

The Campbell twins could identify with the improbable rise of Freddie Steinmark better than anyone. The road to glory for Mike and Tom Campbell was long and pothole-laden. They started at the bottom and worked their way up, centimeter by centimeter.

"My brother and I were absolutely bad football players coming out of high school," Tom Campbell said. "Nobody wanted us—and I mean *nobody*. Finally, Daddy came into our room one night and told us that Darrell [Royal] said we could come out for football and stay as long as we liked. Shoot, they didn't even offer us scholarships."

"Daddy" was Mike Campbell III, the Texas defensive coordinator since 1957 and one of the most coveted assistant coaches in college football. Because of his long friendship with Royal, no one was ever going to convince him to leave Austin. As the assistant head coach, Campbell had a large say in all team matters.

If Mike Campbell III wanted his sons on the Texas team, the matter was already settled. He could not have cared less that their careers at Reagan High School in Austin were so undistinguished that not a single university offered them scholarships. As they said around the high school scene, Tom and Mike were small but slow.

About the only person who believed in them was their mother, Mary Campbell. She told them on the day they left for the University of Texas, "Boys, do me one favor. *Do not fail.*"

When the twins enrolled at U.T., they did not know if they were walk-ons or scholarship athletes. Forty years later, Mike and Tom still believe they spent their entire careers as walk-ons. This was disputed by someone who should know, a guy named Darrell Royal.

"Sure, they were on scholarship," Royal said. "We couldn't have kept them around that long if they hadn't been on scholarship."

Told of Royal's remarks, Tom Campbell said, "Neither myself or my brother ever signed a letter-of-intent with Texas. We never signed anything. So how could we have been on scholarship?"

Scholarship or no scholarship, the Campbell twins could have received a free education because their father was employed at U.T. Regardless, Tom and Mike Campbell could not have been happier in the fall of 1969 as the Longhorns moved toward the second game against Texas Tech. They were starting on one of the best defensive units in the country and teaming with Steinmark, a player they greatly admired. The Campbell twins and Steinmark could have been triplets if Freddie had been their size.

That season, Tom Campbell was the starter at left defensive halfback and Mike held down the rover linebacker position. In many respects, "rover" was a misnomer because Mike Campbell did little roving. Most of the time, he lined up on the weak side of the defense, away from the tight end, and occasionally dropped into pass coverage.

No one in their right mind would have predicted two years earlier that the twins would be candidates for the starting lineup. They were nothing more than glorified dummy-holders. At the beginning of 1967, they were relegated to the "shit drills" in the south end zone of Memorial Stadium. They were about as far from the starting lineup as Montreal to Melbourne. Even their own father barely acknowledged them.

The shit drillers of that era wore blue jerseys and either stood around on the sideline or held blocking dummies. At the end of practice, they sprung into action with "Big Mike" Campbell supervising the shit drills.

"Daddy didn't consider the shit drills to be punishment for being a bad player," Tom said. "He just figured there were many guys in blue jerseys who might be football players. He worked hard to find them."

The shit drills were a facsimile of football, and nothing more. The players were herded through some of the toughest football maneuvers known to football—"eye-openers" and "bull in the ring." They were required to hit, hit, hit, and to keep hitting. As the sun set over Austin, you could hear the pads popping and helmets pounding all the way to the Capitol about a mile away.

What Tom and Mike accomplished in the drills proved to be something of a miracle. Through grit and sheer determination, they proved that anyone could reach their dream in big-time college football. Stuck as low as the tenth string, they began their climb together. A lot of ground was gained through attrition.

"The University of Texas gave out at least fifty scholarships a year," Mike said. "Some players looked around and realized they were never going to play at the University of Texas and they started quitting. Some of them just stopped going to class so they could flunk out."

Compared to the other players, Tom and Mike had nothing to lose. They had come to Texas with virtually nothing and were prepared to leave that way. One key to their success was that so many players were leaving.

"Based on where I was in life, all I wanted to do was make my way to the second or third team so I could get a uniform and stand on the sideline on Saturdays, watching the other guys play," Tom said.

Tom's journey up the roster was a slow one, but he did manage to make the traveling squad for the Arkansas game in Little Rock in 1967. He replaced a third-stringer who had worn the number 84. He found that same number at his locker when he reached the stadium on Saturday. He picked up the game program, hoping to see his picture. He did find number 84—along with a picture of the player he had replaced. That was just the beginning of his frustration.

The next week against Rice in Austin, Campbell intercepted a pass and, for the first time, basked in the spotlight. His teammates hugged him. Even the father who never praised him flashed a quick smile. Then he heard the public address announcer call him by the name of the player he had replaced. His own mother, watching the game from the west stands, did not know that her son had intercepted a pass.

Tom began the 1968 season as the second team rover linebacker. With each passing day, he checked the defensive roster that was written with a grease pencil on the glass outside the equipment room. Tom was not curious to see if he was moving up. Rather, he always figured that his dad was going to move him down.

"My greatest worry was that Daddy would demote me," Tom said. "I walked in and checked the depth chart one day and I looked to see if my name was still on the second string. It wasn't. So I started going down to the third, fourth, and fifth strings. My name was nowhere to be found. So I checked at the defensive halfback positions and I wasn't there, either. So I went back to rover and there I was on first string."

Tom headed straight for his father's office.

"I always called Daddy 'Coach Campbell' around the stadium," Tom said. "But I walked straight in there and said, 'Daddy, there must be some kind of mistake. Your secretary typed up the new roster wrong. You've got me on the first string.'"

"There's no mistake," the elder Campbell snapped. "You're the starter at rover and you will be on the field for the first play against Oklahoma State."

"But Daddy—"

"Don't 'Daddy' me. Don't tell me you're not ready."

"Yessir, Coach, I'm ready," he said. "Thank you very much."

Tom turned and marched out of the office. Yet, it still seemed impossible that he would be introduced with the starters on Saturday in the town where he had grown up for the past twelve years.

One of the biggest reasons that the Campbells rose through the ranks of the roster was that both were fighters. If another player wanted a knuckle sandwich, all he needed to utter were two words: "coach's sons." It ignited a fire inside the twins like nothing else.

"We were obligated to fight whenever those words were spoken,"

Mike Campbell said. "The first couple of years it seemed like we were always fighting. We didn't care who we had to fight and size didn't matter."

Tackle Bob White, who was sixty pounds heavier, decided to test Tom Campbell one day during practice on the freshman field. As the players were warming up, White and another player were throwing a football back and forth. White missed one of the passes and the ball fell into the hands of Tom Campbell.

"Give me the ball! Give me the ball!" White demanded. When Campbell cradled the ball and laughed, White walked toward him in a menacing manner. With White only a few feet away, Campbell punted the ball directly into his chest. He went off like a hot Roman candle.

"He took a swing at me," Campbell said. "So I reared back and clocked him. I bloodied his nose."

The fight was on and players were running from all directions to watch.

"All of a sudden, White realized that I wasn't about to back down," Campbell said. "Pretty soon, all of the other guys realized that, too."

Almost from childbirth, the Campbell twins were fighting each other. They loved pushing each other's hot button. On long driving vacations, it was inevitable that they would start picking at each other in the backseat of the family's Ford station wagon. Before long, Mary Campbell would give up her front seat to sit between her boys in the backseat and referee. Once, when they arrived at a vacation spot, Mike was sent to one end of the campground and Tom to the other.

One day at U.T., Tom returned to the dorm with a golf bag slung over his right shoulder and his girlfriend on his left. He had spent most of the day playing golf and drinking beer. Noting that his brother was a little tipsy, Mike pulled out the needle. He said, "You know, Tom, your girlfriend's got little tits."

Tom took a swing at his twin brother and Mike ducked. Tackle Charles Crawford stepped between them and Tom landed a punch to his jaw. Then Mike ducked once more into his room and locked the door.

"Mike was like a cartoon character giggling behind the door," Tom said. "I challenged him to come out and fight and he wouldn't do it."

Tom pounded and pounded and got no response. So he pulled out his eight iron and went to work. Not only did the club raise a racket, it began to slice huge chunks out of the wooden door. Soon it was pocked from top to bottom. Realizing that he was getting nowhere, Tom retired to his room next door.

"It finally wore me out and I realized it was a bad idea anyway," he said.

The next morning, Tom heard laughter in the hallway and knew the reason why. Not until he walked down the hallway, though, did he see the sign taped to the badly damaged door.

WINTER RULES APPLY.
PLEASE REPLACE DIVOTS.

Later that day, Big Mike Campbell marched up the stairs to the third floor of Moore Hill Hall with Fred Akers. He pounded on Tom's door.

"What is this I hear about you trying to knock a door down," the father said. "I hear you were using your golf clubs. You know, I gave you those golf clubs."

"Yessir, Daddy, you did," Tom said.

"Which one did you use?"

"The eight iron."

"Let me see it."

The father inspected the eight iron and detected no damage. He stuck the club back in the bag.

"You're still going to have to pay for the door," Big Mike said and stormed out.

In the spring of 1968, Tom and Mike were planning to attend the Tri Delta formal with a couple of sorority sisters. They devised a plan of Tom picking up his date first, returning to the dorm to fetch Mike.

After picking up his date, though, Tom somehow forgot about Mike. Tom drove his date straight to the hotel, where the dance was being held and they stayed for over an hour. Suddenly, Tom remembered his poor brother back at the dorm and they went to get him. The threesome then proceeded to grab Mike's date, and they were on their way to the hotel once more.

Sitting in the backseat, Mike began to needle his brother. "You know, Tom, you're the biggest dumb-ass in the Campbell family. I leave you in charge and look what happens."

Halfway to their destination, Tom pulled the canary yellow Cutlass over to the shoulder and the twins jumped out and squared off.

"We were dressed in our tuxedos and all of a sudden we were rolling around in the grass," Mike said. "We fought for a little while, then we started laughing. I'd imagine we looked pretty silly."

They were forever arguing over the canary yellow Cutlass. One car did not satisfy the needs of two college studs. They both had keys, which made matters worse. If Mike ever slipped away, Tom knew where to find him.

In September 1969, Texas fans were still a little nervous about the twins holding starting jobs. Neither were speed burners. The coaches, however, were overjoyed to have Mike at the rover position. In spite of weighing only 185 pounds, he was an excellent run defender and one of the toughest players on the team.

Tom Campbell, on the other hand, was considered too slow to make the transition to cornerback. Still, his father knew that if a receiver beat him deep, Steinmark would save the day.

"I knew in my mind if I got beat that Freddie was going to be there to save me," Tom said. "Freddie was always there."

Against California in the season opener, Tom put all doubts to rest by playing the zone defense to perfection and intercepting a pass. The next day, though, he was surprised when he walked into his parents' house for Sunday dinner and heard his father talking on the phone.

"Look, lady, I know that Tom's no damned good," Campbell said. "But he's all I got!" It was the mother of a Texas player chewing out Big Mike for playing Tom instead of her son.

Big Mike Campbell did not care what the fans thought. He did not care what the parents thought. His secondary was set for the season and the Longhorns were ready to make a push for the national championship.

"It seemed that everyone was always worried about the Campbells," Mike Campbell said. "Most of the coaches wondered if we could play. They were worried that we would screw it up. But once the Campbell twins got on the field, they stopped worrying about us."

In truth, the brothers were quite fortunate to have their dad as a coach. Their rise to the starting lineup would not have occurred if not for his tutelage. During the 1960s, Big Mike Campbell was considered the best college football assistant coach in America. If they were giving out the Frank Broyles Award during that period, Campbell would have picked up the hardware every year.

"I really thought that Coach Campbell was a genius," Scott Henderson remembered. "I was shocked that he never got a head coaching job."

Campbell could be hard on his players, but he was doubly tough on Mike and Tom. Not once in their lives could they ever remember being praised for anything.

"The other assistant coaches had to do a lot of hugging on the Campbell twins," Fred Akers remembered. "Mike could be pretty tough on his boys."

One of the reasons for his leather exterior was that Big Mike Campbell had grown up tough himself in a broken home near Memphis. Each summer, his father picked him up and they went off on a three-month journey that might seem unimaginable to other kids. Mike Campbell II was an American League umpire and therefore on the road all summer. During the Depression, umpires were treated with as much respect as crows in the vegetable garden. They were not even allotted a place to dress at the ball parks.

Mike Campbell sat in a major league ball park each day and watched his dad working. His dad always said, "Find a place to sit where nobody's around you. And don't ever tell *anyone* that you're an umpire's son."

On the Texas practice field, Big Mike Campbell's sarcasm was biting. Everything he said was with a smile. The only person who flinched was his target. Everyone else laughed like crazy.

One day, backup running back Jackie Rushing was trying to avoid being tackled by All-American defensive end Bill Atessis and ran far out of bounds.

"Godammit, Jackie," Campbell yelled. "Why are you running for the stands? You're gonna scare the hell out of the fans."

During goal-line drills one afternoon, Atessis went low in order to halt the progress of the blocker ahead of him. He wound up lying on his belly.

"Dammit, Atessis," Campbell ranted. "I could go out on San Jacinto Street and find just about anybody who'll lay down."

It seemed that Campbell yelled at everyone for every little mistake. Not once in two seasons, however, did he ever raise his voice to Freddie Steinmark.

"My dad was always on everybody," Tom Campbell said. "But Freddie was that good and that smart. My daddy loved Freddie like a son."

To begin the 1969 season, Steinmark was the only returning starter in the secondary at lone safety. Tom Campbell lined up at left halfback with Danny Lester on the other side. Lester had spent the previous season backing up Cotton Speyrer at wide receiver, catching 5 passes for 120 yards. Lester wore his hair a little longer than the others and his teammates described his wardrobe as "hippie clothes." He loved to party and hit the bars with Steve Worster and Cotton Speyrer almost every night. It was not unusual for Lester to be out until closing time, but never miss a beat in practice the next day. Even with a hangover, he could usually beat everyone in wind sprints.

"Danny hardly ever said a word," Fred Akers said. "He could be very quiet. But he was tough and he'd never let you down. Making the starting lineup was a big jump for him. But we knew he could handle it."

After defeating California in the first game of the season, the Longhorns were still ranked number four in the Associated Press poll while Arkansas, in spite of defeating Oklahoma State 39–0 in Little Rock, slipped from second to third. Penn State moved up one slot to number two behind top-ranked Ohio State.

For the Longhorns, there was nothing like a double-revenge game to fire up the adrenaline machine. Texas Tech had upset Texas by the scores of 19–13 and 31–22 the past two seasons. Royal did not need to remind his team of how embarrassing a third straight defeat might be.

"We were running over each other trying to get out on the field for that game," Mike Campbell said. "I was involved in a lot of games at Texas and it seemed we always got the most fired up for the Oklahoma game. But I'd never seen our team as wild-eyed as we were for Texas Tech."

The night before the game, Mike Campbell had predicted to his roommate that he would intercept a pass and return it for a touchdown. Indeed, he did in the second quarter, picking off Tom Matulich and sprinting 26 yards into the end zone as Texas grabbed a 28–0 halftime lead. Tom Campbell recovered a fumble in the first half and the secondary came up with 4 interceptions.

One of the biggest turnovers of the game was provided by Steinmark, who baited Matulich into believing that he was giving up deep coverage to cover the tight end on a quick hook pattern. Steinmark took three steps forward, read the quarterback's eyes, then quickly retreated into the middle of the field. He caught up with the wide receiver just in time to make an over-the-shoulder grab, returning the ball 30 yards to midfield. Once again, Steinmark proved he was the best safety in the Southwest Conference, along with being one of the biggest ball-hawkers in the country.

On a day when Street completed only 3 of 10 passes, the Longhorns still rolled 49–7. Tech coach J. T. King hung his head after the game and said, "They really whipped our butts good." It was merely a sign of things to come.

That Saturday, Penn State barely defeated an average Kansas State team, 17–14. The Nittany Lions fell to sixth in the A.P. poll as Texas leapfrogged Arkansas all the way to number two. The Hogs remained third after thumping Tulsa 55–0. With Texas and Arkansas sitting at 2 and 3, the ABC executives were starting to smile in New York. Their dream matchup was starting to take shape.

Chapter 15

LOOK OUT, FREDDIE!

Freddie Steinmark was soaking his sore leg in the large whirlpool when Scott Henderson sauntered into the training room an hour before practice.

"Hey, Professor, I need a favor," he said.

"Whatever you need, Freddie Joe," Henderson replied. "Just let me know."

"Just keep that big animal off me on Saturday," Steinmark said. "I don't need to tackle Steve Owens twenty times. As you know, I've got a bad wheel. Owens just might run a little guy like me into the ground."

The previous season against Texas, the 6", 215-pound Owens rushed for 127 yards on twenty carries, and Steinmark worked overtime making touchdown-saving tackles. A common sight was Steinmark, the last line of defense, giving up his body to stop Owens, who was en route to the end zone.

The previous season, thanks to Steinmark's sure tackling, the Longhorns did manage to erase a late deficit with a Steve Worster touchdown to win 26–20.

Owens led college football in rushing in 1968 with 1,536 yards, and it was little wonder he was the favorite to win the Heisman Trophy in '69. His streak of 100-yard games had reached eleven. The previous week against Pittsburgh, his bruised left leg had turned purple by halftime, but he kept right on trucking, picking up 117 yards in a 38–7 rout.

"It was a dumb thing for me to do, playing with pain like that," Owens said. "But I wanted to keep the streak intact."

Saturday in the Cotton Bowl, the Texas linebackers would have their hands full against the tough-as-nails tailback who preferred to run over tacklers than around them. If the big basher got loose in the secondary, he was certain to take straight aim at Steinmark. With a 10-yard head start, and a fifty-pound advantage, he might demolish the little man playing with an undiagnosed leg injury.

Henderson thought about what his buddy had said about Owens. "This is what I'll do, Freddie," he said. "If Owens gets past me, I'll yell 'Look Out!' Then you'll know he's coming."

"Gee, thanks, Professor," Steinmark said. "You're a real pal."

Beating Oklahoma was a must if the Longhorns were to continue their march toward a national championship. Otherwise, the showdown against Arkansas in December would be for the conference title and nothing more. Darrell Royal had won 10 of the last 12 against his alma mater, but Texas-OU could be a crapshoot because of the blood hate between the teams that in 1969 were both undefeated. Tickets were always distributed evenly to both schools, and the Cotton Bowl would be split down the middle with the whiskey-addled fans coming off a Friday-night bender on Commerce Street.

It was evident from the opening kickoff that Oklahoma had its mind on business. Oklahoma coach Chuck Fairbanks's game plan was to steamroll the Longhorns with Owens. The Sooners reached the Texas 16-yard line early in the first quarter when Owens blasted off right tackle and Henderson employed everything except a nightstick to stop him. Owens would not go down, so Henderson climbed aboard and pulled with all of his might on the big man's neck and shoulders. The Texas linebacker soon realized he was losing his grip. So, while hanging in midair, he turned his head and yelled toward his buddy, "Look out, Freddie! Here he comes!"

Steinmark might have laughed if the moment had not seemed so grim. He took two steps forward, braced himself, and managed to cut down Owens at the ankles just inside the 10-yard line. On the next play, though, quarterback Jack Mildren scooted around left end, faked Danny Lester off his feet, and boogalooed into the end zone for a 7–0 lead.

Texas struggled to run the ball early in the game and it was obvious that Fairbanks and staff had deciphered the veer option. Simply, the Sooners were clogging up the middle to stop Worster, who had terrorized them with 133 yards the previous season. When James Street tried to complete a pass over the middle to Randy Peschel, OU defensive back Steve Aycock intercepted at the Texas 17-yard line.

Owens went right back to work, hammering the ball four straight times to the 2-yard line. On the next play, he rumbled into the end zone for a 14–0 advantage. Two minutes still remained in the first quarter, and it already looked like a long afternoon for the Longhorns, who were facing double jeopardy. The running game was not clicking and the Longhorns' defense could not slow down Owens. In fact, the Texas defense was already withering in the ninety-three-degree heat. As the game moved into the second quarter, 260-pound defensive tackle Leo Brooks was so exhausted and breathing so heavily that he had to lean on Mike Campbell in the huddle just to stay upright.

"You would have thought it was the first hour of spring practice instead of the fourth game of the season," Campbell said. "Leo was already spent."

Playing the rover position on the weak side, Campbell had made several tackles and knew he was holding up his end of the bargain. The Owens wrecking ball was doing most of its damage on the other side of the offense. Between plays, Campbell looked up to see his replacement, Mack McKinney, trotting onto the field. He could not believe it.

"Mack, why did Daddy send you in for me?" Campbell said.

"I'm not replacing you," McKinney said. "You're going to the strong side to replace Richardson. I'm moving to rover."

Linebacker David Richardson, unable to weather the OU onslaught, was being benched. So on his first play at the new position, Campbell faced the same dilemma as Richardson. His name was Steve Zabel, and he was an All-American tight end who stood 6'2" and weighed 225 pounds.

"After Zabel knocked me around for three or four plays, Daddy called me over to the sideline," Campbell said. "He said, 'It's okay to get blocked by Zabel. I expected that. Just let him knock you backward. Don't let him block you to one side or the other.'"

The plan worked and the Sooners did not score again in the first half. Meanwhile, Street jump-started the offense with some remarkable passing—at least for him. Just one other time had Street been called upon to win a game with his arm and that was the 1968 Oklahoma game.

After a first quarter filled with futility, the Longhorns offense finally gained some traction following a 42-yard kickoff return by sophomore halfback Jim Bertelsen. With Oklahoma in single coverage, Street completed a 35-yarder over the middle to Speyrer. Three plays later, from the Oklahoma 24, Speyrer cut to the right sideline and made an acrobatic over-the-helmet catch in the end zone, cutting the OU lead to 14–7.

With a 25-mph wind behind them in the second quarter, Texas kept passing from the wishbone. Oklahoma monster man Jim Files lost track of Bertelsen as he swung up the left sideline. Street sailed a perfectly thrown pass over his right shoulder for a 55-yard gain. The Longhorns then pounded the ball down the field and Bertelsen scored on a 1-yard run. The Longhorns had managed to tie the game 14–14 in spite of only 30 rushing yards in the first half.

After two short field goals by Happy Feller in the third quarter, and a 45-yarder by OU kicker Bruce Derr, Texas led 20–17 to start the fourth quarter.

The game was still in doubt with slightly more than five minutes to play when Scooter Monzingo lofted a high, wobbly punt into a crazy crosswind. Return man Glen King tried to set himself for the fair catch, but Bertelsen, barreling down the field, was right in his face. Bertelsen bluffed a hit on King and the ball fell through his hands. It was loose on the ground until Bob McKay smothered it. Texas took possession at the Sooners' 23-yard line and needed 5 plays to reach the end zone. Worster put the game away with a 2-yard run with 4:31 to play. Texas led 27–17.

On third down and needing a miracle, OU's Mildren faced a strong pass rush from Bill Atessis. His off-balance throw was intercepted by Tom Campbell and returned 15 yards to the OU 33-yard line. The Longhorns ran out the clock.

On a day when the pass was an operational necessity, Street completed 18 of his throws for 215 yards, and Speyrer hauled in 8 for 160. Again, Street proved that he could come through when all else failed. By using single coverage against Cotton Speyrer, the Sooners challenged a quarterback who understood the odds all too well. Street was not a classic passer, but he was capable of throwing completions all day long to a wide open receiver.

Lou Maysel wrote in the *Austin American Statesman*, "Darrell Royal, who portrays himself as the cowardly lion when it comes to the forward pass, found a new heart here Saturday in the 93-degree heat of the Cotton Bowl."

On his reputation for running the ball, Royal always said, "You have to dance with the one who brung ya." Against Oklahoma, it was more like, "Stop dancing and go long!"

In the next Associated Press poll, Texas was still ranked number two following its thirteenth straight win. Ninety miles away in Waco, Arkansas had pulled off a less-than-stellar 21–7 win over Baylor as Bill Montgomery threw 2 interceptions. Tailback Bill Burnett saved the day with 137 rushing yards and 3 touchdowns.

After four games, these were the top five teams in the A.P. poll: 1. Ohio State, 2. Texas, 3. USC, 4. Arkansas, 5. Penn State.

Freddie Steinmark was limping. Linda Wheeler could see it all too clearly as they walked across campus Monday morning. Two days later, Steinmark had tackled Owens 7 times while registering a total of 18 stops.

"Why are you limping so badly?" Linda said.

"I am not limping," Freddie shot back. Before Linda could say another word, Freddie stopped limping.

"Stop doing that," Linda said.

"Stop doing what?"

"Stop acting like you're not hurt. I know you're hurt."

"I'm getting better."

"No, you're not. You're faking, Freddie. You need to go see the team doctor."

The last thing Freddie Steinmark was going to do on a Monday morning in the middle of October, with the undefeated Texas Longhorns fighting for a national championship, was to consult a physician. It could wait.

Steinmark knew his left leg was aching, but what else was new? If he could just hide the pain for six more games, and walk away with a national championship ring, his life would be complete. Everything was on schedule. If Linda would just get off his back.

It was nothing new that Linda and Freddie argued. These spats were often carried on in front of friends. In these times, they spoke quite directly to each other. Those who knew the couple well wrote it off as old married people with nothing better to do.

"There were times when Freddie and Linda would get into it," Henderson recalled. "But I never saw any meanness. Even when they argued, they showed great respect for each other."

That morning, as they were parting, Linda knew she had lost the argument. She knew Freddie better than anyone. His competitive spirit was never going to allow him to admit he was badly injured.

"Freddie, you need to tell Coach Royal how bad you're hurt," Linda said. "Your leg's been hurting you since the summer. That's long enough for you to do something about it."

"Look, Linda, I'm sitting in the whirlpool every day," he said. "That's hard enough on me. Everybody's watching. The coaches know I'm hurting. They see me every day in the training room. But I want them to think I can still play."

"It's not going to get better until you see the team doctor."

"I promise. I'll do just that right *after* the season."

That afternoon, Steinmark encountered Spanky Stephens in the training room. Having watched Freddie try to hide his limp, the student trainer realized that Freddie was in more pain than he was letting on. Looking back on the situation, Stephens said, "All I had to do was touch that sensitive spot at the end of his thighbone. And he would flinch and grimace. It was hurting him. Really hurting him."

Head trainer Frank Medina had diagnosed Steinmark's injury as a charley horse, but Stephens knew better.

Stephens's unofficial diagnosis was a mylcipis osificus, which was a bleeding in the muscle. He shared his thoughts with head trainer Frank Medina, but got no response.

"Frank rarely responded when anyone else had an opinion on an injury," Stephens said. "That was just Frank being Frank. He was going to do things his way, like he always did."

Getting a handle on Steinmark's injury was not the easiest task. For one thing, he rarely shared with anyone the level of pain he was experiencing. Steinmark was determined to make it to the Arkansas game and was not going to let anything stop him.

"One game Freddie would be fine and the next game he would be hurting," Stephens said. "It went back and forth. That's what made it hard to figure out."

Randy Peschel had little choice about sitting in the whirlpool every day. He suffered the constant pain of swollen hemorrhoids. The swirling hot water helped to coagulate the tissue and allowed Peschel to stay on the field. He could be sure that he would see Steinmark each day in the tub.

"Freddie just didn't talk about his injury," he said. "But I kept asking myself, when is he going to get better? I was hoping the trainers or the doctors would finally do something to alleviate his pain and fix his injury. But as it turned out, they never could figure it out. Freddie kept coming back and coming back and he never could get well."

Because they spent so much time in the whirlpool, Peschel and Steinmark took their share of abuse from teammates and coaches. They were used to the stares and the whispers. They knew the latest joke making the rounds:

"Has anybody seen Peschel and Steinmark?"

"Check the whirlpool. They're in the water so much that they're thinking about going out for the swim team."

The only way Steinmark could get his leg loose enough to practice every day was to spend an hour in the whirlpool. Steinmark continued to tell Coach Fred Akers that his injury felt like a charley horse.

During this period, Stephens said that Steinmark was seeing both team doctors inside the athletic office.

"Freddie was in there a lot seeing the doctors," he said. "But neither Dr. Julian or Dr. Reneau was taking him to be X-rayed. If they had, they would have figured out the problem."

As time passed, Steinmark tried to keep the extent of his pain a secret from the coaches. Still, Akers did not need a medical degree to know that something was wrong with his star safety. Steinmark no longer made the plays that were his trademark during the 1968 season.

"Freddie was known to take some pretty big risks during the 1968 season and we let him do it because we knew he had the speed to get to the ball," Akers said. "That is the reason he had five interceptions. That's a lot for a sophomore. But with the injury, he gave up making the interception and concentrated on making the tackle."

Akers and defensive coordinator Mike Campbell concurred that Steinmark was not his old self. This observation was triply confirmed by Darrell Royal, watching practice each day from his tower. Royal was known for spotting the most minuscule of flaws—errors that no one else could even imagine.

"I never knew what he was doing up there in that tower," Bobby Mitchell recalled. "One day, he stopped me on my way to practice field and told me that I'd made a certain misstep on a running play. I just scratched my head. I think my right foot might have been off by about an inch. But he saw it."

Royal kept a sharp eye on Steinmark and knew that something was wrong. He called Campbell and Akers into a meeting.

"What's wrong with Freddie?" Royal said. "He seems to be slowing down."

Akers said, "He told me he got a leg injury playing baseball over the summer."

Royal looked at Campbell, who said, "I know there's something wrong with the kid. But he's the smartest player I've got. He's staying in the lineup."

That's all Royal needed to hear. He trusted Campbell instinctively. No one knew the Texas personnel better than Campbell. By receiving Big Mike's seal of approval, Steinmark was staying in the lineup.

The coaches' number-one option to replace Steinmark was Rick Nabors, a bigger and stronger safety, but one who lacked his overall maturity and experience. Still, Campbell and Akers would not have hesitated one minute to play the talented Nabors if they felt Steinmark was faltering.

"Nabors was very smart, just like Freddie," Akers said. "The coaches had some conversations about resting Freddie. But it always came back to the fact that Freddie was our smartest guy on defense."

Something else about Steinmark worried Akers, and it had nothing to do with a charley horse or other physical ailments. Simply, Steinmark seemed to be dodging everyone. Akers was used to seeing Steinmark trot out of the locker room and onto the practice field an hour ahead of everyone else. He was always the first to arrive and the last to leave. Before practice started, he was constantly picking the brains of the coaches. He wanted to learn everything he could from the coaches about defensive strategy. He was innately curious about everything around him. As the season moved into late October, though, Steinmark was arriving later for the daily drills, and leaving earlier.

"Freddie started hiding out," Akers said. "He got to where he stopped coming early to practice. On top of that, he wasn't telling the doctors the whole story. He didn't want to talk to me about his injury. When he started avoiding me and everybody else, I really started to worry."

Because the Arkansas game had been moved from mid-October to December 6, the Longhorns had an extra week to rest leading to the game against Rice. It gave Steinmark some more time to recuperate.

Coaches were trying everything to help Freddie cope with the injury. Man-to-man coverage was virtually eliminated in favor of a zone defense, also known as "Cover 3."

In "Cover 3," Campbell, Lester, and Steinmark split the field into three sectors. This took away a lot of responsibility from the single safety and some pressure off his sore leg.

Before long, Akers noticed that Steinmark was not lining up directly in the center of the field. He was cheating to the left or right, hoping to compensate for his sore leg. He made the correct choice most of the time and seemed to know exactly where the quarterback was going with the ball.

"I tell you that the guy had instincts that were very uncommon," Akers said. "It was like his head was inside the offensive huddle. He was just amazing. Normally, coaches would not give a safety the freedoms we gave Freddie. But Freddie could see the field and he knew what was going on. Some guys looked but they could not see. Freddie could see everything."

The bye week did not cost Texas any ground in the Associated Press weekly poll as the 'Horns stayed at number two behind Ohio State. They received five first place votes, the same as they had the previous week. Arkansas did fall one spot to fourth as Tennessee took their place at number three after walloping Alabama 41–14 in Birmingham. Penn State moved from eighth place to number five with a 42–3 defeat of Ohio University.

The lowly Rice Owls, losers of eleven of their last twelve games, would be a timely breather for Steinmark and a few other injured players. The Owls had defeated Texas in 1960 and '65, and tied the Longhorns in '62. However, since the retirement of Coach Jess Neely three years earlier, they were no longer feared as the feisty underdog that could surprise a team like Texas. Neely was a cocky bantam rooster who fired up his teams. He was an offensive innovator and the Rice Owls loved to pass during his twenty-six years as coach.

After his final game against Texas in 1966, Neely walked across the field to the Longhorns' dressing room, where he found Darrell Royal talking to his assistant coaches. Neely stuck his head into the group and said, "I just wanted y'all to know that I'm retiring. I hated you guys all of these years I coached against you. But I also respected your program." With that, Neely pivoted on his heel and walked out the door.

In the fifth game of the season, the Longhorns got off to a rough start against Rice, losing 3 fumbles. One of those turnovers tumbled into the end zone for a touchback. Another Texas drive stalled at the Rice 9-yard line on downs. Still, with a grinder like Steve Worster, the offense eventually started to click. Worster culminated a 32-yard drive, following a Mack McKinney interception, and scored on a 1-yard run late in the first quarter for a 7–0 lead.

Billy Dale and sophomore Jim Bertelsen, splitting time at left halfback, registered back-to-back touchdown runs of 4 yards as Texas took a 21–0 halftime lead.

In the third quarter, Dale scored on a 1-yard run off left tackle as Texas led 28–0. Mike Campbell, who did not start because of a sprained ankle, returned an interception on a broken-field run to the 11, setting up Happy Feller's 24-yard field goal for the 31–0 victory.

In Little Rock, Arkansas, quarterback Bill Montgomery sat out the entire game against Wichita State as John Eichler led a 52–15 victory. The Razorbacks and Longhorns were both 5-0. The top five teams in the Associated Press remained the same.

The phone call from Fred Steinmark came on Thursday night before the SMU game, and Freddie could instantly hear the frustration in his voice. "Freddie, you've got one interception all season and you've already played five games. You had five interceptions last year. What's wrong, big guy?"

"Ah, Dad," he said. "We're playing more three-deep zone this year. Plus, we're so far ahead that Coach Royal's been pulling the first string out in the fourth quarter."

There was a pause on the line. "That's not it," his dad said. "That's not it at all. You're not as aggressive as you were last year. It's that leg of yours. You're hurt, Freddie."

"Okay, maybe," Freddie said. "But, Dad, the coaches are perfectly happy with the way I'm playing. More than anything else, Coach Campbell doesn't want me to give up the big play. And I'm not doing that."

Another pause. "Freddie, have you told Coach Royal how bad your leg hurts?"

"It's okay, Dad. I'm sitting in the whirlpool every day. I'm taking care of my leg."

"Tell you what I'm going to do. If you don't tell Coach Royal how bad it is, I'm going to call him myself."

"It's not time yet."

The Steinmarks were planning to drive to Dallas the next day for Texas-SMU.

"I'll be the judge of how bad your leg is after the game," Big Fred said.

Playing SMU in Dallas created many complex issues for the coaching staff and the entire secondary. The previous year, as a sophomore, quarterback Chuck Hixson had broken all kinds of Southwest Conference passing records: 265 completions on 468 attempts with 3,103 yards and 21 touchdowns. The previous holders of those records went by the names of Bobby Layne and Davey O'Brien.

One problem with Hixson was the graduation of All-American receiver Jerry LeVias, the first black scholarship player in the history of the Southwest Conference.

Against SMU in the first half, it seemed that Texas was playing straight into the Mustangs' hands. As they had done against Rice, the Longhorns lost 3 quick fumbles. SMU marched all the way to the 1-yard line late in the second quarter. Believing his team had an excellent chance of winning in the second half, Fry opted for a field goal and a 10–6 deficit at halftime.

What occurred in the final two quarters was a scene of mass destruction. For the first time in the history of the SWC, all four starting backs—Street, Bertelsen, Koy, and Worster—gained more than

100 yards in a game. Bertelsen and Worster led the way with 137 apiece. Texas also shattered the conference record with 611 rushing yards in the 45–14 victory. After the game, Fry slumped on a stool in the corner of the SMU dressing room and said, "Texas is the greatest football team that I've ever seen and probably ever will see."

Steinmark and the rest of the defensive starters were pulled from the game in the fourth quarter. Again, the Texas safety never did allow a receiver to get behind him. Still, he failed to register an interception, and Hixson managed to complete 20 of 37 passes for 223 yards.

As Freddie walked from the locker room to the team bus after the game, he was met by his grim-faced father. "Freddie, you've lost a step," he said. "There is no question about it. If you don't tell Coach Royal how bad you're hurt, I'm going to call myself."

"Please don't do that, Dad," Freddie said. "I'm going to be all right. I promise you. Just give me a couple more weeks and I'll be fine."

"You won't be fine," Big Fred said. "Freddie, you're getting worse."

In Fayetteville, quarterback Bill Montgomery had never looked better, leading Arkansas to 5 touchdowns in the Razorbacks' first 7 possessions against Texas A&M for a 35–13 victory.

Texas gained ground on number-one Ohio State in the Associated Press. The Buckeyes had defeated Northwestern 35–6, but their margin over the Longhorns fell to a total of 8 points. For the third straight week, Tennessee, Arkansas, and Penn State rounded out the top five.

ABC executives in New York knew that Ohio State would have to lose in order for the dream matchup between Texas and Arkansas to occur on December 6. Three games were left on the schedule.

Chapter 16

A GROWING REALITY

Jones Ramsey was one of the funniest men in college football. Instead of plying his trade at the local comedy club, he was the famous sports information director at the University of Texas.

Jones, who called himself "the world's tallest fat man," once said "There are two sports at Texas—football and spring football."

As the Longhorns prepared for Baylor in the seventh game of the season, news was spreading of a stomach virus in the Texas locker room. Called before the TV cameras to explain, Ramsey said, "Oh, there isn't anything serious about it. The biggest problem was nobody in the sports information department knew how to spell diarrhea."

After the Longhorns rolled to a 56–14 victory over Baylor, Blackie Sherrod wrote in the *Dallas Times Herald*, "the Texas backs ran like there was a men's room in the end zone."

Royal had pulled most of the starters by halftime. Backup fullback Bobby Callison, subbing for Worster, scored 3 touchdowns while Eddie Phillips, the quarterback of the future, scored two more after replacing James Street.

Arkansas defeated Rice 30–6 and the top five teams remained intact. Texas did gain more ground on Ohio State, and trailed the top-ranked Buckeyes by only 5 points in the Associated Press poll.

After most of the home games, Freddie Steinmark, Linda Wheeler, Scott Henderson, and Henderson's girlfriend, Mille, went to a gathering in Austin at the home of David and Gladys Conway. The couple once lived in Wheat Ridge and were longtime friends of the Steinmarks. It was one of the few nonalcohol parties thrown after a Texas victory, so Steinmark and Henderson fit in quite well.

As the evening wore on, Steinmark and Henderson walked to the back patio to talk. Henderson could tell that his friend needed to discuss something important.

"Everything all right, Freddie boy?" Henderson said.

"Not really," Steinmark said. "I need to tell you something that I'm not telling everybody else. You see, my leg's really hurting."

"I know."

"How'd you know?"

"Freddie, you're not playing as well as you did last season. I'm not saying that you need to take a few weeks off. You just don't have your old get-up and go."

"I don't want the coaches to know how bad I'm hurt," Steinmark said. "They're already worried. I know that for a fact. I see how closely they watch me in practice. I've got two more games to go and then we play Arkansas. After that, I can rest for a while."

When Henderson thought of Steinmark, he was reminded of the pain that Mickey Mantle had endured during his childhood and throughout most of his baseball career. Mantle suffered for years with hip, leg, and knee problems. In high school, he was diagnosed with osteomyelitis, an inflammation of the bone marrow. Mantle's shin bone was permanently weakened by the disease in high school. The doctors actually considered amputation, but finally settled on a plan to rest the leg. They told young Mantle to walk on crutches for six months. Mantle quickly threw away the crutches and started playing football and baseball again.

As Steinmark and Henderson sat on the patio, they talked about the trials and tribulations of their hero. As a kid, Freddie had idolized The Mick and patterned himself after the center fielder with the sweetest swing in baseball. Mantle had been Henderson's neighbor for years in Dallas during the off-season. Mantle was around a lot more a year following his retirement.

"You know, Freddie, they almost had to cut Mickey's leg off," Henderson said. "Maybe they'll have to cut off yours."

They both laughed. Then Henderson tried to continue on a more positive note.

"Maybe you should talk to Coach Royal. Like next week."

"I will," Steinmark said. "I will talk to him *after* the season."

The next morning, instead of going to early mass, Steinmark and Henderson decided to change the routine and head straight to the training room. At least Freddie could enjoy some peace away from the prying eyes. Henderson suffered his share of bumps and bruises and could also use some time in the hot whirlpool.

As they walked through the door, they felt certain the training room would be empty early on a Sunday morning as their teammates were sleeping in. They were wrong. They quickly spotted Steve Worster limping around the room. He was black and blue from the tops of his shoulders all the way down to his ankles. He moved slowly across the room like an old man without a cane. The sight of him left both players speechless.

Everyone understood the beating that Worster took each Saturday in the fall. Still, few of his teammates had seen him completely undressed. His body looked like a road crew had taken a jackhammer to it.

Reasons for the bruises were obvious. Worster carried the ball straight ahead without dodging and it took several men to bring him down. Sometimes the collisions sounded like train wrecks. His teammates often wanted to look away. Worster was the heart and soul of the wishbone offense and he carried a great responsibility on his shoulders. If he did not make the tough yards, the Longhorns did not win. Without him, there would be no hunt for the national championship, and, like Steinmark, he played each down as if it were his last.

Steinmark walked slowly toward his close friend, not believing what he was seeing. There was barely a spot on his body that was not bruised.

"Steve, I had no idea—"

"Ah, hell," Worster said. "Remember the day you knocked me on my ass in practice? That's how I got all these bruises."

Steinmark laughed. "Baloney. You've been taking a beating the whole season and I knew it was pretty bad. But I had no idea—"

"Ah, hell, Freddie, it just goes with the territory. After all, you should know."

Henderson was also taken aback at the sight of a black-and-blue Worster. He knew about the toughness of the big fullback because he had to tackle him many days in practice. Still, the sight of his body made him cringe.

"I had never seen Worster completely out of his uniform," Henderson recalled forty years later. "I couldn't believe what I was seeing. He looked like he needed to be in the hospital."

Steinmark climbed in the large whirlpool and gazed across the water at his battered friend. It was obvious what he was thinking. *If Steve Worster can play with that kind of pain, so can I.* Like Worster, Steinmark had endured a number of injuries in his football career. In the midget leagues, he played an entire quarter with a broken arm. In high school, he had played three quarters over two games with a broken leg. As a senior, he had decided against seeking medical attention when he broke his right hand. In his mind, though, those injuries could not compare to Worster's high tolerance for pain.

"I think that seeing Steve that day had a pretty big impact on both of us," Henderson said. "We both knew that we needed to gut it up the rest of the way. Freddie talked about Worster and his toughness the rest of the season."

The next opponent was TCU, a team that had been crushed by number-one Ohio State 62–0 in the second week of the season. Against the Horned Frogs, the Longhorns rolled to a 34–0 halftime lead and Royal emptied the bench. In spite of wholesale substitutions, the Longhorns put up 35 points in the second half for a 69–7 victory. It was Texas' seventeenth win in a row.

In the meantime, Ohio State defeated Purdue 42–14. Third-ranked Tennessee's hope for a national title was destroyed by Ole Miss and quarterback Archie Manning by the score of 38–0. Arkansas moved up to number three and Penn State to the fourth position. The folks at ABC were praying that Ohio State would lose its final game of the season against Michigan. It was their last hope for the Game of the Century to materialize.

Because Texas did not play again until Thanksgiving, the Long-horns were off the following Saturday. Most of the players, includ-ing Steinmark, slept late that day. Freddie was spending as much time off his sore leg as possible.

Players began to saunter into the lounge of the Jester Center around noon and most were not aware that the Ohio State-Michigan game was about to begin in Ann Arbor. The game was not even tele-vised in Austin. So they casually watched a boring matchup between Missouri and Kansas. Missouri was so far ahead by halftime that most of the Longhorns were napping.

Ten minutes later, though, when the scores began to trickle in on Ohio State-Michigan, Texas players started waking up. When Mich-igan went ahead in the first quarter 7–6, it was the first time all season that Ohio State trailed in a game.

Ohio State regained the lead 12–7 on the next drive, but Michi-gan quickly answered to make it 14–12. Late in the second quarter, a 60-yard punt return set up yet another Wolverines' score and a 21–12 lead.

The previous season, quarterback Rex Kern had led Ohio State to a national title. Against Michigan, though, he could not have hit an open receiver with a deer rifle. He threw 4 interceptions and was pulled in the second half. The Buckeyes never crossed the Michigan 44-yard line in the final two quarters. With the 21–12 victory, the Wolverines were headed to the Rose Bowl while Ohio State was moving down the ladder in the A.P. poll. Texas was certain to move to number one.

Darrell Royal had been watching the scoreboard from the press-box at the SMU-Baylor game the past three hours. He jumped out of his seat when he saw the final score of Michigan-Ohio State. He quickly reined in his excitement when the sporting press came run-ning with notebooks in hand.

"I would like to remind you folks that we still have to win three games for us to finish the season number one," he said. "I'm as nervous as a cat. A lot still has to happen. Arkansas, Penn State, and some others have the same opportunity that we do."

Late that afternoon, the lobby of the Jester Center exploded in jubilation when the final score of Ohio State's upset was posted. In Bill Atessis's room, the cards were soon being dealt and the beer flowed at places like the Flagon and Trencher. In New York at ABC headquarters, champagne bottles were being uncorked as the thought of a network-arranged national championship was so close to reality. Texas would need a win over the hated Texas A&M Aggies on Thanksgiving in College Station while Arkansas defeated Texas Tech two days later.

Two days before the Longhorns traveled to Aggieland, Steinmark walked into the training room and tried not to limp. He was looking for Frank Medina.

"Mr. Medina, do you think I could have a knee brace?" he said.

Medina smiled. He liked Steinmark and all of his toughness. Still, he was growing weary of an injury that would not go away.

"What is it now, little Freddie? Do you think you've got a knee sprain?"

"My knee hurts," Steinmark said. "I just thought it might give me some support against A&M."

Steinmark was fortunate that he asked for the brace. In the first quarter, hard-running Texas A&M halfback Larry Stegent blasted through the line and was quickly into the secondary. Steinmark thought about the ferocious sight of Steve Owens tractoring toward him. Just as he had done against Oklahoma, he dipped his shoulder and tried to cut down Stegent at the ankles. This time, it did not work. Stegent ran over him, ramming his knee into Steinmark's bad leg. The knee bent awkwardly and everyone on the defense heard him scream.

Henderson ran to help his friend off the ground.

"Are you going to be okay?" Henderson said.

Steinmark stood up and tested the knee brace. It was bent on one side.

"Look at this," Steinmark said. "If I hadn't had this thing on, I think I'd have a broken leg right now."

Fortunately, the Longhorns scored on 6 of their first 8 possessions in the first half. Jim Bertelsen broke a 63-yard scoring run and, on the end around, Speyrer threw a 37-yard TD pass to Randy Peschel. The starting defense exited the game before halftime and Steinmark was thankful he would see no more of Stegent. The Longhorns barely broke a sweat in a 49–12 victory over the Aggies.

Four weeks earlier, A&M had been run over by Arkansas 35–13 in Fayetteville. So the natural question was posed to Aggie coach Gene Stallings: Who will win Arkansas-Texas?

"Arkansas has a great team, but Texas has the greatest football team I've ever seen," Stallings said. "I'm not so sure that any team in the country can beat them."

Stallings was asked about Steinmark and his will to persevere with a leg injury.

"You want to talk about courage, that was courage at its finest," Stallings said. "That kid Steinmark is the most courageous player I've ever seen. We didn't score a touchdown against Texas and we've got pretty good offense. Freddie Steinmark was the biggest reason for us getting shut out."

Two days later, Arkansas defeated Texas Tech 33–0 in Little Rock. The 'Horns and Hogs were 9–0 and ranked one-two in the country. The dream game was on.

Chapter 17

LAST CALL FOR COURAGE

On the Monday morning before the biggest game of his life, Freddie Steinmark stayed in bed. Bobby Mitchell could never remember his roommate of three years not rising and shining and heading off to class. The mere site of this latter-day Jack Armstrong lying in the sack was like watching John Wayne giving up on a saloon fight.

"Freddie boy, you're either bad sick or that leg's a lot worse than we thought," Mitchell said.

"The leg's bad, Mitch," Steinmark said. "I need all the rest I can get before practice. If I don't practice well this week, I probably won't play against Arkansas. The coaches are close to taking me out. I can feel it."

After nine games, it was evident that nothing was going to heal Steinmark's injury, other than extended rest. Texas trainer Frank Medina had exhausted his small bag of medical aids. He showed Steinmark how to put analgesic balm between gauze and tape and to apply it to the sore area. He also recommended that he elevate the leg at night with a pillow.

Late in the season, when the pain intensified by the day, Medina actually prescribed extra running after practice. Steinmark followed the trainer's advice. As might be expected, it only served to exacerbate his misery.

"Frank Medina told him that he should do some more work after practice," Akers said. "Of course, Freddie was never immune to hard work. He would be out there after practice doing wind sprints. But the extra running did not help him at all."

The U.T. doctors had prescribed Darvon, and the powerful pain-killer was making it easier to get through the day and night. But Steinmark was sleeping only three hours and, at times, he felt as drained as a frat boy coming off a weekend bender.

Over the past few months, Steinmark had become accustomed to the pain and had learned to manage it. He knew his physical limitations and when to take a few shortcuts. Something else had been on his mind recently, though. Why was he feeling so weak?

"Freddie just didn't act the same," Mitchell recalled. "Here was a guy who was always going full speed and suddenly he was slowing down."

For those who loved Steinmark, it was difficult to watch. The previous season, he had been a shining star on a defensive unit that helped save a sluggish program. Linda Wheeler, the love of his life, found it painful to see a proud young man struggle.

"Freddie was hurting bad, and I mean really bad," Linda remembered. "He had trouble walking across campus just to make it to class. If he hadn't sat in the whirlpool for hours, the leg never would have loosened up enough for him to play football. But come hell or high water, he was going to play in that Arkansas game."

Regardless of a downshift in the gearbox, Steinmark was not a burden to the Texas defense. The coaches could hang their hats on one statistic: In nine games, the starters on defense had allowed only 3 touchdowns. Equally as impressive, the Longhorns first team offense was scoring touchdowns on 50 percent of its possessions. The ageless adage, "If it ain't broke, don't fix it," never made more sense.

Furthermore, Texas had won eighteen straight games with Steinmark in the starting lineup. The coaches could not fathom making a change at safety with one of the biggest games in the history of college football coming up.

While most of his teammates were attending class that morning, Steinmark studied his chemical engineering books. His grades were so high across the board that he would not be required to take final exams—a stress reducer, for sure. Renting space inside his head, though, was the Arkansas Razorbacks offense. The passing combination of Bill Montgomery to Chuck Dicus had created numerous problems for the Longhorns in 1968, when Texas won 39–29 in Austin. An excellent case could be made for Montgomery as the best quarterback in the country. Only Jim Plunkett at Stanford boasted more overall talent. Only SMU's Chuck Hixson had put up better numbers.

So refined was Montgomery coming out of high school that Arkansas coach Frank Broyles had flown in a private airplane from Fayetteville to Dallas to sign him. As the coach stepped onto the tarmac at Love Field, a wire-service photographer snapped his picture. If Broyles was flaunting his recruiting victory in the heart of Texas, everyone knew that Montgomery must be the next Joe Willie Namath.

Alabama had courted Montgomery for several weeks, and Coach Paul "Bear" Bryant invited him up to his tower when he visited Tuscaloosa. On the way down the stairwell, one of the Alabama assistants stopped Montgomery. "Gee, Bill, did you know that the only recruit Coach Bryant ever invited up to the tower was Joe Namath?"

In the end, the Hogs outsprinted Alabama and Texas for Montgomery's services because Broyles promised to tailor his offense to his passing skills. He did so by hiring two new offensive coaches.

For the first time all season, the Texas three-man secondary would be severely challenged. Dicus was the leading pass receiver in the conference and, over the past year, John Rees had developed into a solid secondary receiver. No one would ever compare Arkansas to the flimsy passing outfits of Baylor, or TCU, or, Rice, or even Oklahoma. Rover Mike Campbell would spend most of his day in the secondary helping out on pass coverage.

Steinmark put down the textbook and pulled out a dope sheet on Arkansas that had been produced by the Texas coaching staff and presented to the players the previous night. He could never remember a scouting report so lengthy or thorough. In his speech to the team, Royal went out of his way to express his respect for the Razorbacks. This was the same football program that had cost the Longhorns a national championship in 1964, then sent his team into a tailspin with a come-from-behind victory in '65. Frank Broyles was the only coach who consistently gave Royal fits. It was a stone-cold lock that Texas versus Arkansas would be decided in the final minutes.

As expected, Texas had climbed to number one after Ohio State was treated so rudely by Michigan. Arkansas was ranked second, several points behind the Longhorns. This made sense since the Longhorns had beaten their common opponents by 83 more points than the Hogs. According to records of the *Gold Sheet,* the opening Las Vegas line favored the Longhorns by 13 points, something that made Texas All-American tackle Bob McKay laugh.

"I always wondered how they came up with that shit," McKay said. "Hell, I knew if we beat Arkansas, it'd be by one point."

Royal had suggested to a gathering of sportswriters that they call the Texas-Arkansas game "The Big Shootout." Sports pages across the country trumped him by printing bold headlines that trumpeted the event as "The Game of the Century." A hundred years had passed since Princeton and Rutgers had staged the first collegiate football game on November 6, 1869, at College Field at Rutgers University in New Brunswick, New Jersey, and it was time to roll out the hype. Only twice in the last ten years had a team not wearing burnt orange or cardinal red represented the Southwest Conference in the Cotton Bowl. Once again, the conference championship was on the line in Fayetteville. To fuel the fight, the fans of both teams hated each other. Texas fans regarded Arkansans as "shoeless hillbilly folks," and Arkansas fans considered Texans arrogant "tea-sips" with too much starch in their button-down shirts.

Dan Jenkins of *Sports Illustrated* compared Razorback Stadium to a "thundering zoo." No doubt, it would be an eye-popping and ear-exploding experience for every player on the Texas roster. Coach Mike Campbell described Fayetteville as "like parachuting into Russia" because of the mountains, the sea of red in Razorback Stadium, and the sounds of "Wooooo, Pig Soooooie!" Overnight, Fayetteville would be converted from the number-two chicken producer in America to the capital of college football. Radio stations across the state were already blaring what amounted to be the national anthem of Arkansas, a song about a Longhorn getting thumped by a Razorback, titled "Short Squashed Texan."

Texas quarterback James Street had provided some bulletin board material for Arkansas after the Longhorns manhandled Texas A&M in College Station. Street decried the notion that Fayetteville would be louder or crazier than Kyle Field. Royal bristled when he read the quote. "You've never played in Fayetteville," Royal lectured. "It's going to be a lot different."

Royal spread praise about the Razorbacks far and wide. He told the press, "They're gonna come after us with their eyes pulled back like BB's. And they'll be defending every foot as if Frank Broyles has told 'em there's a 350-foot drop-off just behind 'em into a pile of rocks. If you believe that, you're actually pretty hard to move around."

An hour after Mitchell left for anthropology class, Steinmark used both arms to lift his left leg off the bed. Then, as he limped across the room, he spotted a newspaper that someone had slid under the door. On the first page was a photograph of President Richard Nixon beneath the headline that read, NIXON COMING TO BIG GAME. It was official. America's number-one citizen and football fan would be flying into Fayetteville as the self-appointed coronator of college football's mythical national championship.

Steinmark imagined himself being photographed after the game with the leader of the free world. Nah, he thought. If the Longhorns won the game, he would stand in the back of the locker room, avoiding the glare of the TV lights.

Nixon loved football so much that he might have endured a month of Medina Drills just to score a ticket to the Big Shootout. At the height of his political campaigns, Nixon often bragged to the wealthiest of supporters that he played high school football and later at Whittier College. It took him several years to admit that he was not a good player, basically a scrub, but his enthusiasm for the game was boundless.

Nixon would be traveling on the Marine One helicopter to the stadium with an impressive entourage. Razorback Stadium was going to be a circus and Freddie was not about to miss it. After all, he had outlasted the pain through nine games of pure hell.

Chapter 18

THE BIG SHOOTOUT

They landed in Fort Smith, Arkansas, on the day before the big game and traveled by bus along the twisting, narrow, mountainous highway for sixty miles into Fayetteville. The Ozark Mountains were on fire with the blazing colors of early winter, but the ride was a bit comical. Some of the country folks the Texas players spotted along the highway were straight out of the comic strip *Lil' Abner*. No one on the 1969 roster had played a game in the mountains of northwest Arkansas, and they laughed when they saw a farmer in greasy coveralls with tobacco stains down the front.

An edginess permeated the bus as the number-one team in the country rolled toward Fayetteville. Freddie Steinmark and Bobby Mitchell began to share their anxieties. "I'm not afraid to play Arkansas," Steinmark said. "Just afraid of how I'm going to play. I just don't know if my leg'll hold up."

Mitchell said, "Just keep playing like you have all season, Freddie, and everything's going to be fine."

"I'm not so sure I've played that great this season," Steinmark said.

Staying in bed and missing class had given Steinmark more energy. By the afternoon, he was feeling better and it helped convince the coaches he was ready to play. They were eyeballing his every move. They needed to know if he could handle Arkansas's bombs-away offense and keep up with Chuck Dicus.

Bill Montgomery had completed 93 of 173 passes for 1,333 yards that season, almost doubling the production of Texas wishbone signal-caller James Street. Of course, Darrell Royal seemed unfazed that the Longhorns' conservative offense had averaged 8 passes per game.

As the Longhorns' bus pulled into the parking lot at the team's hotel that chilly, cloudy afternoon, Royal felt a sudden sense of dread. All he could hear were the blaring of car horns up and down the busy avenue. The hotel marquee read ATTENTION DARRELL ROYAL. DO NOT CAST YOUR STEERS BEFORE SWINE. Across the street at the Holiday Inn, the marquee read GO HOGS! BEAT NOTRE DAME! For the first time since 1925, Notre had lifted its self-imposed bowl ban and accepted an invitation to the Cotton Bowl on January 1 to meet the champion of the Southwest Conference—the winner of Texas-Arkansas.

The players checked into their rooms and were soon back on the bus for the ride over to the stadium. There would be a brief workout to get acclimated to the stadium's Astroturf and all of the surroundings.

Riding on the team's chartered jet that day was *San Antonio Express-News* columnist Dan Cook. Like many Texans, Cook could not find a flight to Arkansas or a hotel room within five states. The sportswriter was lucky that he did not drive to Arkansas, as gas stations all over the state were refusing service to customers with Texas license plates. Fortunately, he hitched a ride with the Longhorns and would be rooming with assistant sports information director Bill Little at the team hotel.

Little and Cook stood on the sideline that afternoon and watched the players warm up before practice. Little pointed something out that the sportswriter had not noticed.

"Watch Freddie Steinmark," Little said. "He's limping around right now. But when the coaches start watching, he'll stop limping."

Almost on cue, Steinmark ditched the limp when Fred Akers and Mike Campbell came around.

"That's amazing," Cook said. "I didn't know that kid could act."

Steinmark was finding it more difficult to disguise his predicament. One of his best friends, tackle Bill Zapalac, was not helping matters.

"Hey, Ratso," Zapalac yelled. "Man, you are really limping today. What the hell is wrong with you, Freddie Joe?"

Steinmark put his right index finger to his lips. He wanted to yell "Shut up, you dummy!" His new nickname was hardly flattering. "Ratso" Rizzo was the gimpy, greasy Dustin Hoffman character in the film version of the novel *Midnight Cowboy*.

The scene at the pregame practice was straight out of the 1971 novel *The Day of the Jackal*, which was set in 1963. In the distance, a government sniper stood on one of the campus' tallest buildings. On the practice field behind the north end zone, helicopters practiced takeoffs and landings. Secret Service agents lined the sidelines and were easy to spot because of their sunglasses on a cloudy day. Most of the agents seemed more riveted to the action on the field than scouting out the stadium.

Darrell Royal, conversing with defensive coordinator Mike Campbell, surveyed the scene and said, "You know, you work all of your life to get to the big game. Then you get here and it's just weird."

On the bus ride back to the hotel, Royal sat next to Street and presented him with several options for a two-point conversion if the Longhorns needed it to win the game. All of his coaching life Royal had been willing to gamble to avoid the tie. As the bus traversed the rain-soaked streets, the Texas quarterback listened intently to Royal. Then he spoke loud enough for the whole team to hear. "Coach Royal, we aren't going to need a two-point conversion to beat Arkansas. We're gonna beat the *shit* out of this team."

Royal was all too familiar with Street's cocky outbursts. "Listen to me, James," he said. "I know this game is going down to the wire and you need to know every option we've got."

After dinner in a large hotel ballroom, Royal walked to the lectern, cleared his throat, and said, "Let me make one thing very clear to all of you. Boys, there will be a winner and a loser out there tomorrow. We aren't playing for a danged tie."

A cheer went up. A tie, as Bear Bryant once said, was like "kissing your sister," and the 'Horns were in no mood to kiss female relatives.

They had come to Fayetteville to win the Big Shootout and to earn the right to play Notre Dame in the Cotton Bowl. Of course, there was a good reason for not settling for the tie. If the game ended in a deadlock, Arkansas would go to the Cotton Bowl to play Notre Dame by virtue of Texas having gone the previous season. This was according to conference rules.

Texas entered the game with the nation's number-one-ranked scoring offense and the number-two defense, right behind Arkansas. However, this was not a favorable matchup for a 'Horns defense weighted down by a limping safety. An even larger concern was rover Mike Campbell getting stuck in man-to-man coverage against Chuck Dicus, creating a speed mismatch. If Dicus lined up in the slot, he would become Campbell's man-to-man responsibility.

Of all the opposing coaches in college football, Royal knew the tendencies of Arkansas' Frank Broyles better than anyone. They vacationed together in the summer and were known to play fifty to sixty holes of golf a day, driving their cart like a race car and whacking balls until darkness intervened.

Broyles and his Arkansas staff were famous for scouting opponents on film until the wee hours of the morning and to come up the solutions that usually worked. No one on the Texas schedule was capable of finding an edge faster than Broyles.

The last decade of Arkansas versus Texas had been a litany of drama, tension, and adrenaline rushes. It was enough to turn Royal and Broyles into gray-haired old men. In 1959, Texas scored a late touchdown for a 13–12 victory. The following year, Mickey Cissell kicked a 24-yard field goal in the waning seconds for a 24–23 Razorback victory. The Hogs led most of the 1962 game by the score of 3–0 until Tommy Ford scored from the 4-yard line with thirty-six seconds remaining for a 7–3 win. Texas was coming off a national championship in 1963 and seemed unbeatable when the 'Horns and the Hogs met at Memorial Stadium in Austin in '64. Ken Hatfield returned a punt 81 yards for a touchdown and Arkansas stopped the Longhorns' 2-point attempt with 1:27 to play to win 14–13. In 1965, the game went back and forth until Razorback quarterback Jon

Brittenum rallied the offense for an 80-yard drive in the final minutes, completing most of his passes to Bobby Burnett. From the Texas 15-yard line, Brittenum feathered a sideline pass to Burnett, who caught it and stepped out of bounds inches from the goal. On the next play, Brittenum dove into the end zone for the winning touchdown with 92 seconds left. Arkansas had won again, 27–24.

So intense were the two coaches that Royal once accused Broyles of stealing his play signals. They were playing golf in the summer of '65 when the subject came up.

Cruising along in the golf cart, Royal turned to Broyles and said, "Frank, were you stealing my signals last year?" Broyles shrugged, bowed his head, and said, "Yes, Darrell, I was."

Then it was Broyles's turn: "Darrell, were you stealing my signals last year?" Royal smiled and said, "Why, yes, Frank I was. If I can see them, I'm going to steal them."

Friday night in Fayetteville, Royal never went to bed. He was trying to come up with any angle that might turn the game in Texas' favor. Cactus Pryor, the host of Royal's TV show, shared the suite with the coach. In his foreword to Royal and John Weaver's book *Coach Royal: Conversations with a Texas Football Legend*, Pryor wrote, "I would have slept better in a New York city bus. All night long Coach Royal was calling coaches in for yet another brain session. He didn't sleep a wink."

The only way to reach the stadium Saturday morning was by going down Highway 71 the wrong way. Cars going the right way were directed by the police escort to pull off the road. There was no paved shoulder, so some of the cars got stuck in the mud. This made the Arkansas fans even angrier.

Royal and Street sat in the first two seats on the right of the bus. Royal had decided on "Counter 49" as the two-point play. It was one of the toughest plays to defense in the veer option.

After they reached the stadium and dressed for the game, the Texas players were surprised to find that almost every seat was filled more than an hour before kickoff. Fans were sitting in the freezing drizzle, pulling deeply from their antifreeze flasks. They actually cheered the Razorbacks during warm-ups.

Down on the field, word filtered through the ABC crew that President Richard Nixon was on his way to the stadium on Marine One.

Outside on the ever-slickening streets, a taxi cab pulled up to the curb outside the stadium and dropped off two passengers. One man told the driver that he heard Nixon was on his way. "Nixon, huh?" the cabbie said. "Well, that's almost as big as Johnny Cash coming here last year."

The Ozarks were filled with celebrities that day. Billy Graham was scheduled to give the invocation, and the ABC cameras were already combing the stands in search of Glen Campbell, John Wayne, Dan Blocker, Roy Clark, Buck Owens, and Colonel Harland David Sanders of Kentucky Fried Chicken fame. Touring the pressbox during pregame festivities was a sexy blonde, Barbara "Bobbi" Specht, who had recently been crowned the queen of the college football centennial. One of the writers asked Bobbi who she would be pulling for.

"Well, I am from Texas Tech," she said. "So that makes me a Texan."

With a half hour until kickoff, Bill Zapalac once again watched his buddy struggling to cover the Texas receivers in warm-ups. Once more, the big tackle yelled, "Hey, Ratso, what's wrong with you?" Steinmark tried to mute his friend. "Shut up, Zap," he yelled. "The Arkansas coaches are watching."

Sure enough, a couple of Arkansas staff members had already radioed the information down from the pressbox to Broyles. There was glee in their voices. The Texas safety was limping worse than Chester Goode (Dennis Weaver) on *Gunsmoke*.

Street noticed that Freddie was limping and approached him. It was the first time that he had seen Freddie limping that badly all season. As a team captain, Street felt obligated to address the injury.

"Hey, Freddie, we all have hurts at the end of the season," Street said. "I just think you need to focus on the game. Focus on what is ahead of you. You've got to get over that hurt if we're going to beat Arkansas today."

One of the cooler aspects of the ABC broadcasts in those days was the introduction of the starting players on the field just minutes before the game. Sideline reporter Bill Fleming handled the introductions and his voice could be heard over the stadium's public address speakers, cranking the stadium energy to a fever pitch.

Bobby Mitchell was worried as he stood in line for his introduction. Ten days earlier, he had missed the Texas A&M game with an injury and was replaced by Randy Stout. As he stood in line between tackle Bobby Wuensch and center Forrest Wiegand, Mitchell tried to read over Fleming's shoulder. *Was it possible that Fleming would have Stout's name and not mine on his list?* He wanted his friends back in Wheat Ridge to know he was a starter, just like Freddie.

As he moved closer to Fleming, Mitchell said, "Can I see your list just for a second?" Fleming gladly handed it over and Mitchell saw Stout's name and not his.

"Sir, this is a mistake," Mitchell said. "I'm Bobby Mitchell and I'm the starting left guard today."

Fleming smiled and said, "I'm glad you told me." The ABC technicians frantically went to work superimposing LG BOBBY MITCHELL.

A burst of turbulence from the south end of the stadium signaled that the first of the presidential helicopters had landed. They were running late, thanks to the bad weather in Fort Smith, where Air Force One landed from Washington. With all of the bigwigs on board, the army-trained helicopter pilots had lifted off from Fort Smith and circled instead of heading north. This frustrated Nixon, who did not want to miss kickoff. Some of the other politicians were no so concerned with missing a couple of plays and wondered if they should be flying in this weather at all.

As Arkansas's Bill McClard was kicking off, Marine One thropped over the Ozarks, then angled low across a cut in the mountains and landed on a grassy spot just beyond the north end zone.

Enough politicians poured out of that helicopter to form a special session in the Arkansas mountains: U.S. senators J. William Fulbright (D-Arkansas), John McClellan (D-Arkansas), and John Tower (R-Texas), along with U.S. representatives George H. W. Bush (R-Texas), Robert Price (R-Texas), Jim Wright (D-Texas), J.J. Pickle (D-Texas), Wilbur Mills (D-Arkansas), and John Paul Hammerschmidt (R-Arkansas). The White House contingent included Henry Kissinger, H. R. Haldeman, and press secretary Ron Ziegler. Arkansas Governor Winthrop Rockefeller, who had extended the original invitation to Nixon, met the Washingtonians at the chopper and walked in the brigade toward the stadium.

On the first possession of the game, Texas' vaunted wishbone went nowhere. As Nixon strode into the stadium amid a bevy of Secret Service agents and Arkansas State Police, Street faked to Worster and tried to hand off to Ted Koy. The ball came loose, sliding across the slick Astroturf. Arkansas's Bobby Field recovered at the Texas 22-yard line.

On the next play, the Texas fans thought the fix was in. Arkansas wide receiver John Rees made a diving stab at the 2-yard line, but neither foot came close to being inbounds. Still, side judge Shorty Lawson, standing about five feet away with a good view, ruled it a catch. Lawson was from College Station, the home of Texas A&M. Naturally, the Texas fans theorized that Lawson favored Arkansas.

On the next play, Arkansas tailback Bill Burnett dived head-first over the line and into the end zone for a touchdown. The Hogs led 7–0.

As the Nixon entourage was reaching its seats, Arkansas Congressman John Paul Hammerschmidt, wearing a bright red jacket, turned to George Bush and said, "Hell, Bush, we've already scored!"

Nixon was walking up the aisle, just arriving at his row, when he turned and craned his neck to catch a glimpse of Burnett's high-jump act. At the time, the undersized and outdated Razorback Stadium held only 44,000 fans, but the roar that rose up sent shock waves through the mountains.

In the week before the Texas game, Broyles had changed the

Arkansas defense from a 4-3 to a 6-2, also known as the "split six," to combat the run-heavy wishbone. Street could not get any rhythm going on the Longhorns' first two possessions. The Arkansas forward wall stuffed Worster at the line, thus eliminating Texas' biggest weapon.

"It was like they changed everything in their defense," tackle Bob McKay recalled. "I would fire out to block somebody and nobody would be there. It was like I was blocking the wind."

After Texas punted, Burnett and big fullback Bruce Maxwell pounded the ball down the field. Montgomery ran for 8 and 14 yards on the option, and from the Texas 26-yard line, the quarterback stepped under center and noticed that Dicus was facing man-to-man coverage from cornerback Danny Lester. Steinmark was stationed in the middle of the field, preparing to cover the tight end, but Montgomery felt certain he would shift into double coverage against Dicus if the receiver ran a post pattern. Montgomery called the audible because he knew Steinmark was playing on one good leg. Dicus blew past Lester and hauled in the pass at the 3-yard line, just ahead of Steinmark, who threw an errant elbow as the receiver crossed the goal. The scoreboard flashed ARKANSAS 13, TEXAS 0.

On the Texas sideline, Royal hustled over to defensive coordinator Mike Campbell. "Do you think we should take Freddie out?" Campbell nodded and replied, "I'm thinking about it."

Then the coaches spotted a flag on the field. Almost thirty seconds after the end of the play, the back judge determined that Arkansas had committed pass interference. Tom Campbell had somehow finagled a penalty against Arkansas's Rees that wiped out the score. "I just walked up to the official and said, 'Sir, that [John Rees] man was blocking on me and that's pass interference,'" Campbell said. "I figured it couldn't hurt. And the next thing I knew, the official was dropping a flag." Six points came off the scoreboard.

On the Arkansas sideline, the coaches thought it was a make-up call for Rees's controversial TD catch. Broyles's protests fell on deaf ears, though, and on the next play Montgomery was sacked for a 24-yard loss.

The drive died on downs two plays later. Arkansas should have led 14–0 at halftime, but instead held only a 7-point advantage. They had outgained the Longhorns almost 2-to-1, forcing 3 turnovers. It should have been much worse.

In the dressing room at halftime, tight end Randy Peschel told anyone who would listen that he could get open. He spoke with assistant coaches, teammates, and even the trainers. He sought Royal's attention, but that was impossible at such a hectic time. The head coach was huddled with offensive coordinator Emory Bellard, trying to save the season.

It seemed that everyone in the Texas locker room was trying to make adjustments. Mitchell and Wuensch put their heads together and devised a plan to attack the Arkansas defensive right side. Mitchell proposed that he block the tackle in the gap while Wuensch held off the outside linebacker. Or they would call a switch at the line of scrimmage and Mitchell would loop around and block the linebacker.

As Arkansas trotted back onto the field for the second half, Montgomery told himself that he wasn't going to let any more opportunities slip away. Six minutes deep into the third quarter, the Hogs' quarterback found Dicus over the middle. He had shaken loose from Mike Campbell at the 15-yard line. Tom Campbell was again blocked by John Rees, this time legally. Steinmark had one last shot at Dicus near the goal, but the little safety was limping so badly that all he could do was throw a weak forearm. Dicus's run-and-catch covered 29 yards. This time, there was no flag and the scoreboard read AR-KANSAS 14, TEXAS 0.

Arkansas's passing game was shredding the Texas secondary and Steinmark's limp was noticeable to everyone in the stadium, not to mention the thirty million watching on national TV. Arkansas was looking like a sure thing for number one.

As the 'Horns came off the field, Texas defensive coordinator Mike Campbell started yelling at his son, Mike Campbell. "You've got to get closer to number 20 [Dicus]."

"Daddy, I can't get any closer to number 20," Mike said. "That's just not possible."

For the first time all season, Campbell was not getting the deep support that he was accustomed to from Steinmark.

Everything that Texas tried seemed to be wrong. The wishbone was out of sync and the 'Horns defense was confused by the intricacies of the Arkansas passing offense. Time was already running out as the game moved into the fourth quarter.

Looking back on the moment, Montgomery recalled, "We're in a position to win a national championship. We were playing well. We had a terrific defensive game plan. All was right with the world. Then the fourth quarter started."

During a TV timeout at the end of the third quarter, Street stepped into the huddle and saw a team that looked scared.

"Look, guys, we're going to be all right," Street said, clapping his hands. "Just stay steady in here. Listen to me. We're going to be all right."

From the middle of the huddle came the booming voice of Bob McKay. "No, James, we are *not* going to be all right. We haven't moved the fucking ball the whole fucking game."

Street glared at McKay. "Look, Big 'Un. Just worry about blocking your guy and we're going to move the ball right down the field."

On the first play of the fourth quarter, Street dropped back to pass from the Arkansas 42-yard line. Again McKay missed his block, forcing Street to retreat to the 49, where he spotted a seam in the left side of the line opened by tackle Bobby Wuensch.

Heading upfield, Street bounced off two Razorbacks. In the midst of the chaos, McKay headed upfield and threw a clearing block. Street ran through the arms of linebacker Cliff Powell at the 25-yard line, then flashed some foot speed that no one had ever seen. He was motoring so fast that it was hard to tell if he was running for the end zone or the presidential helicopter.

After he crossed the goal, Street realized why Royal had been making such an issue of the two-point conversion.

"When Coach Royal ran onto the field and started waving his arms and telling the offense to stay on the field, I felt pretty good about things," Street said. "At least I was prepared."

Street took the snap, headed left, faked the pitch to Koy, then stopped. He sensed the momentum of the Arkansas defense going past him. Then he veered toward the goal and burrowed his body into the end zone, cutting the lead to 14–8.

It did not take long for Montgomery and the Arkansas passing game to come back firing. The Razorbacks moved all the way to the Texas 24-yard line, where on first down, Royal felt his gut burning. He knew he had made the wrong decision to leave a limping Steinmark on the field. Ninety-nine percent of the decisions regarding the Texas defense were made by Campbell, but Royal could veto *anything*. At that moment, he thought about calling a timeout and substituting Rick Nabors. Steinmark might have been the smartest guy on the field, but he was no longer effective with the bad leg.

As Montgomery retreated to pass, Royal set his eyes on Steinmark. Little Freddie would be responsible for keeping Dicus out of the end zone and, at that moment, he had no shot. Dicus faked to the outside, broke to the inside, and was running past Steinmark when the wily safety grabbed the receiver's jersey with both hands. He stopped Dicus dead in his tracks. A blind man could have seen that Steinmark was holding. When he saw the flag, Steinmark shrugged. *At least I kept them from scoring.*

This time, the Texas coaches were not in a forgiving mood. Royal took two quick steps toward Campbell, and the defensive coordinator held up his right hand. "I know, Darrell. I know." He yelled, "Rick Nabors, get your butt in there for Freddie!" Steinmark limped to the sideline and it seemed to take forever. The fans shook their heads. How had he played so long on that bad leg?

Arkansas was awarded a new set of downs at the Texas 9-yard line. Two plays later, the Razorbacks faced a third-and-goal from the 7-yard line. Broyles wrestled with one of the biggest coaching decisions of his life. Bill McClard, who was 7-of-9 that season, was among the best kickers in college football. A running play surely would have moved the ball even closer for the Arkansas kicker.

Up in the pressbox, offensive coordinator Don Breaux had a different idea. He was in a mood to put Texas away. He relayed a pass play through Broyles's headset. The head coach had plenty of time to veto it, but sided with Breaux.

Broyles was worried about a recent trend of bad snaps on field goals. That is why he did not react when Breaux sent down the call from the pressbox—a sprint-out pass to the left with Montgomery throwing to Dicus in the left corner of the end zone. This type of pass had been so successful for Arkansas the past two years that a Las Vegas "wise guy" might have called it a stone-cold lock. Montgomery didn't have the strongest arm in college football, but his passes were normally so precise as to dot the I in victory. Taking the snap, Montgomery wheeled left, twisted his hips, squared his shoulders, and delivered the pass.

It was intercepted. Sprinting across the field like a bullet was Texas cornerback Danny Lester, who slashed inside Dicus at the sideline and intercepted the ball on the run. He returned it all the way to the Texas 30-yard line.

As it turned out, Steinmark was the hero of the defensive series. If he had not grabbed Dicus's jersey, the Arkansas receiver would have been wide open in the end zone for a certain touchdown and a 21–8 lead.

The real moment of truth would come 5 plays later at the Texas 43-yard line. It would be one of the most memorable plays in the history of college football. On fourth-and-three with 4:47 to play, practically everyone expected the Longhorns to run something conservative. Instead, Royal vetoed the play sent down from the pressbox by Bellard, who wanted a counteroption to the short side of the field. Street trotted to the sideline, then Royal blurted to his quarterback, "Run Right 53 Veer Pass." Street would have the option of throwing to only one receiver, Peschel—perhaps the slowest receiver on the field.

Campbell, leaning over Royal's shoulder, was shocked when he heard the call. He yelled, "Oh my God, Darrell!" Then he turned to the bench and hollered, "Get ready, Defense!"

Even more perplexing were these cold, hard facts: Street already had thrown 2 interceptions, and the Texas turnover count was up to six. Opting for a miracle this late in the game could be disastrous. Why not just run Worster off left guard?

As the day grew darker, and the clouds hovered above the upper rows, Street slowly trotted back onto the field. Suddenly, he stopped, turned around, and said, "Are you sure, Coach?" Street wondered if Royal meant to dial up "Right 52 Veer Pass" to Cotton Speyrer, the fastest player on the team. Royal shook his head and said, "Just call the damn play, James."

As Street approached the huddle, he said, "Randy do *not* look at me. But the ball is coming to you, and this play is going to work." Peschel looked away. Street knew the Arkansas defensive players had been sneaking looks inside the Texas huddle all day. As he spoke, he stared and pointed at Speyrer, hoping the Hogs would think the pass was going his way. Street quietly said "Right 53 Veer Pass." Then he called Peschel by his familiar nickname—"Pasquale." Street said, "Pasquale, if it's not open deep, break it across the middle. We'll get the first down. We've *got* to get the first down. This might be our last chance."

A tick before the 'Horns broke the huddle, McKay said, "You've got to be shitting me!"

As the offense set up, Bill Little, up in the pressbox, silently mouthed the word "Peschel" to Dan Cook, who nodded.

Peschel knew the play was going to work the instant he got set in his three-point stance. The Arkansas defensive backs were leaning forward, prepared to crash the wishbone sweep to the left side. Every player in the secondary took two forward steps before realizing that Peschel was accelerating past them. He was 5 yards behind the defense before the secondary could react.

Street spun and unleashed the pass of his lifetime. Arkansas defensive backs Jerry Moore and David Berner were starting to catch up with Peschel when the ball spiraled down from the gray Arkansas sky. Berner was a half step behind Peschel and Moore was on his left shoulder. As Berner leaped, he felt the ball tick his left ring finger.

The high, arcing pass looked at first to be a dream and nothing more. Somehow it sailed beyond four outstretched Razorback hands and into the arms of Peschel, who wobbled and fell at the 13, the ball firmly in his grasp. The stadium fell deathly silent. Peschel turned and saw a Texas male cheerleader doing backflips across the playing field. It all seemed surreal.

On the next play, Ted Koy made a quick cut to the inside and fought his way for 11 yards down to the two. That run alone negated his two fumbles. On the next play, Jim Bertelsen powered his way into the end zone behind blocks by Bobby Wuensh and Mitchell. If not for the quick hands of holder Donnie Wigginton, the kick would have failed. The backup quarterback snared the high snap and got the ball on the tee quickly. Happy Feller swung his leg and Texas led for the first time 15–14.

No doubt, this was the nightmare from hell for Arkansas. Then the fans looked up at the scoreboard clock and were reminded that 3:58 was still left to play.

Rain was beginning to fall when Montgomery started completing passes again. The Arkansas quarterback had been given one last chance to vanquish the ghosts. He exuded confidence and Royal could feel his gut aching again. Steinmark was back on the field and the entire game seemed like a crapshoot.

After three straight completions, Arkansas was at the Texas 39-yard line, facing second-and-three. McClard calculated that the Razorbacks needed to gain 14 more yards to get into his range. At the moment, it would have been a 56-yard kick, almost impossible into a stiff wind.

When Arkansas broke the huddle, Mike Campbell again drew coverage on Dicus. From the rear, his brother Tom yelled, "Push him to the outside, Mike. Don't let him get loose."

Tom Campbell was covering John Rees as he burst up the field and cut to the right sideline. Campbell said to Rees, "I've got you this time."

The second that Rees planted his left foot, Tom Campbell planted his left foot. In the ABC broadcast booth, Chris Schenkel said, "That Texas defender is in the receiver's hip pocket." Not only was Campbell in his pocket, he was counting Rees's cash. When the pass arrived, Campbell stepped in front of the receiver and pulled the ball to his chest. The game was over with ninety seconds to play.

At the final gun, the pain finally died in Steinmark's leg. It was a moment frozen in time. Numbed by the excitement and all the adrenaline, Steinmark danced with his teammates along the sideline. Then he took off running at full speed for the dressing room. When he came upon Worster, he yelled, "Why are you crying?"

"No, Freddie," Worster said. "Why are *you* crying?"

Steinmark could barely explain the emotional roller-coaster ride of the 1969 season. One moment, his left leg was racked with pain, and the next he was looking up at President Nixon standing behind a microphone on a platform set up inside the Texas locker room. This was the national championship the Longhorns had lived for.

In the corner of the Texas dressing room, Steinmark stood with a tear rolling down his cheek. Bobby Mitchell put his arm around his shoulders.

"Freddie, we finally made it," Mitchell said. "Can you believe what just happened?"

"This is why we came to Texas, Mitch," Steinmark said.

Then the leg began to ache again. Steinmark bent over in agony. He could barely enjoy the celebration.

Gathering on the stage were the three Texas captains—Glen Halsell, Koy, and Street. Royal reached down and lifted Randy Peschel by the shoulder pads and helped him onto the stage. Then he kissed the tight end on the cheek. Peschel led the team in the Lord's Prayer, and Royal did a quick interview with ABC's Bill Fleming, who had called it "one of the greatest games ever played."

Royal disagreed. He shook his head and said, "We just kept turning the ball over. I just don't know what to say."

During a steady downpour at the end of the game, Nixon was one of the few people in the stadium not to wear a hat. The makeup that had been applied to his face at halftime before a TV interview was now running. Still, the President felt like a man thriving in his element. He wanted an entire nation to know that he possessed a geninus-level football IQ. He stepped to the microphone and said,

"One of the great games of all time without question. I was up in the booth, the ABC booth, at halftime and incidentally I've got to brag a little. They asked me what was going to happen in the second half, and I said, 'Both teams are gonna score,' but that I thought what would really determine the second half would be whether Texas had the ability in the fourth quarter to come through. And you did!"

That is when Nixon played to the cameras. An aide handed him the presidential plaque that he would present to the champions of college football.

"What convinced me that Texas deserves this plaque is the fact you won a tough one," he said. "For a team to be behind 14–0, and then not to lose its cool and go on to win, that proves you deserve to be number one, and that's what you are!"

Nixon handed the plaque to Royal, and the coach turned the inscription toward him so he could read it. Nixon quickly grabbed the plaque and wrested it away from the coach. He pointed the inscription toward the TV cameras. He wanted thirty million TV viewers to see his little creation. In the meantime, the Longhorns whooped to the high heavens.

A half hour later, as Steinmark walked to the team bus in the freezing rain, he stopped to say hello to Marie Henderson, Scott's mother.

As he walked away, Marie Henderson said to her son, "Freddie doesn't look good."

"I know," Henderson said. "But at least he's going to tell the coaches and the trainers on Monday just how bad he's hurt."

The plane ride back to Austin seemed to take about three minutes. Players and coaches could see the Bell Tower on campus glowing orange with a huge white "1" in the middle. The pilot announced that more than 20,000 fans were waiting at the airport and some had made a mad dash onto the runway. They would have to circle a couple of times.

As the players descended the stairwell onto the tarmac, some were apprehensive about wading into the sea of tightly bunched, well-lubed fans. The wall of burnt orange seemed impenetrable. Players were actually disappearing from sight after descending the stairwell. One of the most miserable souls was James Street, who suffered greatly from claustrophobia. A female grabbed the collar of his shirt and tried to kiss him. Fortunately, Bobby Wuensch was close by and delivered one last clearing block.

Freddie searched the airport for Linda. When he found her a half hour later, he lifted her high with both arms and spun her around. They rode together in Scott Henderson's GTO to a party put on by local boosters and politicians on South Congress. Freddie grabbed the first beer offered to him as he walked through the door. This shocked everyone, including Linda.

"I just want to see what it feels like," Freddie told everyone, hoisting the can. "You know I've never done this before."

Freddie desperately hoped the alcohol might kill his pain. He was on his eighth beer when he ran into Reverend Fred Bomar of St. Peter the Apostle Church, a Roman Catholic parish in southeast Austin. Freddie knew that Father Bomar was a regular drinker and wanted some advice on how to handle the stuff.

"Go slow," Bomar said. "If your body isn't used to alcohol, it can catch up with you pretty quick."

Freddie was disappointed the beer did not relieve his pain. Curfew for everyone was two A.M. Leaving the party, Freddie slipped on a stair and the pain jolted through his left thighbone. It was like fire shooting through his leg. He sat down and choked his leg with both hands. He turned to Henderson. "Why does it never go away, Scott? This thing is just killing me."

Freddie needed some rest. Then he could begin his conditioning work for Notre Dame in the Cotton Bowl. Facing the Fighting Irish and Ara Parseghian, the man who had turned him down for a scholarship, was going to be fun. First, though, he was going to have to face Darrell Royal.

Chapter 19

DAY OF RECKONING

Monday morning, Freddie Steinmark limped across the burnt orange carpet toward the long oaken desk. It was his first visit to the Darrell Royal domain in three years, since his high school recruiting trip. Players who stayed out of trouble rarely suffered the consequences of these one-on-one encounters. Freddie had avoided the sins of the campus and the sins of the city.

Still, he was feeling a mixture of guilt and sadness. He had not been totally honest with his head coach about a serious injury that had practically ruined his season. He was ready to confess, and, hopefully, to gain some forgiveness. Most of all, he wanted to fix his injured leg for the Cotton Bowl in twenty-four days.

"Coach, I'm a lot more hurt than I've been letting on," he said.

"I was afraid of that," Royal replied. "You know we've had our eyes on you for quite some time. I know that Coach Campbell and Coach Akers asked you if you were hurt bad. But you never told them that you were."

"I didn't tell them, Coach, because I wanted to keep playing," Steinmark said. "Oh, I really didn't know how bad I was hurt until after the Texas A&M game."

"You probably should have gone to the doctor for X-rays," Royal said. "All you had to do was say the word."

"I know. But I wanted it to wait until after the season. That's what Scott Appleton did."

"I know that's what Scott Appleton did," Royal said. "But we don't encourage players to play with a broken ankle or a bum leg."

Royal reached for the phone.

"I'm calling Frank Medina. I want you to go by there and get a doctor's slip. I want you to go see Dr. Joe Reneau for X-rays. I want you to go now."

Freddie borrowed the Ford Galaxy from Linda and drove the five miles to the offices of Dr. Joe Reneau, who, at the age of thirty-eight, had recently gained the title as the team physician for all of the Texas sports teams. He had replaced Dr. Jerry Julian, who had been elevated to orthopedic surgeon at the university infirmary.

Thirty minutes after taking the X-rays, Reneau returned with the negatives of Steinmark's injured left leg and placed them in a brown envelope.

"I'll send these pictures over to Dr. Julian, who can look at them later today," Reneau said.

Hearing Dr. Julian's name raised a red flag with Freddie. Surely, this meant that there was trouble with his thighbone, known as the femur. The femur is the longest bone in the body. It is one of the two strongest along with the temporal skull bone. Freddie had thought for months that his injury was either a charley horse or a deep bruise.

"I'll take the pictures to Dr. Julian," Steinmark said to Dr. Reneau. "I'm going right by there anyway. "

He had driven no more than three blocks when the curiosity forced him to pull the Ford Galaxy to the side of the road. He slowly lifted the X-rays from the envelope. The pictures were not very clear, but holding them to the light, Steinmark could see a hump on the thighbone, where it met the knee. He thought about the phrase "curvature of the spine," and wondered if there was such a thing as a curvature of the femur. One thing was certain: the bone was not right. Waiting on the X-ray results was not going to be fun.

His head was still spinning when he took Linda to the Texas-Ole Miss basketball game that evening at Gregory Gym. The football team would be introduced as national champions at halftime.

Sitting on the east side of the gym during the freshman game, Steinmark kept watching the front entrance and hoping that

Dr. Reneau would show up. As the freshman game ended, he spotted the doctor taking a passageway underneath the floor bleachers.

"There's Dr. Reneau," Freddie said to Linda. "I've got to go get the verdict."

"Who's Dr. Reneau?" she said. "And what does he have to do with you?"

"We'll find out soon," Freddie said, smiling weakly.

When Steinmark reached the entrance to the varsity basketball dressing room, he spotted Dr. Reneau talking to Frank Medina. They were speaking quietly with their heads together. No doubt, this was urgent business. Freddie wasted little time approaching the doctor when the conversation ended.

"Dr. Reneau, how's my knee?" he said.

"Just fine, Freddie," he said.

"What about the curve in my bone?" Freddie asked. "I took a look at the X-rays and could see some kind of curve."

Dr. Reneau looked him solemnly in the eye. "That's what we're worried about, Freddie. You just might have a bone tumor. It looks like it might be, but we can't tell. I want you to come to my office in the morning."

Reneau kept talking, but Steinmark no longer heard the words. His mind was on another planet. The word "tumor" sent a shattering pain through his skull. Surely his chances of playing in the Cotton Bowl were out the window. A tumor was associated with cancer and cancer could mean extended health problems, or even death. While growing up in Wheat Ridge, adults talked in hushed tones about this disease. Steinmark knew little about it. Head down, he walked away slowly and headed back up the bleachers toward Linda.

"The first thing I noticed was that he was pale," Linda recalled four decades later. "He was really limping. It was like he was in more pain than I ever saw. I put my left arm around him and I could tell he had sweated through his shirt."

Their eyes met and Freddie said quietly, "Linda, they say I have a tumor in my leg. I'm in trouble. I don't know what to think."

"Oh, my God," she said. "Do they think it's cancer?"

"They didn't say. But we're going to do some X-rays in the morning. I've got to say this is not sounding good."

Steinmark placed his left hand on his knee and started to squeeze. Never before could he feel a bump on the bone, but this time he did. He put Linda's hand on his knee.

"Feel that?" he said.

"I don't feel anything," she said.

"Don't give me that, Linda. Don't tell me you can't feel that hump."

Freddie and Linda watched the first half of the varsity game in silence, enjoying not a single second of it. At halftime, the football team was called down to courtside. Not surprising, James Street was handed the microphone. Street called each teammate by the nickname he had given them. As Steinmark walked across the floor, trying not to limp, he heard "Fast Freddie Steinmark" followed by applause. The pain was killing him, but he smiled anyway. He always smiled.

Freddie and Linda left the game in the third quarter and walked back to the dorm. Linda tried to cheer him up. "It could just be bone chips. Freddie, I've heard of floating bone chips. Maybe that's what's wrong."

"The way that Dr. Reneau looked at me, I don't think so," he said. "At least I'll know something in the morning. I'll let you know something."

Freddie wanted to be alone. So he said good-bye to Linda at the women's wing of the Jester Center and took off for a walk. His first stop was the Catholic Student Center that was empty and dark inside. Freddie sat on the front row and said his prayers. Before long, he was crying. Bawling, actually. The words from Reneau had hit him straight in the heart. Everything he knew about the injury was beginning to crystallize in his mind. He knew why the pain would not subside and why the long hours in the whirlpool did not help. His father was right. He should have talked to Coach Royal much sooner.

The silence of the chapel was more than he could handle, so Freddie started walking again, this time toward the southern edge of campus. He reached the Littlefield Fountain and sat on one of the stone benches. He gazed at the cascading water. He focused on the European-style leaping horses that seemed poised to vault from the fountain. Over the top, he could see the 307-foot University of Texas clock tower that lorded over the campus. Two nights earlier, as the Texas charter flight returned from Arkansas, Steinmark marveled at the sight of the orange-lit monstrosity with the number "1" straight down the middle. It was one of the most beautiful sights of his life. He wondered if he would ever see it again.

A couple of students walked past, and one started yelling, "Great game, Freddie! Boy, you were fantastic out there against Arkansas." They came over to shake his hand. Freddie's grip was limp and he seemed to look straight through them. They walked away in silence, not knowing what was eating the little guy.

Steinmark sat down to think some more. It was past ten o'clock and the campus was still. Linda was not far away. His fellow teammates were either studying or playing Bourre inside the Jester Center. Almost everyone he knew in Austin was minutes away. Still, he had never felt more alone.

He stood up, wiped away the tears, and headed back to the dorm. Unlocking his room, he realized that Bobby Mitchell was still out, so he closed the door and picked up the telephone. He needed to talk to his father.

Big Fred answered on the second ring.

"Dad, I need to talk to you and I don't want you to tell Mom," he said.

"What's the problem, Freddie?"

"It's my leg, dad. It's a lot worse than we thought. The doctors X-rayed it today and they told me it might be a tumor."

"God, Freddie, I knew it might be bad."

"Please don't tell Mom."

"I won't." They hung up.

When the phone rang five minutes later, he knew who was on the other end of the line.

"Freddie, it's your mom," Gloria Steinmark said. "Tell me what's wrong."

He told her the story of the X-rays, and described the hump where the thighbone met the knee. When he used the word "tumor," she began to cry. He told her there would be more X-rays in the morning and that he would call when there was more news.

Freddie turned off the lights and laid down to sleep and realized there was little hope of even dozing. His heart was pounding. So he got up and took his last Darvon.

The next morning at five o'clock, Randy Stout got up to study for a final exam and carried his books into a small study on the first floor. A little before seven, Steinmark slipped out of his room wearing blue jeans and a T-shirt.

"Where are you going this early in the morning, Freddie boy?" Stout said.

"My leg is really hurting," Steinmark said. "I'm going to get some more X-rays. I should be back before you know it."

Spanky Stephens picked up Steinmark at curbside and drove him to the infirmary. Dr. Joe Reneau was waiting at his office with a grim expression. He had already notified Dr. Charles A. LeMaistre, the university's vice chancellor, that they might need the private university airplane to transport Steinmark to Houston's MD Anderson Hospital.

After completing more X-rays, Reneau gently delivered the news to Steinmark. In both sets of X-rays he had found a clear spot about the size of a golf ball in the middle of the femur, near the knee. The bone should have been completely solid, but it was not.

"We're sending you to MD Anderson in Houston," Reneau said.

Going to MD Anderson meant nothing to Steinmark. He had never heard of the hospital or anyone named M. D. Anderson.

"It's the biggest cancer hospital in the world," Reneau said without a smile.

Stephens received a phone call from the infirmary and was told to hurry back. He would be transporting Steinmark to the airport.

Stephens carried the title of student trainer, but was as much a part of the team as anyone wearing the burnt orange. He was around the players night and day and roomed and Randy Peschel. He went to the bars and the churches with them and knew most of their secrets. He was even invited to the steak fries that featured plenty of beer at the Catholic rectory on the southeast side of town.

Upon learning that Steinmark was headed to MD Anderson, his heart fell into his shoes. It was like learning that his brother had cancer.

"Like everybody else, I loved Freddie," Stephens said. "I saw him every day. We had classes together. It was really tough for me that the training staff never could figure out exactly what was wrong with him. On the day I picked him up, I was about the only person on campus that knew he had a bad problem."

His instructions were to drive Steinmark back to the dorm to pick up toiletries and some clothes. They returned to the Jester Center and Steinmark picked up another pair of jeans and a shirt.

"Maybe you ought to take a few more things to wear," Stephens said. "You might be back tomorrow. But you never know about these things. It could take a few days."

On the drive to the airport, Stephens said that Steinmark was not overly talkative, but seemed to be taking the news in stride.

"For someone who had basically been told that he had cancer, Freddie was doing okay," Stephens said. "I don't think he was any more depressed than anyone else. But that's just the way that Freddie handled things."

Stephens knew precisely where the University of Texas hangar was located, at Bergstrom Airport, not far from campus. The two-engine four-seater was already warming up when they arrived. Steinmark almost threw up when he saw the airplane. Flying in large commercial airliners was enough to make his stomach do somersaults. This little plane would be rocking and rolling all the way to Houston.

Steinmark looked at his friend and said, "Spanky, why don't you come with me? That would make the trip a lot easier."

"I don't think they'll let me, ol' buddy," Stephens said. "But I'll get there just as fast as I can."

Seconds after Steinmark boarded the plane, the door was shut and the plane began to taxi.

"They put Freddie on that airplane and they were gone in a hurry," Stephens remembered. "They wanted to get him there pretty fast."

Linda had heard nothing from Freddie all morning in spite of placing several calls to his room. She went to the Jester Center cafeteria at lunch and could find no one who had seen him. She was desperate and on the verge of tears. This scenario was especially strange since everyone always seemed to know where Freddie was at all times. He was like a neon light with his bright smile and cheerful manner.

Linda spotted Stephens near the mailbox and ran toward him. Spanky always seemed to know the daily gossip around campus.

"Spanky, where's Freddie?" she almost pleaded. "I haven't seen him since last night. He didn't call this morning. I don't know what to think. "

"I just drove him to the airport," Stephens said. "They put him on the university plane and took him to MD Anderson in Houston."

"What is MD Anderson?"

"It's the biggest cancer hospital in the world."

Linda gasped. She turned and looked into the parking lot. She thought about firing up the Ford Galaxy and taking off for Houston. Being from Colorado, though, she had no idea where Houston was. Turning around and around, she finally spotted Scott Henderson, schoolbooks in hand, heading to class.

"Scott, they took Freddie to a cancer hospital this morning and it's called MD Anderson," she said. "This really looks bad. What are we going to do?"

A native Texan, Henderson knew all about MD Anderson Hospital and its reputation. He quickly reached into his pocket and pulled out the key to the GTO.

"Let's go to Houston," he said. "Get in the car."

They were soon rolling along the two-laned Highway 290 toward Houston. Driving fast, Henderson knew they could be there in about three hours.

En route to Houston, Steinmark took a seat next to Texas deputy chancellor Dr. Charles LaMaistre, who oddly enough had once viewed the X-rays of Mickey Mantle's legs when he was stricken by osteomyelitis.

"Your X-rays look a lot like Mickey's," LaMaistre told Freddie.

Freddie did not know whether to laugh or cry. At least Mickey was still alive.

The speed with which the plane reached Houston was alarming. Minutes after they arrived at Hobby Airport, the whirlwind gathered more steam. They were met on the tarmac by Dr. Bob Moreton, the assistant director of MD Anderson. They were driven in his car to an apartment complex called Anderson Mayfair across the street from the hospital. As Freddie toted his small bag into the apartment, he knew that he would be staying for a while. Why else would he have an apartment?

At the hospital, doctors and nurses were soon coming at him from all directions. Everyone was pleasant. Still, they were all in such a hurry. The newest patient was informed that MD Anderson was a branch of the University of Texas. Then came the realization that he was getting so much attention because he actually played for the Texas national championship team. *Maybe they brought me here to talk about the Big Shootout.*

Within an hour, Steinmark was informed by chief surgeon Dr. Dick Martin that a biopsy would be performed in the next day or so. Dr. Martin broke the news so casually that Steinmark wondered if it was just another procedure that the doctor performed on his lunch break.

While Steinmark settled into his new environs, friends and family members hustled to catch up. Linda and Scott Henderson would arrive soon. His mother and father, Fred and Gloria Steinmark, were scheduled on a flight from Denver that night.

After their arrival in Houston, LaMaistre caught a commercial flight and traveled to New York for the National Football Foundation Awards at the Waldorf Astoria Hotel. Royal was there, along with the three captains, to accept the MacArthur Trophy as the national champion of college football. Just before the banquet began, LaMaistre guided Royal into a private room.

"Coach, I've got some very bad news," LaMaistre said. "Freddie Steinmark has been checked into the MD Anderson Hospital in Houston. As you know, it's a hospital that focuses on cancer. They've taken X-rays and they're certain it's cancer. They're not going to say that until they go in and do a biopsy. But if it's benign, it will be the first time this has ever happened with these kind of X-rays. The early prognosis is not good."

Royal turned pale. He could not speak. When he did, he said, "This just can't be happening."

Edith Royal was standing close to her husband and felt his pain. She had never seen him this distraught. Royal walked away, turned around, and said to Edith, "We knew he had some kind of injury. But we had no idea that it was cancer."

Royal stepped back to consider the situation. "We'd better call in the captains and tell them. Then I want to get on a plane to Houston. I want to be there tonight."

Ted Koy, James Street, and Glen Halsell were quickly summoned. Within minutes, they walked into the same room where the news had been delivered to Royal. When he saw his coach's expression, Koy thought that one of his children had died.

"I had never seen Coach that devastated," Koy said. "When he told us what was going on with Freddie, we all stopped breathing at once."

The news was starting to spread. Bill Little received a call that night from Dr. Reneau, who said, "Freddie has cancer and it doesn't look that good."

At first, Little thought he was talking about Freddie Akers. He could not imagine how a nineteen-year-old could contract this kind of disease.

Fred and Gloria Steinmark arrived in Houston late that night. When Gloria saw Freddie, she almost fainted. Her health was not that good to begin with. She had recently undergone three blood transfusions for bleeding ulcers and everyone worried about whether she could endure the strain of seeing the pride of her life in such a physical demise. She began to sob uncontrollably.

Royal arrived in Houston late Tuesday night and was picked up by Willie Zapalac. He arrived at the hospital bright and early Wednesday morning. Dr. Dick Martin was happy to see him. The doctor planned to spell out the details of the surgical procedure that afternoon to Freddie. The young man would need the moral support of his coach.

Upon his arrival, Royal was led into a meeting with Drs. Moreton, Martin, and Dr. Clifford Howe, the head of the department of medicine. They met in a huge boardroom on the seventh floor that would eventually be converted into a waiting room for friends and family.

Dr. Martin told the men that he feared Steinmark's tumor was an osteogenic sarcoma, also known as osteosarcoma. It was a bone cancer that afflicted mostly children and young adults. It represented about 20 percent of all bone cancers. It occurred most frequently between the ages of fifteen and twenty-five, and mostly affected long bones, like the femur. The symptoms included intense pain for a long period of time, especially at night.

Steinmark had suffered almost all of the symptoms. The only way the cancer could have been revealed was through X-rays. That is why he had played the entire 1969 season with so much pain.

Royal looked at the doctors and said, "If we'd X-rayed earlier, could we have caught this? Could we have avoided a possible amputation?"

"Not likely," Martin said. "Even if we caught it all the way back in June, we still would be facing a bad situation. We might still have needed to amputate."

Dr. Martin informed the gathering that he was going to break the news gently to Steinmark, hoping to keep his spirits up. "I will be talking to Freddie in a few minutes and I don't plan to give him such a grave report. I want him to go into surgery with a brave attitude. Besides, there is a very slight chance the tumor is benign. Let's just pray that it is."

At three o'clock on Wednesday afternoon, Dr. Martin and Royal walked into Freddie's hospital room. Wearing pajamas, Freddie was sitting on the bed with his legs crossed and his back leaning against the wall. Nothing in his expression revealed that he was frightened. Dr. Martin sat in a chair next to the bed and Royal leaned against the far wall, his arms crossed, his face pale with red splotches creeping onto his cheeks. This worried Freddie. This was how Royal always looked an hour before game time when the nervous anxiety cooked his arteries.

As Martin talked about the biopsy procedure, Royal started to pace. He looked at the floor, shaking his head. Steinmark had seen this demeanor so many times before. He knew his coach was dying inside.

Martin informed Freddie that he would perform the biopsy early Friday morning.

"Freddie, there are several possibilities," Martin began. "One is that it's not a tumor at all. I doubt we are going to find that it's not a tumor since the X-rays have revealed that it is. It could be a blood clot or osteomyelitis, or something like that. Or it might be a benign tumor. If that is the case, we'd drain it and you'd be fine."

After several minutes of explaining the peripheral possibilities, Martin plunged to the heart of the matter.

"If I discover it's cancer, I am going to amputate your leg," he said, his expression never changing. "That is our only hope of saving you."

Steinmark looked straight into the doctor's eyes. He tried to read Dr. Martin for anything that might tell him more.

The young man never blinked. He did not duck his head or drop his gaze. He absorbed the news with a calm resolve. He somehow believed he had been given a puncher's chance to beat the cancer.

Royal could not believe the cool demeanor of the young man.

"I remember being as nervous as hell as I'm listening to Dr. Martin talk," Royal recalled. "But Freddie sat there like the good soldier. He never changed expressions. I knew he was a courageous kid, but this was an act of courage that was out of this world."

When Martin concluded his talk and left the room, Steinmark set his eyes on his coach. Royal knew he was on the spot.

"Coach Royal," Freddie began, "I don't believe that Dr. Martin told me everything. I know they told you and you won't lie to me. What is it?"

It was a predicament that Royal, at first, did not know how to handle. At times, Royal could seem as distant as the Milky Way to his players. He did most of his coaching from a tower above the practice field. He let the assistant coaches do most of his communicating with players. He let Frank Medina dole out the punishment for breaking rules. The players, in turn, barely knew him.

Steinmark, on the other hand, was someone Royal knew intimately. He did not mind letting his guard down around him. Freddie was just like him, having grown up small and tough with few material possessions. He was more like a son than a player. That is why he did his best to tell him the truth.

"Freddie, we've been through some tough spots together," the coach said. "Both of us have been behind in life and we've come back. We've never given up. I'm not giving up now. I know that you're not giving up. Let's just see what happens."

Freddie actually smiled. "Right now I'd settle for losing a leg if it would save my life."

Forty years later, Royal said he still regretted not telling Freddie everything he knew. He agreed with Dr. Martin that Freddie needed to carry a flicker of hope into surgery. On the other hand, he wanted this player to know the truth.

"If the doctors weren't going to tell him, I didn't feel like it was my position to do it," Royal said. "I wish I could've. It was a very tough position to be in."

Chapter 20

A LIFE FOREVER CHANGED

At 6:30 on the morning of surgery, Freddie Steinmark's hospital room was filled with friends and family members. Linda Wheeler, with her blond hair and blue dress, stood next to Freddie's bed. On the other side, Fred and Gloria Steinmark quietly watched their son sleep. Nana Marchetti, the maternal grandmother, had flown in the previous day. Standing next to the wall was Father Fred Bomar, the priest from Austin. Darrell Royal fidgeted with his tie in a corner by the window.

"He doesn't look good," Gloria Steinmark said. "The doctor told me he lost twelve pounds in three days. He can't eat."

The previous night, the nurses had given Freddie a sleeping pill and it proved to be the knockout punch. He was so groggy when they wheeled him out of the room that he barely noticed the gathering of loyal supporters, or the tears.

Everyone in the room was aware of the odds. Fred and Gloria Steinmark had listened to the presurgery evaluation from Dr. Dick Martin late Wednesday afternoon, and were joined in the hospital boardroom by Royal, who heard the speech for the second time.

Wednesday, Bomar had heard the news of Steinmark's pending surgery from Spanky Stephens and called Freddie that night. The two were fairly familiar with each other. Bomar was the orange-blooded priest who threw steak fries for the players on Thursday nights at the Catholic rectory. Steinmark had attended the dinners with his roommate, Bobby Mitchell, and Scott Henderson and that is how he became acquainted with Bomar. On Saturdays, the priest stood on the sideline at the Longhorns games with a full-access pass. Royal often invited Bomar to practice. When he was not watching practice in the tower, the coach occasionally stood next to Bomar. Royal figured that a few more prayers from a friendly priest could not hurt.

The night before the operation, Bomar asked Freddie to repeat an old-time prayer called the Memorare. As it turned out, it was one of Freddie's favorites, one that he had written on a holy card as a kid and kept in his pocket:

> *Remember, O, most gracious Virgin Mary,*
> *That never was it known,*
> *That anyone who fled to thy protection,*
> *Implored thy help or sought thy intercession,*
> *Was left unaided.*
> *Inspired with this confidence,*
> *I fly unto thee . . .*

The night before the surgery, Linda called her mother, Marion Wheeler, in Wheat Ridge and broke the news about Freddie. She tried to be as gentle as possible, hoping to hear a kind word of support. Never before had she needed her mother so much.

"Linda," Marion Wheeler began, "you need to give up on Freddie. You need to get ready to move on with your life. He's not going to make it."

Linda could not believe what she was hearing.

"Mother," she said, "you don't know what you're talking about. You're not a doctor. Freddie is a fighter and he'll fight through this. He's fought all of his life and he'll make it. I love Freddie and he *is* going to live."

Linda hung up the phone before more hurtful words could be spoken.

Friday morning, Scott Henderson returned from campus, where

he had taken a quick final exam the previous day. Bobby Mitchell had ridden to Houston with him, and the two arrived in the waiting room around eight A.M. The place was getting crowded. Royal was joined by assistant coaches Willie Zapalac and Fred Akers. Several of the Steinmarks' friends, including David and Gladys Conway, were there.

The group sat together in utter silence. The clock on the wall seemed frozen. The fate of Freddie would soon be revealed. Royal paced the floor, repeatedly saying, "I can't believe this is happening to a great kid like Freddie Steinmark. I just cannot believe *this.*"

At nine o'clock, a door opened. Gloria and Fred Steinmark were summoned into the next room. Dr. Martin and Dr. Howe were ready to reveal the biopsy report. The others waited to hear the news. It was delivered with Gloria Steinmark's scream.

Minutes after giving his report to the parents, Dr. Dick Martin began to amputate Freddie's leg at the hip. The doctor had discovered a hole at the end of the thighbone that had been completely devoured by cancer. The golf-ball-sized clear spot that showed up on the X-rays represented the hole. In essence, the final inch or so of Steinmark's leg possessed no bone. He had practiced and played football for weeks with nothing except muscle supporting the leg. Six days earlier, in the national championship game against Arkansas, Steinmark had played heroically on a bone ravaged by osteosarcoma. Limping badly, he had helped the defense keep Arkansas scoreless in the final twenty-five minutes of the game.

In the waiting room, Darrell Royal sat in the corner with his head in his hands. Henderson and Mitchell hugged each other and fought back tears. Fred Bomar walked around the room, telling each person, "Be strong. Let's pray that he lives. This game is not over. Most of all, remember, this is not a funeral. We can't let Freddie see how upset we are."

Linda Wheeler stood alone in another world. She wondered how much time she had left with him. A nurse walked into the room and put her arm around her. She led Linda out into a private hallway.

"Just pray that he's going to be okay," the nurse said. "This is the beginning, not the end. The cancer is gone. Hopefully it will never come back."

"I know," Linda said.

The two talked at length. Linda was anxious to return to the waiting room. She was beginning to gather herself.

"There's one more thing I need to tell you," the nurse said. "Freddie's going to be a different person. It happens to all amputees. They go through personality changes. He's going to need you more than ever."

Linda thought about Freddie turning into another person. She could not fathom it. Her boyfriend was so strong-willed, his beliefs so firm and everlasting, that he would forever be her Freddie.

"I will keep that in mind," she said. "Thanks for telling me."

News outlets across the state were banging the drums before noon. A statement from the hospital read in part, "The tumor of the left femur, or thighbone, was found to be malignant. It was necessary to remove the left limb at the hip."

Bobby Wuensch, the soft-spoken tackle who terrorized opponents, was driving along the south freeway in Houston when the news came over the local news station. He pulled the car to the shoulder of the road and cried.

Few of Steinmark's teammates even knew he was at the hospital until hearing the news on the radio. With Royal and the team captains out of town, the line of communication had broken down. Scott Henderson was about the only player in the loop and he had spent most of the week in Houston. With no practices or team meetings to attend, the Longhorns had been celebrating like madmen since the victory over Arkansas.

"Everybody was going to the bars at four in the afternoon and staying until closing time," Scott Palmer recalled. "We had no idea what was going on with Freddie. We didn't even know he was in the hospital."

When Palmer and Bill Zapalac returned to their room after lunch on Friday, the phone was ringing. It was Palmer's dad, Derrell Palmer, who had played eight seasons of pro football at defensive tackle in the late 1940s and early '50s. The elder Palmer had just heard the news about the amputation.

"They took off Freddie's leg," the father said.

"Daddy, you've got to be kidding me," Scott said, bursting into tears. "I didn't even know Freddie was in the hospital."

"It's cancer, son. It's not good."

Palmer and Zaplac laid down on their beds and cried. The celebration was over in Austin. In the next few hours, the campus turned deathly silent. That night in Austin, the U.T. bars were quiet. The same kind of atmosphere permeated Texas A&M University some ninety miles away.

"Our campus was dead quiet, too," recalled former baseball player Butch Ghutzman. "Everybody at Texas A&M was stunned to hear the news about Freddie Steinmark. I loved the guy."

The news was met with a mixture of sadness and anger. Upon hearing a radio report, Tom Campbell dropped his head and wiped a tear away. Then he said to his brother, Mike, "This just stinks. God, I wish they could have saved his leg. It just shouldn't have happened to Freddie Steinmark. There are some other guys it could have happened to and that would have been okay with me. Freddie lived his life better than anyone. This is just not fair."

An hour after the surgery, Fred Akers was on the phone to the other U.T. coaches.

"The doctors said that a lesser man's leg would've snapped," he told them. "It's just a miracle that he was able to play for as long as he did. That young man got everything out of his body that you could possibly get. That was an act of courage that we will never see again."

———

Freddie opened his eyes and saw through a gray haze the ghostlike face of Father Fred Bomar. He suddenly realized the news was bad. He had requested through Dr. Bob Moreton that a priest be present if the amputation had been necessary.

"Freddie, you're waking up and your surgery is over," Bomar said. "You're going to be with us a long time. Everything is okay."

When Freddie seemed to doze, Bomar shook him. "Do you know what this means, Freddie?"

Freddie's eyes blinked three times. "They took it off. Oh shit! They took it off."

He fell asleep again.

Three hours later, when he was visited by his mother and father in intensive care, Gloria Steinmark was still emotionally distraught, but holding up better. Freddie knew that for the sake of his mother he had better show a little sense of humor.

"Well, I guess it didn't turn out to be bone chips, after all," he said.

The next day, when Uncle Joe Duncan came by, Freddie said, "Didn't they pass a rule that amputees couldn't play football this year?"

Duncan didn't know what to say, but told him not to worry about football at a time like this.

That Saturday, Linda walked slowly into the room wearing a bright red dress and a smile. Freddie knew the amputation had been tougher on her than anyone. She could cry at the thought of a moth dying. From her expression, though, Freddie knew she was doing better than anyone might have expected.

"Hi, Hot Dog," she said. They talked for a while and Linda said, "As soon as you get out of the hospital, we'll go parking." It surprised Freddie that Linda was smiling.

Steinmark was visited by the Texas captains—Ted Koy, James Street, and Glen Halsell—after they returned from New York with the MacArthur Trophy. Around four o'clock Sunday afternoon, the call came from President Richard Nixon. Eight days earlier, after the Arkansas victory, Freddie could remember looking up at the stage and seeing the president. His life had changed dramatically since that moment. He never expected to get a call from the president, much less at the hospital.

"Freddie, I just want to tell you that you are one of the finest young men I've ever met," Nixon said. "We all admire your courage and heart. You made some outstanding plays against Arkansas. You saved the day when you stopped Dicus. I just want you to know that it won't be the same not seeing you at the Cotton Bowl. But your life is going forward now. Just as soon as they get you upright, I'm going to bring you to the White House. What do you think about that?"

Freddie's world was still blurry. Still, he managed to say, "You can count on it, Mr. President."

Fred Steinmark told a UPI reporter, "The call sure picked up my boy a bit. His eyes got real big. I'm not sure what the exact words were. He's getting along real good. He's taking it like a champ—a lot better than I can take it. He has a lot of energy. Darrell Royal instilled a lot of things in my boy."

Sitting in the waiting room, Mitchell and Henderson were dreading the trip to see Freddie. They had talked about it for two days. Late that afternoon, the two reached the door to his room and stopped. They waited for Freddie to see them.

"Come on in, boys," he said, waving. "There's nothing to be afraid of."

Mitchell and Henderson walked toward the bed and suddenly realized that Freddie was smiling. Laughing, actually. Thirty minutes later, Mitchell and Henderson returned to the waiting room with big smiles.

"We thought we were going to have to go up there and cheer Freddie up," Mitchell said. "As it turned out, he was making us laugh."

On the way to Freddie's bedside, Royal tried to think of a million things to say to cheer him up. As it turned out, he needed no speech.

"Hey, Coach," Freddie said, "I hear you might be looking for a one-legged kicker. What do you say?"

"Freddie, if you can kick one-legged, I'll have you on my team any day. But even if you don't play another down of football, son, you've had a great career. You started twenty-one straight games. You played on two Southwest Conference championship teams. You played on a national championship team. Freddie, you were one of the greatest players I've ever coached. God knows you were the most courageous."

Chapter 21

THE COMEBACK

Freddie Steinmark, wearing blue pajamas, sat upright on his bed with his back leaning against the wall. His crutches were propped against the mattress. With Linda Wheeler by his side, he was eating a huge breakfast that included sausage, pancakes, eggs, along with biscuits and gravy. Freddie needed to gain weight fast. Ten days after the season, he was down to 128 pounds.

For the past half hour, he had been waiting for Dr. Bob Moreton. It was time to start the comeback. His mind was clearing fast and he was focused on the future. A man with only one leg needed to be prepared for the next move.

Moreton strolled into the bright room expecting to find a sad young man. Amputees were known to lapse into a depression that lasted two or three months. The psychological pain could be the most devastating. After losing a limb, most wanted to stay in bed for weeks. Not Freddie Steinmark. His crutches were handy and he was sitting on go.

"Hello, Dr. Moreton," Steinmark said with the old Freddie smile. "I need to discuss some plans with you. I know that my surgery was only five days ago, but I want to start planning for the Cotton Bowl. I want to walk out on the field on my own. I want to stand on the sideline for the whole game. More than anything else, I want to be with my teammates."

"Whoa," Moreton said. "That's next to impossible, Freddie. The Cotton Bowl is fifteen days from now. You've not been out of this bed yet. You still haven't been in a wheelchair. Your prosthesis won't be delivered for at least three weeks. It'll take at least two weeks on a prosthesis to get your balance. You've got a long way to go."

Freddie pulled the sheets off his legs, spun on his backside, and lifted his right leg with his arms, dropping it over the side of the bed. He slid the crutches beneath his armpits and started to motor across the room.

"Look, Dr. Moreton," Steinmark said. "Not many people know this, but I've been going to the bathroom on my own. I'm sick of the bedpan and I'm sick of the catheter."

"You shouldn't be doing that," Moreton said. "You could rip your stitches. Plus, that's got to hurt."

"It does," Freddie said. "But if I'm going to make it to the Cotton Bowl, I've got to start practicing now. You see, I'm already in training."

Hours later, Steinmark rode a wheelchair down to the fourth floor as part of his accelerated rehabilitation process. Dr. Moreton had informed the staff that Freddie would be on a faster schedule than the rest. He was not to be treated as your typical amputee.

A major psychological hurdle for any amputee was to see one's reflection in a full-length mirror for the first time. Steinmark was lifted from the wheelchair by two attendants. He walked with the aid of crutches to the front of the mirror. He seemed to be admiring himself.

"You know," he said, "I don't look bad for a one-legged Mexican."

The next two weeks, Steinmark brightened everyone's life inside the place. Just being around him could lift anyone's spirits. His mother was already overcoming the shock of the amputation. One day, Gloria Steinmark sat down on the edge of the bed and smiled at her son.

"You know, Freddie, you are such a good boy," she said.

"No, Mom," Freddie said. "I'm just okay. God is good."

Somehow his mother held back the tears.

Teammates and former Texas players streamed into the hospital. Scott Henderson and Bobby Mitchell spent almost the entire month of December around MD Anderson. Also coming from Austin were Rick Nabors, Bill Zapalac, Mike Dean, and Bob McKay. During the Christmas break, Houston players like Bobby Wuensch, Donnie Wigginton, and Bill Atessis made the trek. Corby Robertson, who was in the process of opening the Olympia Boys Camp in East Texas, made several trips to the hospital.

"I was going to the hospital thinking that everything was going to be feeling pretty grim," Robertson said. "As it turned out, Freddie was the one making everybody laugh."

Fred Akers continued to recruit the southeast section of Texas and was spending a lot of time in Beaumont and Port Arthur. When his day ended, he often jumped in his car and drove the ninety miles to the hospital.

"The first time I went to see Freddie after the operation, I spent a lot of time preparing a pep talk," Akers said. "When I got there, Freddie gave me a pep talk. He was giving everybody pep talks."

Akers arrived at the hospital late one afternoon and found no one in Steinmark's room. He decided to wait, figuring that Freddie was down the hall for a physical examination, or getting more X-rays.

Time passed and Akers began to worry. The room felt empty and he could not imagine the last time anyone had been there. Was Freddie dead? Surely, someone would have called him

He stuck his head into the hallway and searched for a nurse. She was walking his way with a clipboard in her hand. She did not look happy.

"I sidled up to her," Akers recalled. "I was very worried at the time. I said, 'I'm sorry, ma'am, but I haven't been here in a few days. If Freddie'd died, I wanted to be here with him. Did Freddie die?'"

The nurse smiled and said, "Come with me."

She led Akers across the room and pulled open the curtains. "Look down there on the parking lot."

There was Freddie on his crutches, practicing getting in and out of the backseat of a parked car, preparing for the Cotton Bowl.

"Bless his heart," Akers said. "He'd just had his leg cut off, and he was already back in training. Nothing was going to stop that kid."

Freddie seemed to be all over the hospital. One day he visited the children's ward and was told that most of the kids would have no visitors or gifts for Christmas. He reached into his wallet and found a hundred dollars. He gave eighty dollars to Linda and asked her to buy gifts for the kids. She returned with coloring books and small toys and kid-sized footballs.

It seemed that everyone wanted to see Freddie. The administrators of MD Anderson made it clear that the news media would not be allowed into the hospital the first two weeks after the surgery. The local Houston TV stations were badgering Dr. Moreton. Another broadcast outfit from Denver had practically demanded an exclusive interview with Freddie.

Returning from lunch one day, Father Fred Bomar was accompanied by Jack Agness, a reporter from the *Houston Chronicle*. Hospital personnel figured that since Agness was with Bomar, he must be a friend of the Steinmark family. Agness and Bomar stood around Freddie's bed for about fifteen minutes, and the reporter asked a few innocuous questions, like "How has the whole experience been for you?"

Steinmark smiled and said, "Everybody has just been so nice to me. I could never find the words to thank them all."

In the next day's *Chronicle*, Agness wrote a story that contained little news and was basically a kiss on Freddie's cheek. The reporter quoted Steinmark as thanking everybody.

The result was a firestorm that raged through the hallways of the hospital. Bomar was warned by Dr. Moreton never to bring a reporter into the hospital again. A security guard was stationed outside of room 415-West and, for the next week, only family and friends were allowed in.

"Father Bomar was starting to take over and I could tell it," Linda Wheeler said. "He and Freddie were not that close before this whole ordeal. But I could tell that he was up to something."

A few days later, Freddie received a letter from Chicago running back Brian Piccolo. On November 28, fifteen days before Steinmark had lost his leg, a grapefruit-sized tumor had been surgically removed from Piccolo's chest. Like Steinmark, Piccolo had been rolling through the Bears' 1969 season when he suddenly realized halfway through postpractice wind sprints that he could barely breathe.

After the surgery, Piccolo still held out hope that he would live a long, productive life after football. This letter to Steinmark was published in Jeannie Morris's book *Brian Piccolo: A Short Season*:

Dear Freddie:

Although I don't know you personally, we have a lot in common. This is why I'm writing you this letter. My football career, just as yours, was brought to a sudden halt by cancer, mine in the form of a tumor directly below my breastbone. The tumor popped up from nothing to the size of a grapefruit in a period of about three months. I had my surgery November 28th at Memorial Hospital in New York and missed the last five games of the season. I watched your game against Arkansas from my hospital bed when I was recovering from surgery and then read about your problem a few days later.

I guess that I, more than any other football player, know how you felt. I spent a lot of time thinking about you and praying for you in those days and that's when I decided I would write. Fred, I'd mainly like to share with you my feelings since my operation, simply that our lives are in God's hands, just as they were before our illnesses were known. And I shall never stop praying to God for the strength to carry out the plans He has laid out for me.

I know that you are a courageous young man and I hope this letter might be of some help to you. Perhaps some day we may meet one another. I'm sure we would have much to talk about.

Best of luck to you, Fred.

Your friend,
Brian Piccolo

Two years later *Brian's Song,* a movie about Piccolo's life and his relationship with Gale Sayers, would be released. It became one of the most popular sports movies in the history of the genre.

Like Piccolo, Steinmark was worried that his cancer would rear its ugly head once more. No one knew the impact of having an osteosarcoma in the leg for so long. Dr. Dick Martin had informed his fellow doctors that he worried Steinmark's time might be short. That news, however, had never been directly delivered to the patient.

One afternoon, Steinmark tried to dig the information out of Bomar.

"Did they get all of the cancer, Father Bomar?" he said.

"The doctors told me they got all of it," Bomar said. "You will leave this hospital in a couple of weeks with a clean bill of health."

Linda Wheeler was happy that her mother was traveling to Houston to see her and Freddie. It was a show of support. Maybe her mother would apologize for hurting her feelings so badly the night before the surgery.

They met in the Steinmarks' makeshift waiting room on the seventh floor. Linda instantly knew that her mother was not bearing good cheer. Marion Wheeler had been gathering information on osteosarcoma from her brother, Dr. J. P. Keller, a physician in Duncan, Oklahoma. The news she brought to Houston was more salt for the wound.

"Linda, there is something you need to know," her mother began. "I just talked to your uncle J.P. again and he tells me that Freddie has little chance of surviving this cancer. I wanted you to know that. There really isn't much hope for Freddie, dear."

Linda wanted to scream.

"Mother, this has got to be the most awful thing that you have ever done to me," Linda said. "Freddie is trying to make a comeback. The doctors are trying to save his life. And you come down here and ruin it all."

Linda walked away from her mother and promised herself that

she would never talk to Marion Wheeler again. She planned to live a long and happy life with Freddie. They were still planning to get married. Nothing was going to stop them.

Forty years later she remembered her anger. "My mother had the capacity to be a horribly cruel person. It was one thing to dislike Freddie, and yet another thing to be that cruel to her daughter. That was such a traumatic moment. It took me a long time to get over that."

Linda returned to Freddie's room and tried to close the door on her mother's words. In the meantime, Marion Wheeler was telling anyone who would listen that Freddie would never survive.

Around the Steinmark circle, everyone dreaded the coming of Christmas. What joy could be found in watching a one-legged Freddie unwrapping gifts? Still, they did their best with what they had. For the first time, Freddie's siblings Sammy, twelve, Paula Kay, fourteen, and Gigi, fifteen, came to Houston. Linda stayed over for the holidays. On Christmas Day, the party grew even larger with the addition of Longhorn locals Bobby Wuensch, Bill Atessis, Scott Palmer, and Donnie Wigginton. After holding mass at his Austin church, Father Bomar made the three-hour drive to Anderson Mayfair and did mass again, completing the doubleheader. Everyone ate turkey in the Presidential Suite of the apartments.

"It was actually a very happy Christmas, considering everything," Linda Wheeler said.

During his stay at MD Anderson, Steinmark would receive more than 12,000 letters. There were so many flower arrangements in his room that visitors complained they could not breathe. The plants were robbing the oxygen. Arkansas quarterback Bill Montgomery and Chuck Dicus collected more than 10,000 signatures on a get-well card sent to Steinmark. He was invited to attend the Hula Bowl in Hawaii; even though he could not attend, the game was dedicated to him. He took a tour of the year-old Astrodome, where he told a group of reporters, "I'll be back in classes next semester. Then I hope to go to law school after graduation. More important, I will

be in the Cotton Bowl on New Year's day when my team runs onto
the field."

With less than a week until the big game, no one doubted that he
would make the Cotton Bowl. Steinmark was gaining more strength
by the day. Nothing, however, made him as happy as a visit from
Darrell Royal after Christmas. In spite of the team's preparation for
Notre Dame, Royal had made several trips to Houston.

"Freddie, I want you to consider staying in football," Royal said.
"I sure could use you as a freshman coach just as soon as you think
you can handle it. I know what it would mean to the young players
to have you around."

"That is the greatest offer I've ever heard in my life," Steinmark
told Royal. "I can't wait to start coaching."

Steinmark was already filled with enough energy to walk all of
the 240 miles to Dallas.

Chapter 22

OH HAPPY DAY

"He didn't want to go to the Cotton Bowl to show off. He didn't want to go to the Cotton Bowl to bring attention to himself. He just wanted to show people that Freddie Steinmark was all right. He wanted to show people that he was still whole."
—LINDA WHEELER

The Cotton Bowl tunnel leading from the dressing rooms to the playing field was long and shadowy. As the players tore down the dark alley just minutes before kickoff, they could see virtually nothing ahead. Then, just as they burst onto the playing surface, the sunlight hit their eyes, transforming the world into a sea of burnt orange. They could hear the bands playing the school fight songs.

Most said that the trip down the tunnel was exhilarating to the point of raising marble-sized goose bumps. All except Mike Campbell, who made his first trek as a starter before the Texas-Oklahoma game in 1969.

"Everybody said it was like running on air," Campbell said. "Not me. I was so damn scared that I felt I was running in concrete shoes. I never thought I was going to get to the sideline."

Freddie Steinmark had dashed down the tunnel three times with some of the best teams in America. He was moved to tears each time. He played two of his best games against Oklahoma in 1968 and '69. Against Tennessee in the Cotton Bowl Classic on January 1, 1970, he made a lasting impression on national TV with an interception and three long punt returns.

Exactly one year later, Steinmark was making his fourth trip down the tunnel, this time on crutches, this time quite alone. Twenty days from the amputation, he was buttoned up in a long brown coat. His trousers were pinned to the hip on his left leg. He wore only one Riddell football shoe. His aluminum crutches squeaked with each step.

The young man could barely see the playing surface on his way down because of the sun's rays bouncing off the shiny, wet grass. It had rained for four straight days in Dallas, but January 1 broke as clear as the Rocky Mountain mornings of his childhood.

Down the tunnel, Freddie was moving so slowly that he wondered if he would make it. Then his right foot felt the familiar grass and he knew he had arrived. Standing on the edge of the shadows, he peered into the bright light, shaded his eyes with his right hand, and flashed the Steinmark smile.

Few people in the raucous crowd knew he was coming. Many peered down at the tunnel, waiting for the teams to run onto the field. In the distance, bands played, pom-poms shook, and twirlers twirled.

Anticipation was roaring through Linda Wheeler's arteries. For the last half hour, she wondered where Freddie could be. Then she saw him.

"There's Freddie!" Linda yelled from her seat in a special section of the pressbox. "There he is!"

Suddenly, friends and relatives and everyone in the stadium saw him. They were on their feet. As he began to walk slowly through the wet grass, the chant went up from the end zone. "Freddie! Freddie! Freddie!" They were seeing firsthand the determined young man they had read about in the newspapers. This was the Freddie Steinmark who Darrell Royal said was the most courageous player ever. This was the Freddie Steinmark, who, by God, was going to the Cotton Bowl come hell or high water. There he was, arms pulling like pistons, eyes straight ahead, his body moving in a machine-like manner. "Freddie! Freddie! Freddie!"

An hour earlier, Steinmark had crutched into the Texas dressing room amid much anxiety. About 80 percent of the players had not seen him since the Arkansas game. Practically no one had set eyes on the one-legged Steinmark. James Street, a team captain, said, "I was actually worried about what kind of effect it would have on the team. I was wondering if his presence was going to be a downer."

Bobby Mitchell had known Freddie longer than anyone. They had battled shoulder to shoulder to win a state championship. They had stood arm-in-arm after winning the Big Shootout. But the last twenty-five days seemed impossible to describe.

"It was all so weird," Mitchell said. "One minute, we were all riding this big roller coaster. We were way up in the air when we beat Arkansas. The next minute, they cut Freddie's leg off and we all hit the bottom."

Everyone wondered what the scene would be like when Steinmark entered the Texas locker room. The day before the game, a Dallas reporter asked Darrell Royal if Freddie might be a distraction for the team. "Wouldn't it be more practical if Steinmark watched the game on TV?" the reporter asked.

"Why, that would be like saying that Freddie could not go back to his own home," Royal responded. "I don't guess anybody not connected with athletics can understand it. But a team is just like a family. If Freddie feels like he is strong enough to come to the game and be with us on the sidelines, if that's what he wants, then that's exactly where he belongs."

A few days before the Cotton Bowl, Steinmark asked Royal that no one make a big deal of him. He did not want a "Win one for the Gipper" speech.

Steinmark had ridden to the stadium in a limousine and was dropped off at the large double gate behind the south end zone. He quickly headed for the dressing room on the left side of the tunnel. Notre Dame occupied the locker room on the right. He casually walked into the room and started making his rounds. He stopped at every locker, shook every hand. Halfway around, he found a locker marked STEINMARK with the number 28 below the name placard. His full uniform and helmet were waiting for him.

"I got chills just watching him," James Street recalled. "He was walking around like he was about to suit up. If anything, he lifted the team up. Way up. He was saying things like, 'I want you to beat these guys' asses!'"

His teammates rubbed his head, tousled his hair, and hugged him like a long-lost brother.

"The one thing that Freddie wanted to do was beat Notre Dame," Street said. "They had turned him down when he came out of high school. Watching him walk around that day at the Cotton Bowl, you would've thought he was getting ready to play in the game. In five minutes, he was just back to being one of our teammates. All of a sudden you realized just how much you missed him."

As he moved across the locker room, within earshot of Steve Worster, Freddie began to talk louder. He wanted to fire up his friend.

"Have you guys been reading the newspapers?" he said. "Have you been seeing some of the stupid things the Notre Dame players are saying about Woo? They are saying that he can't play a lick. How dumb are those guys?"

"What are you talking about?" Worster snapped.

"You can read it for yourself," Freddie said, tossing him the *Dallas Times Herald* sports page.

Worster sat down to read and his face turned crimson. To a man, the Notre Dame players said Worster was the most overrated player in the country. Upon finishing the article, he threw the newspaper to the ground and stomped on it. He was now ready to play the game of his life.

Fifteen minutes before kickoff, both teams began to receive final instructions from their coaches. Notre Dame head coach Ara Parseghian was feeling good about his chances of beating the Longhorns. Notre Dame was ranked ninth with an 8-1-1 record, the lone loss coming in the second week of the season to a Purdue team led by All-American quarterback Mike Phipps.

"I really thought we could beat Texas," Parseghian remembered. "We hadn't played any bums all season."

The winning percentage of Notre Dame's opponents in 1969 was 52.5, while Texas had beaten weaker opponents, winning only 43.5

percent of the time. Notre Dame had defeated teams from all over the country while Texas picked on the likes of Baylor, Rice, Texas Tech, and TCU. A cynical view on the East Coast, and in the Midwest, said that Texas was the number-one-ranked team because of a cupcake schedule.

Royal didn't care. He was coaching a team with the nation's longest winning streak of nineteen games. They were not about to be embarrassed by a bunch of Catholics from a small, private university with a campus that was covered with three feet of snow half the year. Royal, like a lot of people, lacked respect for Notre Dame because Parseghian went for a tie against Michigan State in 1966 to remain number one.

With kickoff approaching, Royal stood in front of the team and said, "They are bigger than us. Some people say they are stronger than us. But I don't think anything can stop us today. Let's go out and make it twenty in a row."

Royal could feel a knot in his throat as Randy Peschel led the team through the Lord's Prayer. The coach had one last thing to say before they hit the door. He gathered the team around him and said, "Guys, I want you to go out there and do *one* thing for me. I want you to win a game ball for Freddie."

The locker room fell silent. Players could see the emotion in Royal's eyes. Then came the hollering and the clattering of cleats on the concrete steps leading to the tunnel.

It was inevitable that Royal would say something about Steinmark. The players, however, needed no reminder of what they were playing for. Steinmark had been in their thoughts and prayers for weeks. They were going to beat Notre Dame, and they were going to do it for Freddie Steinmark.

On the sideline, waiting for the team, Steinmark was surrounded by the press as he talked with Lyndon Baines Johnson, a close friend of Royal's. Cameras clicked and Freddie smiled. Standing beside him was his brother, Sammy, who, along with the rest of the family, had stayed in Texas for the game.

The week leading to the Cotton Bowl, Royal had offered Steinmark a wheelchair, but he replied with a resounding no. He was going to stand with his friend, Father Fred Bomar, who had ditched the priest smock and was wearing a cowboy hat and boots.

All eyes were on him in the final minutes leading to the game. Reporters lofted questions his way.

"What are you going to do after the game?"

"I'm going to celebrate the victory with my family," he said.

"After that?" another asked.

"Well, I'm getting my prosthesis on Monday and I'm going to start walking on it. Then, on January the twelfth, I'm going to walk across the stage at the football banquet in Austin and pick up my letter jacket."

The reporters scribbled furiously.

A cannon rolled near the tunnel and the Texas players, dressed in burnt orange jerseys with white helmets, came streaming out of the tunnel. The Texas contingency occupying the west stands and the south end zone went berserk. For the first time since January 1, 1964, they were watching their beloved Longhorns run onto the field at the Cotton Bowl as the number-one team in the country.

Each player that ran past Steinmark touched him. Shutters worked overtime. Father Bomar stood close by just in case Freddie slipped on one of his crutches and started to fall.

In the past few weeks, since defeating Arkansas in the "Game of the Century," Texas had collected three national championships: the MacArthur Bowl, President Richard Nixon's plaque, and the U.P.I. top ranking. The only meaningful prize left was the number-one ranking in the A.P. poll. That vote would come after the bowls. In order to sweep all titles, Texas would need to defeat Notre Dame, otherwise Penn State was poised to jump to number one. The Nittany Lions had been invited to the Cotton Bowl to meet the Southwest Conference champion. Coach Joe Paterno, however, opted for warmer weather at the Orange Bowl. Paterno was still wringing his hands that his undefeated Nittany Lions team had not received a plaque from the President. Down in Texas, they were laughing at Paterno.

The Cotton Bowl power brokers could not have been happier.

Texas had been ranked number one since late November. The Fighting Irish, one of America's glamour teams, had not played in a bowl game in forty-five years, since the days of the Four Horsemen. The last six years, Parseghian had campaigned for the university to drop its nonsensical stance against bowl games. He had finally convinced Notre Dame president Rev. Theodore M. Hesburgh to halt this archaic policy.

When Notre Dame thundered down the tunnel and started warming up on the east sideline, the Texas players thought they were living in the land of the giants. Parseghian had built the Fighting Irish into a big, corn-fed Midwest-style team similar to the Big Ten teams. His schedule demanded big men on both sides of the ball. Defensive tackle Mike McCoy was a monster compared to most of the college players of the day. He stood 6'5", weighed 270 pounds, and would cast a large shadow over Texas right guard Mike Dean, who was six inches shorter and weighed 195 pounds.

Just before kickoff, Parseghian allowed his eyes to drift over to the Texas sideline. He focused on the small youngster leaning on crutches, one leg missing.

"Let me tell you that I felt some real sympathy for that courageous young man," he recalled. "I knew what he had been through and it was too bad he wasn't playing that day."

After the first snap, Steve Worster blasted for 15 yards off right guard. Dean had knocked McCoy to the ground and both were still lying there. Tackle Bobby Wuensch walked up to McCoy, grabbed his face mask, and yelled, "Listen to me, you son of a bitch. This little boy right here is going to kick your fat ass all day long!"

If the Longhorns thought they could out-trash talk the Fighting Irish, they were wrong. Between plays, a verbal assault normally ensued from the Catholic side of the ball.

"I had never heard such cussing in my life," Mike Campbell IV remembered. "Even their coaches were cussing us. If you got knocked out of bounds on the Notre Dame sideline, you could be sure that you were going to get an earful. Even the priests were yelling at us."

Campbell said that when Texas players returned to the huddle after a play, the Notre Dame players tried to jostle them.

"They were always trying to cut us off," Campbell said. "They would bump into you and try to piss you off. They were poorly behaved."

Early in the game, the wishbone came out punching, but it was Notre Dame that grabbed a 10–0 lead. A 54-yard touchdown pass from Joe Theismann to Tom Gatewood let the Longhorns know how much they missed Steinmark. Not once all season had any receiver gotten open deep past the secondary.

Once more in a big game, the Longhorns allowed the opposition to build a lead. That season, they had trailed Oklahoma 14–0 after one quarter, and Arkansas held the same advantage going into the fourth quarter. So there was every reason to believe that the Longhorns would come back.

Worster continued to pound the center of the line as McCoy was consistently flattened by Dean. The entire offensive line was bulldozing a basic four-man front. Notre Dame had not made one change to its defensive schemes in the month-long preparation. It was the same 4-4-3 alignment that the Texas offense practiced against every day. The teams used the same defense concocted years earlier by Notre Dame defensive coordinator Johnny Ray.

The wishbone gained serious traction late in the second quarter, when Worster did most of the heavy lifting. Jim Bertelsen slammed the ball into the end zone from the 2-yard line, cutting the deficit to 10–7. The Longhorns were on the verge of taking the lead in the final minute before halftime. With Texas facing a fourth-and-one at the 7-yard line, linebacker Bob Olson stuffed little Billy Dale one inch short of the first down. The Irish led 10–7 at half.

As the third quarter began, Steinmark moved up and down the sideline, patting his teammates on the shoulder pads and yelling words of encouragement. He truly felt a part of the team. The offer from Royal to help coach the defensive backs during spring drills made him feel more wanted than ever.

The feeling on the Texas sideline throughout the third quarter was that Notre Dame, with its enormous size advantage, was getting the best of the Longhorns. That is why Steinmark stepped up his pep talks. Early in the fourth quarter, the wishbone finally began to gain traction. Street drove Texas 78 yards, straight down the middle of the field. The Irish defense was finally beginning to bend. At the 3-yard line, Street faked into the line to Bertelsen and five Irish defenders tackled him. Dodging that pile, Ted Koy burst into the end zone and Texas enjoyed its first lead 14–10. The 'Horns had chewed 8:10 off the clock.

Theismann had steadily picked apart the Longhorns' pass defense all afternoon. The Texas defense continued to feel the absence of Steinmark. After moving the Irish to the Texas 24-yard line, Theismann spun away from three defenders and threw another touchdown pass to a wide-open Jim Yoder.

Royal wanted to accomplish two things simultaneously on the next possession. First, he wanted to relentlessly drive the ball down the field on short bursts while keeping it out of Theismann's hot hands. With 6:10 to play, the Longhorns started at their 24-yard line. The game possessed much of the feel of the Arkansas rally. As the sun faded over the west side of the stadium, Street kept the Longhorns grounded. They moved all the way to the Notre Dame 10-yard line, where they faced a fourth-and-two with slightly more than two minutes to play.

Street trotted to the sideline. The coach and the quarterback stood side by side as a famous photo was snapped. Royal talked into a headset as Street stood by his side. The quarterback looked into the eyes of the coach and waited for the call. Behind them, the scoreboard read TEXAS 14, NOTRE DAME 17. *Click, click.* There was 2:26 to play. *Click, click.*

Everyone knew the once-predictable Royal was a different man since the Arkansas game. If he would turn James Street loose with "Right 53 Veer Pass," why wouldn't he ask the gambling gods for one more spin of the roulette wheel?

Royal surprised his quarterback again when he said, "Left 89 out." It would be a pass to Speyrer near the left sideline. Again, Street wanted to ask why, but kept his mouth shut as he started jogging away from his coach.

Street stepped into the huddle and told the players, "This just might be our last chance. Stand tall. We'll get this done."

With 73,101 fans screaming their lungs out, the tension inside the Cotton Bowl was thicker than a Baptist hymnal. On the sideline, Steinmark stood on one leg and yelled louder than anyone. The Texas fans had every reason to believe that Street would come through again. He had already converted three fourth-downs on the drive.

Still, no one in the stadium knew that Street held a secret plan. The play called by Royal required him to roll left. If he spotted a hole between the Irish end and the linebacker, though, he intended to shoot the gap and run the 3 yards for a first down. Forget "Left 89 out."

In the blink of an eye, Street knew his idea would never work. Coming away from center, he tripped and stumbled backward. Sweeping the end for 3 yards was no longer an option. The Irish defenders had the angle on him. Street suddenly thought he was going to fall. He put his hand out to brace himself against the ground, but pulled it back. The Notre Dame linemen were all over him. He released the ball across his body and the ball spun nose down. Parseghian was so certain the pass was going to be incomplete that he grabbed Theismann by the jersey and started calling the next play.

"I called a quarterback keeper," Parseghian recalled. "I knew that Joe could get us out of the hole."

Parseghian suddenly was confused by the roar of the crowd. He could not figure out why the Texas players were jumping up and down. Then he saw the side judge spot the ball at the 2-yard line and signal a first down toward the goal.

What Parseghian missed was one of the greatest shoestring catches ever. Speyrer had somehow twisted away from his shadowing defender, Clarence Ellis, and dived under the ball. He stabbed the rock three inches before it smacked the ground.

After the game, a reporter asked Street why he had thrown the pass low and away from the receiver. "Hell, bud, how in the hell would you have thrown it? Speyrer was covered. If I throw it good, it's intercepted."

It took Billy Dale three times to ram the ball into the end zone. He finally made it behind a clearing block by Bobby Wuensch, and Texas led 21–17 with 1:08 to play.

Still, no one doubted that Theismann could bring them back. He was on his way to breaking the Cotton Bowl passing record with 238 yards. Before Theismann could get going, though, everyone would have to endure a three-minute TV timeout.

As the Texas kicking team lined up during the commercial break, Mike Campbell took his place on the far end of the long line, next to the Notre Dame bench. Again, the Fighting Irish were barking and cussing at him and he did not appreciate it. So he flipped the bird to the Notre Dame sideline and made sure Parseghian saw it.

Forty years later, Parseghian confirmed that he witnessed the obscene gesture.

"Yes, I remember something like that happening," the coach recalled.

After the kickoff, Theismann moved the Irish in thirty seconds from their 23-yard line to the Texas 39. He called a timeout with :38 on the clock. On the next play, he rolled right and once again located an open receiver. Tight end Dewey Poskon was waving his hands at the 18-yard line. Theismann delivered the pass with the tip of the ball slightly up. It sailed over Poskon's fingertips—and who else would be waiting for the ball? Tom Campbell saved the day and sealed the Longhorns' second straight dramatic victory with a last-minute interception. Instead of stopping out of bounds, he threw a shoulder into an Irish player.

On the Texas sideline, Royal walked over to Steinmark, hugged him, and kissed him on the side of the head. He lifted him off his feet.

"We got 'em Freddie, we got 'em," Royal said. "How do you feel about that?"

"One of the greatest feelings of my life, Coach," Steinmark said. "This is the happiest day of my life."

Teammates pounded Freddie on the back and rubbed his head.

As the sun sneaked over the horizon minutes later, an orange glow permeated the evening. The celebration was on and it would soon spill into the Dallas streets.

As Parseghian jogged to the middle of the field to shake hands with Royal, he veered left and patted Steinmark on the shoulder.

"You hang in there, young man," he said. "You've got a lot of living to do."

Leaving the field, Steinmark was stopped by *Dallas Morning News* sportswriter Randy Galloway.

"You've gotta be tired as hell," Galloway said.

"Things were so exciting that I didn't have a chance to get tired," he said. "As a matter of fact, I feel so good that if I had another leg I could play the game all over again."

As he trotted toward the dressing room, Tom Campbell clung to the game ball like an oversize chunk of gold. The sight of his father waving him over was a bit shocking. Was he finally going to compliment his son on something in life? Tom felt his heart accelerate.

Big Mike looked proudly at his son. "You know, Tom, I don't know what you're planning to do with the rest of your life. But whatever it is, you should do it on national television."

Tom Campbell could only shake his head and laugh. After all, his championship-saving interceptions in the final minute against Arkansas and Notre Dame had come on national TV. Exactly one year earlier, he had intercepted a pass and been named the defensive player of the Cotton Bowl against Tennessee. Again, on national TV.

Campbell threw his left arm around his dad.

"You know, Daddy, it's been a helluva lot of fun playing for you," he said. "I might even miss you a little."

They laughed and ran side by side off the field.

When all the players were inside, and the doors sealed, Royal walked up to Tom Campbell's locker. He was still holding the football.

"Is that for Freddie?" Royal said.

"You danged right it is," Tom said, smiling.

At the far end of the room, a stage had been set up. Royal walked up the steps, turned, and gazed out at his national championship team.

"I can't tell you how much I love you all," he told the players. "I'm afraid that if I talk too much longer, I'm going to choke up."

No one in the room had ever heard Royal choke up. When he spoke those two words, though, he actually did. Tears never before witnessed by his players rolled down his cheeks.

Royal gathered himself and held up the game ball. The only words he could bring himself to say were, "Here it is, Freddie. Come on and get it."

Steinmark was standing in the back of the room. Every head turned. He was smiling, waving, and pumping his way to the front. The cheer from inside the locker room could be heard all the way to downtown Dallas. He reached the stage and accepted the game ball from Royal. He looked out at his beloved teammates and said, "I love you all. I am never going to forget you guys. I'll never forget all the fun we had. I will be with you the rest of my life."

Playing football was over for Freddie Steinmark. It had been taken away by a surgical saw. In fourteen years of organized football, from the second grade through his junior year at Texas, he had participated in a grand total of seven losses. He had won his final nineteen at Texas. Freddie Steinmark was a winner. Yet the biggest game of his life was still on the horizon.

Chapter 23

CELEBRATION OF LIFE

"I never saw Freddie cry. He never showed emotion because he didn't want to distract us. He sure didn't want us to feel sorry for him."
         —SCOTT HENDERSON

On a brisk winter evening in 1970, as darkness settled over the city formerly known as "laid-back Austin," the downtown streets jolted to life. Voices split the silence as the crowd swept along the sidewalks toward the Municipal Auditorium. Twelve days had passed since the crowning victory over Notre Dame. Still, the cheering went on.

Darrell Royal had come up with a splendid idea to celebrate the 1969 football season. They would throw a Texas-style barbeque, inviting celebrities, politicos, country music stars, and regular fans. It seemed that everyone wanted to rub shoulders with star quarterback James "Slick" Street, fullback Steve Worster, and the Campbell twins. Here was a chance for autographs and pictures to be taken with Coach Royal. Most of all, they wanted to hug the neck of Freddie Steinmark, a young man who lived in their hearts.

Steinmark's goal that night was to walk across the stage on his new prosthesis and to pick up his letter jacket. It was a physical act that seemed impossible. He had lost his leg exactly one month earlier. The prosthesis had arrived only eight days ago.

As the doors swung open that night, thousands spilled into the building, hustling down the aisles toward the best seats. It would not take long for the fire marshal to seal the doors as six thousand people were already inside. An energy filled the hall that was similar to game day. They had come to worship in a different manner from years past. Previously, they were forced to endure long, boring speeches from some of Austin's biggest windbags. Royal wanted to breathe new life into the night, so this time they would serve barbeque ribs, chicken, and brisket, along with beans, onions, cole slaw, and potato salad. Suits and ties were banned in favor of boots, jeans, and cowboy hats. The public was invited at five dollars a throw. Royal, a vision of Roy Rogers in his burnt orange hat, shirt, and bandana, stood high on the stage and smiled as the largest crowd he could ever remember settled into the seats.

Heads turned as Lyndon Baines Johnson strolled through a side door with Lady Bird on his arm. He wore his trademark cut-down gray Stetson, and Lady Bird was decked out like the queen of the rodeo. Unlike the man who would succeed him in the White House, Lyndon never claimed to be a football genius. He was the anti-Nixon in more ways than one. He rarely went to the stadium, or watched the games on television. Richard Nixon liked to dial up Washington Redskins coach George Allen and suggest plays. So obsessed with football was Nixon that he once named an assault on North Vietnam "Operation Linebacker." That was not LBJ's style. He didn't know a football playbook from *Playboy* magazine. He once said, "I am not a fan of football, but I am a fan of people, and I am a fan of Darrell Royal because he is the rarest of people."

A wave of electricity rolled through the drafty hall that night as the fiddles of the "Pflugerville Five" began to wail. It was often said in Texas that these kinds of events usually attracted all hat and no cattle, but not this time. Along with LBJ, the place was packed with some real home-grown beef. Governor John Connally was smiling from ear to ear, and sitting next to him sat a dark-haired up-and-comer who possessed that undeniable look of ambition. His name was George Herbert Walker Bush, a freshly minted U.S. Congressman. Mingling in the crowd was Cactus Pryor, the Austin comic and the host of Royal's weekly TV show. He was named for an Austin theater that was operated by his father, Stinky. As he climbed the stairs to the lectern that night, you could see that twinkle in Cactus's eye. He was there to explain the controversial yet ingenious call that Royal had made against Arkansas in the Big Shootout.

Of course, everyone in the hall remembered that Texas trailed

14–8 with six minutes to play and faced a fourth-and-three near midfield. The logical call was a running play from the powerful wishbone. This is how Pryor recreated the conversation between Street and Royal on the sideline:

Royal: "James, I think this year we should throw a barbeque."

Street: "Are you sure, Coach? A barbeque?"

Royal: "Yeah, we need a *really* big barbeque."

The crowd thundered with laughter.

Backstage, Scott Henderson and Freddie Steinmark were hard at work. Standing in the chilly semidarkness behind the curtains, they could hear the crowd laughing at Cactus Pryor's one-liners. They listened to the Pflugerville Five as they played the "Black Mountain Rag," then broke into "The Eyes of Texas." Six thousand fans stood and sang their hearts out to the school song.

Heads were bowed minutes later when Randy Peschel approached the lectern. "God, we all pray that we can be as brave as Freddie Steinmark," he said. "Thank the Lord he is with us tonight. Amen."

People in the audience looked around and wondered where Freddie was. They did not know that he was practicing one of the most challenging tasks of his entire life. At that moment, Henderson was coaching Freddie to walk on his prosthesis, along with lending moral support. This was not going to be easy. During a practice run, Freddie took a misstep and fell. All of Henderson's muscle was needed to wrestle Freddie back up.

"It's all right," Henderson told his buddy. "I've got a plan when we get on the stage. I'll walk behind you to your right. If you need to fall, fall to the right. If you fall left, Freddie, you'll fall off the stage. That's when we've got a heckuva mess."

They both laughed.

Ten days earlier, Steinmark had received the shiny new prosthesis that he thought would repair his dignity. It came with a velvet-lined carrying case. Freddie could not have been more proud. At first, it was like balancing yourself on a broom stick. In a couple of days, though, he was walking. Doctors still warned him that hobbing across a stage was risky business.

As the presentation of the letter jackets was about to begin, the Texas players started gathering backstage. They were humbled to see Freddie inching his way along on the new leg. They knew how important it was for him to walk without crutches. From the look in his eye, though, it all seemed like life or death.

The players lined up in alphabetical order and, one by one, walked across the stage toward Royal, who handed out the prized posses-sions. Reaching the H's, the coach skipped Scott Henderson. When he called out Cotton Speyrer's name, a smile spread across Royal's face. Instead of handing over the jacket, he tossed it toward the ground. Speyrer dove and caught it on one knee, just as he had done against Notre Dame.

At last, it was Freddie Steinmark's turn. A silence fell over the crowded hall. Royal paused, realizing that something the size of a golf ball was stuck in his throat. He looked to his left to see a smil-ing Steinmark standing just inside the curtain. Royal could feel his heart pounding as he smiled back.

"Ladies and gentlemen," the coach said, "this is an emotional mo-ment for all of us. Come on, Freddie. Come get your letter jacket."

He started slowly, tentatively. Then the crowd spotted him at the edge of the stage, in the dim light, and the roar went up. Freddie was smiling, all right. But it was clear from his ever-widening eyes that he was nervous. Henderson tried to appear casual, but his eyes were firmly locked on his friend. With each step, the cheers grew louder. Suddenly, the crowd rose to its feet. Freddie was barely making it across the stage, but, at least, he was making it.

Sitting on the front row, Linda Wheeler's cheeks were flushed, but she smiled through the pain. Her blond hair was pulled back and her face looked angelic in the far-reaching stage lights. All of her life she had been called a crybaby. She was making a brave effort to stay composed. But as she watched her boyfriend inch across the stage with that enormous smile, the tears came rolling down. There was nothing more she could do. She remembered how hard Freddie had worked to get here.

Linda Wheeler was not alone. Some of the biggest brutes to ever play college football—the likes of Bob McKay, Bill Atessis, and Bobby Wuensch—wiped away huge tears. On the stage, Royal held his composure, but it was not easy. Royal handed the letter jacket to one of his favorite players of all time. At that moment, he realized why he had chosen to coach. These inspirational moments made his career worthwhile. The Freddie Steinmarks drove him to coach, to teach, to believe, and to succeed.

Forty years later Royal recalled, "That was the most emotional moment I ever went through in my life. I will never forget it."

Henderson helped Freddie slide his right arm into his new letter jacket, then pulled it into place on his shoulders. All the while, the cheering grew louder. Steinmark and Henderson were smiling, but they never heard the crowd. Their minds were riveted on the journey. They were happy that Freddie had made it, even happier it was over. Legendary sportswriter Dave Campbell penned these words the next morning in his *Waco Tribune* column:

> Unaided, a slim, cheerful, awesomely courageous figure, face split by a grin, hobbled across the stage, big Scott Henderson at his side, and the applause started in the back of the big coliseum and it swept forward and it overshadowed anything else that drew applause Monday night. On and on the applause went, and there wasn't a dry eye in the house. Even Cactus Pryor, the seasoned old trouper, had to turn his head away. The ovation for Freddie Steinmark continued until Darrell Royal held up a hand, so he could continue. Unforgettable.

That night, they cheered one of the greatest teams in the history of college football. More important, they had come to celebrate the life of Freddie Joe Steinmark.

Chapter 24

FREEDOM

Linda Wheeler was confused when Freddie called to invite her to dinner two nights before Valentine's Day. He suggested they go to their favorite restaurant, a place they normally reserved for the most romantic day of the year.

Linda tried not to worry about the timing. After all, Freddie was adjusting rapidly to life on one leg. The prosthesis was rough on the incision, but it made him feel whole again. After two months of chaos, his life had settled back into a normal rhythm of classwork, studying, and dating Linda. Freddie was spending a lot of time around the weight room at Memorial Stadium as his teammates geared up for the grueling Medina Drills. Lifting weights with the guys made him feel like part of the team again.

In September, he would start coaching the incoming freshmen. It could not replace playing football, or competing for another national championship team. Still, the opportunity to work with the young guys was another reason to smile. What made him feel even better was that Darrell Royal had encouraged him to hang around the team as much as he liked.

One of the two biggest changes in Freddie's life was his brand-new metallic blue Grand Prix, courtesy of Cecil Tindall, a San Antonio Pontiac dealer and one of the biggest Longhorns boosters on the planet. At Freddie's request, Tindall's body shop had repainted the top of the Grand Prix from black to white, and the dealer threw in a top-of-the-line stereo system. One special piece of equipment was a dashboard switch to dim the headlights. In those days, it was located on the floorboard, worked by the left foot.

Steinmark's first duty as a car owner was to drive to the university traffic department and obtain a parking permit for disabled persons. He was on crutches, not using his artificial leg, and his pant leg was pinned up. The girl behind the counter looked at him impersonally.

"Is this a temporary disability?" she said.

"I would like to think so," Steinmark said, "but I'm afraid it's not."

Steinmark's second biggest adjustment was moving into the rectory that was part of Father Fred Bomar's sprawling complex known as St. Peter the Apostle Church. The rectory was like a small college fraternity house with five bedrooms and five bathrooms. It was the perfect size for entertaining guests and Bomar hosted steak fries that included plenty of beer for the football players on Thursday nights.

Linda hated the distance that the rectory placed between herself and Freddie. Instead of living around the corner from each other at the Jester Center, Freddie was now out on the southeastern edge of town, where the deer roamed. It was not a place where Linda felt comfortable and she was not so sure that Father Bomar wanted her around.

Linda disliked the rectory from the moment she saw it. A month earlier, she had ridden in Father Bomar's car with Freddie and his parents from MD Anderson to the Austin church complex. On the day Freddie moved in, she was amazed at her boyfriend's bedroom that included a brand-new burnt orange carpet, a double bed, bookshelves, a desk, and lamps. Bomar's connections all over Austin were clicking. A furniture dealer had donated everything in Freddie's room under the condition of anonymity.

When they reached the rectory, Bomar handed Freddie the keys to the new Grand Prix. It was the priest who had contacted Tindall about arranging for the shiny new car. When Freddie saw it, his eyes lit up like pinballs. Never in his life had Freddie owned an automobile. It represented a newfound freedom. While Freddie smiled like a kid with a new toy, Linda began to worry. Was she already losing her boyfriend to a hot new car and a proverbial frat house?

Since the eighth grade, they had strolled arm in arm through life. They did not need money or a fancy car. Now Freddie possessed both. Thanks to Bomar helping to arrange the Freddie Steinmark Fund, Freddie also carried plenty of cash money in his pocket.

Steinmark and Bomar had become acquainted just a few months earlier when Freddie started going to the steak dinners at the rectory. At the request of Freddie's father, Bomar became the young amputee's personal assistant. In effect, he served as Steinmark's landlord, bodyguard, and travel guide. Ordained as a Catholic priest in 1960s, Bomar was thirty-four years old. It took him nine years to rise to the position of pastor of St. Peter the Apostle Church. One of the best days of his life was when Steinmark moved into the rectory.

"He had a great attitude after he lost his leg and he expected the same thing out of me," Bomar recalled. "I remember him coming down to breakfast in the morning and eating his bowl of cereal. I remember him jumping in that new car and driving off to class. He was happy. That kid had a great attitude. I loved that kid."

While Bomar and Steinmark were settling into this new arrangement, Linda was on the outside looking in. She felt pushed to the side. She could no longer be certain of when she would see her boyfriend, or how often. On the Texas campus during the past three years, they had either walked to the movie theatre, or double-dated with friends like Scott Henderson and Bill Zapalac. Now that Freddie owned wheels, his options for entertainment were endless.

Two nights before Valentine's Day, Freddie drove Linda to the restaurant and they received the kind of star treatment they were getting accustomed to. Everyone recognized him wherever he went. They were escorted to their favorite table.

When Linda looked at Freddie, she saw something different in his eyes. She sensed something serious on his mind. They made small talk, then Freddie cleared his throat and looked at her sadly.

"Linda, I don't know how much longer I'm going to live," he said. "They say that I'm cancer-free right now. But that can change. I'm hearing through the grapevine that some people think I won't live for more than a year. If that's the case, I don't have much more time."

Linda nodded. She did not know what to say. She certainly had no idea where this conversation was heading.

Exactly two months had passed since Freddie's surgery. Linda had noticed few changes in her boyfriend since the loss of the leg. He was the same Freddie—forever upbeat and living in the moment. Tonight, though, he seemed so different.

Freddie cleared his throat again. She could see his eyes moistening.

"Linda, I might not make it," he said. "You, on the other hand, have a long life ahead of you. We are going to live two different lives. I think we should break up."

It came out of the blue. At first, Linda denied she heard it. She had never imagined them breaking up. They had been going steady since the eighth grade. They had been talking about marriage since high school.

In a soft voice, she said, "Freddie, are you kidding?"

"No, I'm not, Linda."

"Have you been thinking about this for a while?"

"I've been thinking about it a lot."

A vision of the nurse back at MD Anderson flooded Linda's memory. Her words came back to Linda. *Freddie is going to be a different person. It happens to all amputees. They go through personality changes. He's going to need you more than ever.*

So many thoughts were going through Linda's mind that she could not keep track.

"Freddie, maybe you should think about this," she said. "You've been through two months of hell. Every time you turn around, there's another traumatic experience. Most people lay in bed after they lose a leg. You've been running all over the place. You haven't had time to think."

Freddie looked down. "Linda, I've thought about it a lot. I think this is the best thing for both of us."

Linda began to cry. Her life had been upside down the past two months. Losing the love of her life, though, was a tragedy she never saw coming.

Freddie drove Linda back to the dormitory, then headed back to the rectory. On Valentine's Day, Linda received a dozen roses from Freddie. She opened the card and read, I WILL LOVE YOU FOREVER. Never had she been so confused.

Scott Henderson was shocked when he heard the news. Freddie had shared with no one his plan to end the relationship with Linda. When the breakup occurred, Henderson knew that his friend was suffering from more stress than anyone knew.

"Freddie was acting like everything was fine, but he was losing some self-assuredness," Henderson remembered. "He tried to be the same, but he wasn't. He might have been saying to himself that, 'Hey, I'm going to die. I might as well live the good life.'"

Back on January 5, the doctors at MD Anderson had given Steinmark a clean bill of health and sent him on his way. Still, Steinmark never felt they were telling him the whole truth. He had researched bone cancer and found it far more deadly than he realized. An osteosarcoma could spread quickly and inflict fatal damage. A pulmonary metastasis could be quick and devastating to the lungs. Even heavy doses of chemotherapy could not derail it.

"Freddie was acting as brave as he possibly could," Henderson said, "but I really think he was scared. That was the biggest reason that he broke up with Linda. He did not know where his life was going, or how much longer he was going to live."

Henderson blamed himself for not stepping in and convincing Freddie to stay with Linda. In the midst of all the turmoil, he did not know what to do.

"I probably should have kicked Freddie's butt and told him that he was wrong about Linda," he recalled. "I wish I had. Maybe I could have stopped it. Isn't that funny that I feel that way now? I should have said to Freddie, 'Hey, you're giving up the best thing you've got going for you.' I think that Linda would have stood by him until the end of his life. I think that Linda understood him better than anyone. Some guys need a good female to keep them going in the right direction. Linda was that person for Freddie. I just think he was happier when he was with her.

"It was a sad day when they broke up."

Chapter 25

SHOWBIZ

America reached out to Freddie Steinmark and pulled him close in a warm embrace. He became an overnight hero. The White House called. The *Today* show booked him. His photo appeared in virtually every newspaper in the country. A major publisher offered a book deal.

As President Richard Nixon had promised, Steinmark was invited to the White House in February as part of the American Cancer Crusade. The national chairman of the 1970 campaign was actor Fess Parker, one of the biggest Orange Bloods on the planet.

On the morning of his visit to the White House, Steinmark and Father Fred Bomar were delivered by limousine to the White House and given a tour. After a brief reception, they were ushered into the Oval Office. Freddie wore a light gray suit with orange and gray pinstripes and he walked with the aid of a brown cane. In his left hand, he carried a football that had been autographed by the entire Texas team.

"You had faith in us," Steinmark told the president that day, "so we would like you to have this token of appreciation."

"Well, thank you, Freddie," Nixon said. "That is very nice that you would bring that along for me. Tell the guys back in Texas that I appreciate it very much."

Freddie nodded. "There's one more thing I'd like to say, Mr. President. When you called me in the hospital, well, it meant a whole lot to me."

"You needed a lift," the president said, putting his hand on Freddie's shoulder. "You're up and going and you don't need any help now. It's good to see you trying to help other people."

After the meeting with Nixon, the limousine whisked Steinmark and Bomar to the Virginia home of Gene Fondren, a former Texas legislator who was the general counsel for the Texas Railroad Association in Washington. That night, the same limousine shuttled Steinmark, Bomar, and Fondren into Georgetown for a night on the town. One of their first stops was an upscale disco on M Street with disco balls that glowed like meteorites sailing through the night. The pulsating boom-boom-boom lured Freddie onto the dance floor. He removed the prosthesis and boogeyed like a wild man on one leg. He was blessed with plenty of flight attendants ready to shimmy. The Commodores kept the hits coming all night.

"We walked into the place and there were a lot of airline stewardesses in there," Bomar said. "They were all interested in dancing with Freddie. They were all having a ball. Freddie was tossing them down. I couldn't remember if it was bourbon or scotch. But he was tossing them down."

It was not the first time that Bomar had seen Steinmark drinking since the night of Texas's victory over Arkansas. After splitting with Linda, he started making the rounds at the Austin bars with some of his Texas teammates. It was still a bit of a shock for his friends to see him drinking beer.

"When Freddie started drinking, it was like the pope started drinking," Mike Campbell IV said. "Of course, just about everybody on the team had a beer from time to time. But you just didn't see it very much from Freddie. But I can tell you that he was enjoying life."

Bobby Mitchell could not believe the drastic swing in his friend's personality. Sometimes he thought Freddie was a completely different person.

"Freddie always went by the book," Mitchell said. "He did what he was supposed to do. He was always responsible. He didn't walk on the wild side until he had his leg amputated and he broke up with Linda. Then he began to drink for the first time and to party. It was surprising."

Back in Austin, Linda Wheeler was hearing the stories about Freddie and Bomar. A photograph of Freddie and the President appeared in the *Austin American-Statesman*. Bomar's name was all over the wire-service story.

"I was so mad at Bomar for going to Washington with Freddie when it could have been his parents making the trip with him," Linda recalled. "Bomar edged his dad out of that. Or his dad and mom. What was Bomar to the family? He was nothing to the family. He was not the family priest or anything. He was always getting his picture and his name in the newspaper. We always read in glowing terms about the fine work of Father Fred Bomar."

Leaving Washington the next day, Steinmark and Bomar flew to New York for his segment on the *Today* show. First, though, they planned to visit Bachelors III, one of New York's hottest nightclubs formerly owned by New York Jets quarterback Joe Namath, the most famous bachelor in America.

The previous summer, Namath had been forced by NFL commissioner Pete Rozelle to sell Bachelors III. A league security investigation lasting three months had revealed that the place was crawling with big-cigar gambling types and members of the New York Mafia, a clientele not suitable to the image of the NFL, or one of its most popular quarterbacks. It was not the first time that Namath had associated with known mobsters. The quarterback was informed by Rozelle that he could either sell the bar or be suspended. To Rozelle, it just did not seem right that Joe Willie Namath in his full-length fur coat was traveling with the mob.

At first, Namath announced his intention to retire, then weighed his bank account against his jet-set lifestyle. He changed his mind before the start of training camp.

All of this did not deter Bomar-Steinmark.

"Freddie could dance better on one leg than most people could on two," Mike Campbell said. "To see him moving around on the dance floor like that was one of the most amazing things that I've ever seen."

The next morning, Steinmark and Bomar were sitting in the Green Room at NBC at 30 Rockefeller Plaza. The priest was reading over the script handed to him by a producer that contained the questions that host Joe Garagiola would ask Steinmark. Bomar was furiously editing when Garagiola walked in.

"Look," Bomar told the host, "I have to go over everything that Freddie does because we always have concerns about libel. There are some things that you can't use here."

Garagiola was known for his off-camera cynicism. He said with a sneer, "If you don't like it, just scratch it out."

"That's what I intend to do," Bomar replied.

Later that day, Steinmark and Bomar met with Roger Donnelly, an editor at Little, Brown, about publishing an autobiography. The idea had been kicked around for several weeks and more than a few New York editors were calling. Dallas sports columnist Blackie Sherrod, a close friend of Bomar, was the logical choice to co-write the book with Steinmark.

In the spring of 1970, Linda Wheeler still held out hope that Freddie would call. She was confused by the dozen red roses on Valentine's Day and the words on the inscription. She wondered if Freddie might someday have second thoughts and come back.

On a day when the dogwood trees bloomed, and the scent of honeysuckle was fresh in the air, Linda realized it was time to give up on her ex-boyfriend. On her way to class one morning, she spotted Freddie strolling across campus with a Texas coed close by his side. It was one of Linda's sorority sisters from Delta Delta Delta.

"I was sad," Linda recalled. "But I remember saying to myself that I wanted Freddie to be happy. If I couldn't have him, I wanted him to be happy with whomever he was with."

It was soon widely known around Austin that Freddie was playing the field.

"I think that Freddie got more girls with one leg than the rest of us did with two," Scott Henderson remembered. "It was one of the most amazing things that I ever saw."

One night at the Flagon and Trencher, Mike Campbell was with his girlfriend when he ran into Freddie and his date. They drank well into the night and, typical of young college students, began planning a road trip.

"Ah, hell, let's go to Mexico," Campbell said.

"I'm all for it," Freddie replied.

Because Freddie was driving the new Grand Prix, the four-hour trip to Laredo seemed like a cruise across town.

"All I remember is that everyone, including the girls, were fired up," Campbell said. "We all wanted to go to Mexico."

Freddie would drive the first leg of the trip, and the others would take their turns. Passing through San Antonio an hour and a half later, Freddie realized that his three companions were fading. Soon, they were fast asleep. Campbell was snoring. Once again, Freddie's common sense took over and he turned the car around and headed back to Austin.

The trip he planned to New Orleans for spring break was a totally different matter. Even when Scott Henderson cancelled on him, Freddie decided to go anyway.

Rolling east through Houston, Steinmark stopped to pick up one of his best friends, Scott Palmer, a junior Longhorns tackle. Knowing that New Orleans would not be a cheap place during spring break, Palmer's parents gave him a hundred-dollar bill. Steinmark was still flush with cash that kept rolling into the Freddie Steinmark Fund.

Steinmark and Palmer were going in style. After the seven-hour car ride, their first stop was at the Playboy Club in the French Quarter. Because it was a private club, the Playboy "key" was provided by a rich Texas alumnus. As Steinmark and Palmer took seats at their table in the dining room, they found themselves surrounded by a bevy of buxom bunnies in low-cut outfits. The bunny-eared girls were informed that Steinmark was to be treated as a celebrity. You would have thought a couple of rich oil barons had walked into the club. In 1970, Hugh Hefner's gentlemen's clubs were still considered quite racy. The women could not be touched, but that did not mean they were not showing off plenty of cleavage. Steinmark and Palmer would have plenty to brag about when they got back to Austin.

Later that night, when they walked into Pat O'Brien's, the duo was quickly approached by a group of Texas Tech cheerleaders. Palmer recognized a couple of the girls from the sidelines when the Longhorns played the Red Raiders. Tech was renowned for its beautiful women, and Texas for its national championships. The girls were instantly impressed with the boys from Austin.

"Freddie ended up with the best-looking cheerleader in the bunch," Palmer remembered.

When it was time to leave New Orleans, Steinmark and Palmer suddenly realized that they had spent so much money that they had thirty-five cents between them.

"We couldn't even buy a Coke," Palmer said. "If not for Freddie's gas card, we couldn't have made it back to Texas."

When Linda heard about Freddie's gallivanting, she figured it was Bomar's influence. She knew about the Thursday night parties at the rectory and the girls who were invited. They came from the Texas campus and from Bomar's former church in Temple. It was not difficult to find women who wanted to mix with a bunch of Texas football players.

"There were always plenty of girls around the rectory," Bobby Mitchell said. "But they were not necessarily our girlfriends."

In spite of having only one leg, Freddie became a magnet for all of the women visiting the rectory.

"Bomar had no good motives," Linda said. "He was just so transparent to me. Freddie's upbringing was one hundred percent totally Catholic. It was unimaginable that someone could be a priest and not be good. Freddie just couldn't see it. There was something symbiotic about the relationship between Freddie and Bomar. I knew that Bomar was feeding him some kind of bullshit from the Bible, or whatever. I don't know what it was. But Freddie was weak at the time and he needed some support and this man was supposed to be giving him that support. Freddie's parents were in Denver. We were broken up. Freddie wasn't a football player anymore. There was a big gap and Bomar was supposed to fill it. It looked right on the outside because you had a priest and a young man trying to get his life back together. But this whole thing wasn't right on the inside."

Not everyone on campus subscribed to Linda's assessment of Bomar. David Ballew, who played halfback, cornerback, and safety at Texas from 1969–71, and lettered on the '70 national title team, said that Bomar did his fair share of directing students in the right direction.

"There are a whole lot of doctors and lawyers who give Father Bomar a lot of credit for their success," he remembered. "I happen to think that he inspired a lot of people. He was there for me when I needed him, and he was there for a lot of people."

Ballew also praised Bomar for his community service, especially in the hospitals.

"There were a whole lot of strangers that Father Bomar did a lot of praying for," Ballew said. "He spent a lot of all-nighters at the hospitals helping people."

No doubt, Linda Wheeler had more of a personal stake in the Bomar-Steinmark relationship. She said she firmly believed that Bomar was the reason for the couple's breakup.

"I don't know if he directly told Freddie to break up with me," Linda said, "but he did counsel Freddie on it."

Bomar denied having anything to do with the couple's split.

"I did not break them up," Bomar said. "Freddie decided to break up with Linda because he wanted to spend more time with his teammates."

Bomar cited one more reason for the two parting ways.

"She didn't want to share Freddie with anybody, not even his teammates," Bomar said. "So he started going out with other girls on a regular basis and he started having a really good time. He was dating a lot of different girls."

Sitting in a ringside seat to this tug-of-war was Scott Henderson. He continued to be Linda's friend and saw her occasionally around campus. He was also spending some time at the rectory because of Freddie.

"I'm not really sure that Father Bomar ever had a conversation with Freddie about Linda," he remembered. "I'm not so sure that Father Bomar took over Freddie's life. I think that some of those decisions were Freddie's. I do know that Bomar said to Freddie, 'Women can be a little different.' And yes, he did enable Freddie to start dating other girls."

After years of seeing Freddie and Linda basically inseparable, Mitchell could barely accept the sight of his friend with other women.

"When I saw him with other girls, it was very strange and very unsettling," Mitchell said. "But I kept asking myself, what would I do if I was in his situation after losing a leg? I might have done the same thing."

The parties at the rectory became the talk of sorority row. Some of the Texas coeds with steady boyfriends were getting worried. They wanted to know what was going on at Bomar's frat house.

Quarterback Eddie Phillips, slated to be the starter in 1970, had been going steady with the same girl since their days at Mesquite High School. One afternoon, Phillips approached Bomar and said,

"Father, I'm going to come out to the rectory tonight to see you. Would that be okay?"

"Just come on out," Bomar said.

That night, Phillips left a farewell note on his girlfriend's bathroom mirror. Then he moved into the rectory for several days.

"Some people said that I broke up Eddie Phillips and his girlfriend," Bomar said. "I didn't even know Eddie until he came up to me and said he was coming out to the rectory. So how could I have possibly broken them up?"

Bomar, who was about a dozen years older than the players, was practically a member of the Texas Longhorns team. He was a close friend of Darrell Royal's and received V.I.P. treatment whenever he showed up at practice, or attended a game. Players were coming and going at the rectory like a bus stop. The Thursday night bashes drew big crowds.

"He provided a place to stay, a place to eat, a place to drink," Mitchell said. "He wanted the fellowship and the camaraderie. For lack of a better word, Father Bomar was a jock sniffer."

Bomar loved to break bread with the players, and to drink with them at Happy Hour. While most of the players drank beer, he was a scotch-and-soda man.

"Father Bomar was one of the greatest fans who ever lived," Bill Atessis said. "He thrived on being that. He could also drink with us better than anyone we knew. He was a wild man for a priest. We had a good time at the rectory. If you were young and you could go out there and drink for free, wouldn't you? He also made sure the girls were there, too, and that was a pretty big draw for the guys."

Bomar admitted that he drank frequently in the late 1960s and early '70s and that beer and booze were always available at the rectory for the players.

"I enjoyed a scotch and soda at the end of the day and pretty soon I was doing it on a daily basis," he said. "When I was out on my boat, I liked Lone Star beer. I can tell you there would have been a lot more Lone Star in this world if not for me. I know that Linda probably thought I drank too much back then, and I probably did.

There certainly wasn't any scandal or anything. But I did a lot of drinking."

Scott Henderson, who lived at the rectory in the late spring and early summer of 1970, said he noticed that Bomar was a problem drinker.

"Father Bomar had a serious drinking problem and he finally got some help," Henderson said. "He never drank during the day. But after he finished his duties around the church, he would drink very, very heavily and pass out."

Two years after graduating from Texas, and during a brief stint with the New England Patriots, Atessis returned to Austin one summer and looked up Bomar. The priest took off the collar and put on regular clothes. They went to a strip club and drank several rounds.

"Every time the waitress came around, I said, 'Do you want another drink, Father Bomar?' He finally said, 'Stop calling me Father.'"

Bomar said he quit drinking for Lent in "1972 or '73." He said that he never again drank beer or scotch again, but he occasionally enjoyed wine.

"The drinking just made me too depressed," he said. "I can't handle that. I had to stop drinking beer because it made me too heavy. Plus, I get up at five in the morning and that's hard to do when you've been drinking."

To his credit, Henderson said Bomar did an excellent job of counseling Steinmark, along with some other Texas players. A couple of players had gotten into debt with local bookmakers and Bomar convinced them to stop betting on sports.

"I think his heart was in the right place most of the time with the players," Henderson said. "I know that he had Freddie's best interest at heart. It just didn't look that way to some people, especially the girlfriends of Texas players."

Forty years later, Bomar said the bottles of bourbon, scotch, and vodka from the 1970s still filled the cabinets at the rectory. He insisted, though, that he did not touch them. At the time, he still had not decided what to do with the leftover booze.

"I can't give it to the young people and the old people don't drink it anymore," he said. "I guess they'll just have to drink it at my funeral."

Ironically, Bomar died after suffering a head injury from a fall on August 11, 2010, about two weeks after making that statement. The funeral mass was held at his church five days later.

Chapter 26

NEW LOVE

Linda Wheeler felt lonely in late spring of 1970. Her phone had stopped ringing. Out of respect to Freddie Steinmark, no one on the campus was going to ask her for a date.

Knowing that Linda could use an escort to the spring formal, one of her sorority sisters came up with an idea.

"Look, there is one guy on this campus who might not know about Freddie," she said. "He is a premed student and I really don't think he's much of a football fan. His name is Richard Meehan."

When she saw Meehan's fraternity picture in the Cactus yearbook, she instantly said yes. He was handsome and a close friend of Scott Henderson, and the two were fraternity brothers in Delta Tau Delta. So he couldn't be too bad.

"Richard Meehan was very smart and very handsome," Henderson said. "He had a lot going for him. He was quiet. He was someone who Linda would appreciate. He was a very nice guy. I don't think he knew a whole lot about football. But I can assure you that he, like everyone on that campus, knew who Freddie Steinmark was."

Linda liked Richard from the start. One date led to another, and by the end of the spring semester, they were an item around the U.T. Greek system. She was looking forward to coming back from Denver for the fall semester and seeing him some more.

———

Freddie was staying in Austin for the break, and it would be the summer to remember. Why not? His May checkup at MD Anderson revealed not a trace of cancer. The sky was still the limit for this one-legged man. Freddie was going to live each day as if it might be his last.

Five months after the surgery, his hair was down to his shoulders and his new "mod" wardrobe was filling up the closet, thanks to the cash flow from the Freddie Steinmark Fund. He had sold the Grand Prix and bought a brand-new burnt orange Corvette with the $5,000 advance from Little, Brown. Steinmark and sportswriter Blackie Sherrod were beginning to do interviews on the new book, scheduled for release in the summer of 1971.

Freddie smiled his way through every day, and if the amputation still haunted him, he never let on. Golf was first on his agenda that summer. There were no one-legged golfers at the Austin Country Club, but Freddie was not deterred. Besides, he was a people magnet, and the first person to offer assistance with his game was none other than legendary swing coach Harvey Penick. At the time, Penick was tutoring a couple of high school whiz kids named Ben Crenshaw and Tom Kite, who would soon enroll at the U.T.

Penick was sixty-six years old and still coaching the U.T. golf team when he ran into Freddie. He was a golfing legend around Austin. Here was a man who had been offered the head professional's job at Austin Country Club before he graduated from Austin High School. He had coached the Longhorns team for the past thirty-three years.

Penick gained instant respect for Steinmark. He could not comprehend how a man on one leg could maintain such balance. He could draw back the club, swing, and follow through without bobbing or weaving. The strength of his right leg was the work of a lifetime of athletics. Steinmark did not wear the prosthesis when golfing.

More important, Freddie possessed the mind and willpower to accomplish anything he decided to try. He was a picture of confidence. He bounced on one leg like a pogo stick as he approached the ball.

"Freddie could really hit the golf ball," Mike Campbell said. "What was amazing is that he didn't get tired."

It had been eight years since he had swung a club on two legs. His first nine holes on a tough track at Austin C.C., he shot a 53. That number would be whittled down to a 46 by the end of the summer.

Steinmark and Tom Campbell were sharing a golf cart one day when they were rolling down the fairway in pursuit of one of Steinmark's stray shots. Normally the procedure was for the golfer on the passenger side to lean down and pluck the ball from the fairway while the wheel man drove by slowly. Steinmark reached down for the ball just as Campbell accelerated and whipped the steering wheel to the left. Freddie was thrown out of the cart.

"I looked back and saw Freddie bouncing on that one leg fifty times," Campbell said. "I couldn't stop laughing. When I went back to pick him up he said, 'Why did you do that?' I said, 'Because I knew you could handle it.'"

They laughed about it for the rest of the day.

With golf mastered, Steinmark's next big step was waterskiing. Father Fred Bomar's boat was on Lake Belton in Temple, the home of his former church. The Saturday afternoon ski trips drew large crowds.

Several years had passed since Steinmark had skied on two legs. Adjusting to the one ski was not as easy as returning to the golf course. He fell down so many times that the boat almost ran out of gas. Typically, he never gave up and by the end of the summer was one of the best on the lake.

James Street was relaxing in his dorm room late one afternoon when Freddie walked in. His hair was still a little wet and there was a towel around his neck.

"You could tell that Freddie had been swimming," Street said. "He said, 'I've been out at the lake. Went waterskiing.' So I said to him, 'Freddie, is it hard to swim with just one leg?' Without even smiling, he said, 'It's not half bad if you don't mind swimming around in circles.'"

As Street recalled the story several years later, he shook his head.

"Here's the amazing part," Street said. "That was not a scripted answer. It was not like somebody wrote it for him. He was not trying to be a comedian. He was out at that lake and he was swimming in circles and having fun. That was the attitude that Freddie took about life. Everything in his life was *good*. You knew it was good if he didn't mind swimming around in circles."

That summer, a group of Texas players traveled about fifty miles northwest of Austin for the dedication of a new country club in Marble Falls. Again, Street's job was to introduce the other Longhorns.

Street grabbed the microphone and said, "Have you ever noticed how Freddie Steinmark walks? It's like he's on his last leg." Everyone laughed, including Freddie. In fact, he was the one laughing the loudest.

Like Steinmark, Street became a graduate assistant when his playing days ended with the Cotton Bowl win over Notre Dame. One of his self-appointed duties was to hide Steinmark's prosthesis.

"Freddie would look and look and look around the locker room, and he could never find that fake leg," Street said. "Then he would walk up to me and say, 'Where is my damn prosthesis, Slick?'"

A group of players was riding with Freddie down to San Antonio for the grand opening of a chicken restaurant owned by former Texas great Tommy Nobis. Freddie liked to drive fast and it wasn't long before a police officer flipped on his lights. Freddie pulled over and waited for the officer to approach the car. When the cop arrived, the players in the back started yelling, "Arrest his ass! Arrest his ass!"

Mike Campbell was one of the guys in the backseat. "The cop thought we were crazy," Campbell said. "The cop finally asked him to get out of the car. When he saw the missing leg, he figured out who Freddie was. He let him go."

The Texas baseball team made the College World Series in 1970 and reached the semifinals before losing to Florida State. When the team returned from Omaha, Spanky Stephens went looking for his buddy, Freddie Steinmark. He found him at a bar just off Guadalupe.

"I walk in and Freddie is there with three girls," Stephens said. "I was feeling pretty good at the time because I had just been hired as a full-time trainer at Texas and I was about ready to start."

Stephens had forgotten, though, that he would need a place to live. The Jester Center was no longer an option. On a first-year trainer's salary, he would need something fairly cheap. He explained his situation to Steinmark.

"The next thing I know, Freddie goes up to the bar and asks for the phone," Stephens said. "He calls Father Bomar and asks if I can move into the rectory. He comes back and tells me that I can move in the next day. Freddie was my good friend."

The parties at the rectory that summer were often nonstop. With the players no longer under the watchful eye of Darrell Royal, they were ready to rock. Bobby Mitchell lived most of the summer of 1970 at Bomar's place.

"The rectory was fun and it was free," Mitchell said. "All summer long, my friends were going there. There were parties. It was like a fraternity house. There were people coming and going. It was entertaining. You never knew who was going to walk through the door next. It could be players past and present. Of course, it could be girls. Father Bomar always had a connection to girls."

Mitchell, however, was spending most of his time with his girlfriend, Honor Franklin. When she heard what was going on at the rectory, she demanded that Mitchell retrieve his autographed picture that he had given the priest.

"I just had a feeling that the other shoe was going to fall on Father Bomar," Mitchell recalled. "Honor and I both felt that something was going to come out about this whole façade that he had going on. On the one hand, he was a Catholic priest, and on the other hand he was sponsoring all of these other activities. We just didn't want to be a part of it anymore."

In July, Bomar came up with the best blind date ever for Freddie. The busty blonde from Texas Tech was quite thrilled to go out with one of Texas' biggest celebrities.

"This girl was absolutely gorgeous and hot," Henderson said. "I just sat there and wondered why I couldn't hook up with a girl like that. Then I realized that it was Freddie we were dealing with here. Here was a guy who could walk across campus and girls would throw their phone numbers at him. He was a celebrity. Girls were chasing him."

Henderson also knew something about Freddie that no one else did. Freddie was starting to repeat the same sad phrase every day. *I miss Linda.*

"All the time that he was going out with other girls, Freddie missed Linda," Henderson said. "He always held out the hope that they would get back together. I encouraged him. I really hoped it would happen."

The hardest part of Steinmark's life was traveling to MD Anderson every two months for checkups. Given a choice, he would have taken a beating with a rubber hose. He did not sleep for two or three nights leading to the trip. The doctors were telling him not to worry. Freddie, though, felt like a ticking time bomb.

Bomar and Steinmark returned to Houston in early July. There were the usual X-rays and blood tests. Freddie seemed more nervous than ever. The two went to lunch and the doctors told them to check in with the hospital before heading back to Austin.

That afternoon, Freddie was on the phone with one of the doctors when Bomar heard him say, "Oh, my God!"

They quickly returned to the hospital and caucused with Dr. Dick Martin, Dr. Bob Moreton, and Dr. Clifford Howe. Their heads were down as they began to share the results. Two spots had been found on his lungs.

Osteosarcoma was one of the most aggressive forms of cancer. Doctors knew from the day of the amputation that, in spite of removing all of the cancer from his leg, it might someday metastasize through the circulatory system.

Bomar asked the doctors if it would be all right if Steinmark accepted an invitation to attend the annual Chicago Charities College All-Star Game played at Soldier Field. The game, which dated to 1934, pitted the best collegiate players against the Super Bowl champions. Texas would be represented by Bob McKay and Ted Koy as the collegians squared off against the Kansas City Chiefs.

Dr. Martin removed his glasses and looked at Freddie intently. "Keep playing golf," he said. "Keep waterskiing. Go to Chicago for the game. But when you get back, we need to do some more X-rays."

That day, driving back to Austin, Steinmark did not talk for the first hour and a half. Finally he told Bomar, "The cancer's in the trunk of my body. This is just like Brian Piccolo. I will have a year or less."

An embryonal cell carcinoma had been found in Brian Piccolo's chest cavity in late November 1969, a couple of weeks before Steinmark's amputation. His season with the Chicago Bears was over. The aggressive form of lung cancer was removed by surgery and the doctors gave him a clean bill of health. He was considered lucky.

In February, Piccolo believed he was on the road to recovery when his fingers located yet another lump on his chest. More surgery followed and his condition began to deteriorate. On June 16, at the age of twenty-six, Brian Piccolo died. Less than seven months had passed since his initial operation.

On his way to Chicago a month after Piccolo's death, Steinmark thought about him many times. He had wanted to meet the man who had written him such a touching letter. Steinmark was already learning that you had to move fast to beat cancer.

The weekend at the all-star game in Chicago was the usual whirlwind of appearances and long limousine rides. He was introduced to the crowd of 65,000 fans at halftime and interviewed on national TV. He told everyone the same thing: "This has been the greatest year of my life."

Steinmark could not wait to get back to Austin. Without telling Bomar, he jumped into the burnt orange Corvette and tore off for MD Anderson. He prayed that the spots on his lungs had vanished.

Once again, his prayers were not answered. The spots were still there and the doctors told him to stick around. In two days, he would begin the horribly painful process of chemotherapy.

Steinmark checked back into the hospital for five days of pure hell. It was the most painful ordeal of his life, other than losing his leg. The doctors told him that his hair would soon start to fall out. He could never remember feeling more weak. On the drive back to Austin, he could see his hair gathering on the dashboard and the seat. His life was changing, and it was not for the better. The man who refused to cry in front of others, broke down in tears.

Steinmark returned to the rectory and told Bomar the cancer had spread. Late that night, he had a long conversation with Spanky Stephens about how cancer had changed his life.

Stephens was still haunted with the realization that he could have acted faster and possibly saved Freddie's leg. The doctors were saying that it did not matter when the osteosarcoma was discovered, Freddie's limb was going to be amputated regardless. Still, Stephens hated to see what his good friend had gone through and, in some ways, blamed himself.

Late one night, when the others were already in bed, Stephens and Steinmark started to talk. Most of the lights were off in the rectory.

"Freddie," Stephens said, "I am torn between two things. First, I wish we could have gotten the cancer earlier. But if we had gotten it earlier, you wouldn't have enjoyed all of those experiences during the sixty-nine season. It's damned if you do, and damned if you don't."

Steinmark smiled. It was something he had contemplated many times during the past six months.

"Spanky, let me tell you this," Steinmark said. "I don't care if I live to be thirty, or if I live to be a hundred. I would have never given up that season with the national championship team. That was the greatest season of my life. It is what I lived for. Spanky, I would have played that whole season even if I knew I had cancer in my leg. I would have never told the doctors or the trainers. It was that important to me. If I could do it over again, I would've done the same thing."

Stephens was on the verge of tears.

"I don't know how you made it through the season," he said. "That is the greatest accomplishment I've ever seen in my life. You are something else, Freddie."

The next day, Steinmark sought out Scott Henderson, who had been on an NCAA-sponsored tour of Vietnam the past two weeks. The trip had been a bummer. Henderson could not get over the looks of sadness. The Americans knew that no one appreciated them, not even the Vietnamese they were trying to protect.

He did not know his sadness was about to grow deeper. His best friend walked into his room at the rectory on crutches and sat down on the bed. Steinmark looked Henderson in the eye and said, "Scott, I'm not well. The doctors at MD Anderson gave me a bad report. The news is not good."

Chapter 27

REUNITED

The first week of September, Linda Wheeler was on a date with Richard Meehan and loving life once more. For the first time since enrolling at U.T., Linda enjoyed a complete freedom. She was finally away from the dormitory scene and living in a new apartment. The relationship with Richard was blooming and she planned to invite him up.

She was riding with Richard back to the River Hills Apartments, south of campus. As the car pulled alongside the curb, she could see through the darkness an orange Corvette parked in front of them. She could also make out the personalized license plate on the back: UT 28. *Oh my God, it's Freddie.*

Linda tried to remain composed. She pecked Richard on the cheek and said, "I think I'd better go up alone. I will call you."

As she walked through the Austin night, Linda felt numb. She had not spoken to Freddie since the night they broke up.

"Freddie was not happy that Linda was seeing Richard Meehan," Henderson remembered. "He thought that Linda had a steady and did not like it at all. I knew she was going out with Richard, but I didn't now how serious they were."

As she approached the front of the apartments, Linda spotted Freddie sitting on the stairwell leading to her door.

"Well, hello, Hot Dog," she said.

Freddie did not hesitate.

"Linda, I'm sorry," he said. "I miss you. I still love you."

"I think we should talk," Linda said. "Why don't you come inside?"

They made casual conversation about what they had been doing the last few months. Freddie talked about playing golf and water skiing. Linda recounted a trip to Mexico City as part of her Spanish studies.

Finally, Freddie said, "I want us to get back together. Linda, I made a big mistake. I don't know why I did it."

"I know why you did it," she said. "You let that damn Father Bomar get control of you. He talked you into breaking up with me. He talked you into doing a lot of things."

"I don't know," Freddie said. "Everything seems pretty confusing."

Linda smiled and said, "Okay, Freddie, this is what we need to do. You have to make a choice here. It's either me or Bomar. I'm going to sit here and think about us getting back together. In the meantime, you go see Bomar."

The next day, Steinmark went to the rectory. He told the priest how much he appreciated everything he had done the past eight months.

"I need you to know that Linda and I are getting back together," he said. "I made that decision last night. It's final."

Talking with Henderson later in the day, Steinmark reconstructed his conversation with Bomar.

"Freddie told me what Bomar said," Henderson remembered. "Bomar told him he should not go back to Linda. He said, 'Freddie, you should stay away from her.'" Bomar said he told Freddie, "You just don't know how women are."

That night, Freddie told Linda that he was moving out of the rectory and that his association with Bomar was over. He also told Linda that Bomar had advised him to stay away from her.

It was not long before Linda was making a trip to the rectory to see the priest. It was a day that she had looked forward to for quite some time.

"I walked into the rectory and called Bomar on what he had done," Linda said. "I called it like I saw it. I never called him names, but I called him on what he was doing. I let him know I could see right through it. He just didn't know what to do with me."

Linda said she remembered telling Bomar, "You are just a man to me. You're a very flawed person. To take advantage of Freddie like this is just wrong. How could you do this?"

Bomar later denied that the conversation ever took place.

"I really don't have anything bad to say about Linda," Bomar said. "She was a fine girl and very dear to Freddie. But I do know that women will be women. I've never been married, but I know that. Linda never had a face-to-face talk with me. That is a lie if she says that. I still don't understand why she is still so angry at me."

Henderson and Steinmark had for the past few months discussed the possibility of moving into an apartment together. They packed their stuff and moved into a singles apartment on Riverside Drive, not far from Linda.

Linda informed Richard Meehan that she was going back to her former boyfriend. She told Richard that she still loved Freddie and had thought about him constantly since the night they broke up.

In spite of the time away from each other, Linda and Freddie returned to their happy routine, only this time they did not argue as much. The relationship began to gain new momentum. After a seven-month separation, Freddie was different. His hair and side-burns were long and he had given up on the painful prosthesis that rubbed against his scar.

"One day he put the prosthesis back in the carrying case and said, 'I'm out of here,'" Linda recalled. "He was walking on crutches all of the time and his arms were just enormous. All of a sudden he looked like a weight lifter. I could not imagine that his arms could get that big."

Some of Freddie's changes struck Linda as odd. Freddie did not talk about religion and his studies as much. He had given up on the engineering degree and wanted to go to law school. She could also tell that the chemotherapy was starting to drain his body. He was going every month to MD Anderson and dreading every minute of it. Adding to the misery was the horrible phantom pain he suffered in the amputated limb.

"He was agonizing in pain over that lost leg," Linda said. "It was just terrible."

They went to a Neil Diamond concert one night in Austin. Returning to Linda's apartment, Freddie reached up to scratch his head and pulled out a handful of hair. He knew what was happening. The chemotherapy was ravaging his body and claiming his hair.

"Just look at me, Linda," Freddie said. "I look like a damned hippie walking around with this long hair. I need to do something about it."

Freddie did not want anyone to know about his hair loss. He certainly did not want the Texas players or coaches to find out. So he hatched a plan to get his head shaved by someone on the team. Otherwise, everyone at the stadium would surmise he was hiding his cancer.

Freddie chose his friend Bobby Wuensch to handle the duty. Wuensch might have been the nicest man on the Texas team. He was a hard-hitting, 240-pound offensive left tackle, yet he was so easy-going off the field that he might have been confused with a tuba player. He might walk a mile to save a dying cricket. He lived in wonder of the world. The night before the Big Shootout in Fayetteville, he got up from his bed at three in the morning and stood barefoot outside in subfreezing temperatures because, like a little kid, he was mesmerized by the falling snow. His roommate Bob McKay had to talk him back into the room.

On the day of the shaving, Steinmark leveled with Wuensch. He told him that the chemotherapy was causing his hair to fall out. His cancer was back.

"I don't want everybody to know why we're doing it," Steinmark told his friend. "We're going to say that this is part of the team hazing for me becoming a coach. What do you think?"

"Pretty doggone smart, Freddie," the big man said.

Wuensch loved all of his teammates, and the love was always

returned. When he talked of his admiration for Steinmark forty years later, his voice broke.

"Freddie was pretty easy to love," Wuensch said. "Any of his teammates would have been proud to shave his head."

On the day of the shaving, Steinmark walked into the locker room and handed Wuensch the barber's sheers. Then he announced to the freshmen that they were about to witness a case of full-blown U.T. hazing.

"All new graduate assistant coaches like myself are supposed to get their heads shaved," Steinmark said. "Today is my day. Of course, I'm lucky to have a friend like Bobby to do it."

Wuensch felt an emotional lump in his throat. He ran the sheers over Freddie's head two or three times and the floodgates opened. Fat tears rolled down his cheeks.

"I cried and I didn't feel there was anything wrong with it," Wuensch recalled. "It's one of the most emotional things that I ever went through. I cared that much about Freddie."

When the shaving was completed, Wuensch leaned over and kissed his friend on his bald head.

For Freddie, it was tough to watch the Texas Longhorns tearing through the 1970 season, winning game after game. Upon signing with Texas, he had dreamed that he would be in the starting lineup every Saturday. Taking his place was Rick Nabors, and he was playing well. Ironically, Nabors had also taken over Freddie's bunk at the Jester Center as Bobby Mitchell's new roommate.

There were ten new starters on offense and defense. The biggest change was Eddie Phillips replacing James Street at quarterback. Ohio State had opened the season at number one with Texas ranked second and Arkansas sitting fourth. Again, the Arkansas-Texas game had been moved from mid-October until early December with the hopes that ABC could televise another national championship game.

Early in the season, Steinmark spent a lot of time around the varsity team in the locker room and watched some of the games from the sideline. Texas rolled through California and Texas Tech by the combined scores of 91–28. In the third week, the Longhorns were heavily favored against UCLA, ranked thirteenth. With ten seconds to play, it looked like the 22-game winning streak was about to end. The wishbone had been stifled all day and Phillips looked confused. The Longhorns trailed 21–17 with the ball at the UCLA 45-yard line. Facing third-and-nineteen, they were at the end of the road. On the final play of the game, Phillips threw blindly toward Cotton Speyrer, who caught the tipped ball and turned on the burners. In a matter of seconds, the clutch Texas wide receiver would pull off another miracle, going the distance and scoring the winning touchdown. The scoreboard read TEXAS 24, UCLA 21.

Unranked Oklahoma debuted its own version of the wishbone the following week as Texas ran over the Sooners 41–9. It was starting to look like another national championship run.

Linda and Freddie were walking across campus one afternoon in mid-October when he felt something sticking in his throat. He spit and saw blood splattered all over the sidewalk. They both looked at each other in dismay.

"Does that look good to you?" Freddie said.

Linda almost fainted. "I've got to get you to the hospital right now," she said.

She drove him to Brackenridge Hospital in Austin, where the doctors drained the blood from his lungs. The cancer was growing. The doctors at Brackenridge advised him to get back to MD Anderson as quickly as he could.

The trips to Houston were becoming more and more difficult. It did not matter that the doctors and nurses were treating Freddie like the biggest collegiate football star since George Gipp, who inspired the phrase, "Win one for the Gipper." Freddie was in a life-or-death situation. This was no longer about losing a leg and trying to adjust. This was about survival.

It was Linda's first trip back to the hospital since Freddie was discharged in early January, and she was still amazed at how the doctors and nurses dropped what they were doing to help her boyfriend. Everyone appreciated Freddie's prayers and his grateful nature.

That day, it was time for a round of X-rays and blood tests to be followed by more chemotherapy. Dr. Martin and Dr. Howe held the X-rays to the light and studied them. Freddie and Linda could tell from their sense of urgency that his cancer was worsening.

"We need to pick it up on the chemotherapy," Martin told them. "You've got more than two spots on your lungs. I think we can get rid of them. But we're going to have to increase the dosage."

"I don't know if I can take anymore," Freddie said. "I feel bad. My hair is gone. Just look at me."

The doctors could not remember a single discouraging word from Freddie. They instantly knew that he was losing mental strength, as well as physical stamina. They had no choice in the matter, though. The chemotherapy doses would be increased. During treatments, he was moved into one of the offices, where he could be alone. The chemicals were injected through a long needle into his back.

"All of this was so hard on Freddie that I could not even describe it," Linda said. "He got so sick. But at least he got to suffer by himself. All of the other patients were out in this big room. There was no privacy for them."

Freddie needed to rest for almost half the day before they could walk out to the car in the parking lot and drive back to Austin. Returning home was never easy because Freddie always knew he was coming right back.

All they could do now was pray for a miracle. Cancer had become the monster now controlling his life.

Chapter 28

LOVE STORY

During the Christmas holidays of 1970, everyone wanted to see the movie about Oliver Barrett IV and Jennifer Cavelleri. A Harvard student from a filthy-rich family, Oliver could not have cared less about Ivy League traditions. This in spite of the fact that his father, a famous lawyer, had gone there. He fell in love with Jenny, a working-class music student from Radcliffe College, and the couple never looked back.

One night, Oliver took Jenny to dinner at his family's mansion. When the Barretts looked down their noses at Jenny, Oliver decided to marry her anyway, forgoing the family money that would send him to Harvard Law School. Oliver's father severed ties with his son. With Jenny working as a schoolteacher, the couple struggled to pay Oliver's way through law school. Still, he finished third in his class. He took a job with a respected New York firm. Jennifer and Oliver were well on their way to a beautiful life together.

At the time, Freddie and Linda were too busy with cancer and college to read the movie reviews for *Love Story*, released about a week earlier. They never inquired about the story line. They simply jumped in the car and headed to the movie theater. They had returned to Denver for the holidays and were ready for a good movie that might allow them to escape their depressing lives.

"It was all the rage," Linda said. "We went to see it because everyone else was going to see it. But we walked into the theater not knowing the premise."

The movie, written by Eric Segal and directed by Arthur Hiller, starred Ali McGraw as Jenny and Ryan O'Neal as Oliver. It opened with the line, "What can you say about a twenty-five-year-old girl who died? That she was beautiful and brilliant. That she loved Mozart and Bach. The Beatles. And me." When Oliver apologized for an angry outburst, the signature line was delivered by Jenny. "Love means never having to say you're sorry."

What unfolded on the screen that night was a story that Linda and Freddie were living: A passionate and tender love is interrupted by a terminal illness. Just as Jenny and Oliver's lives are ascending to fairy-tale status, she is stricken with leukemia. Oliver has to borrow money from his father to pay medical expenses, but it is too late. Jenny asks Oliver to embrace her tightly before she dies.

Linda and Freddie were rendered speechless by the end of the movie. They walked from the crowded theater into the cold Denver night. Snow was falling. It swirled and gathered on their clothes. Freddie turned to Linda, leaned on his crutches, and said, "We just watched our future."

"I know," Linda said.

They hugged and cried.

A couple of days later, Freddie popped the question. It might not have sounded like a marriage proposal to most people, but it did to Linda.

"My family knows some people in the diamond business," he said. "Let's go see them."

Looking back on the day, Linda said, "When you date someone for that long, and go through that much stuff together, it was just implicit that we were going to get married. We knew what we were going to do."

Linda began to make plans. They set a date of May 23, 1971, one day following graduation ceremonies at U.T. They bought a white Italian wedding suit for Freddie with white boots. Linda began to sew her wedding dress. Invitations would be going out in a couple of months.

A few days later, Linda called her mother. She knew the conversation would not be pleasant.

"Freddie is going to die," Marion Wheeler said. "We all know that."

Crying, Linda hung up the phone.

A couple of hours later, the phone rang again and it was Linda's sister, Genie.

"I just got off the phone with Mom," Genie said. "She said, 'I wonder how Linda is going to feel on her wedding night when she sees Freddie's scar?'"

Linda smiled and shook her head. "Tell Mother that I've already seen the scar."

On January 1, a nation turned its eyes to the Texas-Notre Dame rematch at the Cotton Bowl. Texas had whipped Arkansas 42–7 in "Big Shootout II", mostly because Darrell Royal adjusted the blocking schemes to combat the radical Hogs 6-1 defense alignment of a year ago. Riding the nation's longest winning streak of thirty games, the Longhorns were ranked number one in the country. Notre Dame stood sixth with a 9-1 record.

Freddie and Linda watched the game in Denver and cheered their hearts out. Still, it barely felt the same. Freddie had not been around the team for several weeks and lacked the strength to even think about standing on the sideline at the Cotton Bowl. He was drained by chemotherapy and depressed by what he was seeing on TV. Notre Dame threw a nine-man line at the Texas offense in an attempt to stop Steve Worster and it worked. The big, hammering fullback gained only 42 yards on 16 carries and fumbled three times.

"We were not going to let Worster do what he did to us the previous year," Ara Parseghian remembered. "We didn't change our defense one bit the previous year. You could be darn sure we weren't going to make that mistake again."

The result was a 24–11 victory for Notre Dame as the defense took most of the credit. What most people overlooked, though, was that Worster was a beaten and bruised man. Rib cartilage had been torn loose against Baylor and reinjured in the TCU game. He suffered a hip pointer against Texas A&M and a bruised shoulder versus Arkansas.

Eddie Phillips amassed 323 yards of total offense against Notre Dame, but spent the last nine minutes of the game on the sideline with concussion symptoms. It was a hard way to end a string of three glorious seasons. The nation's longest winning streak of thirty games was over. No one felt worse about it than Freddie Steinmark.

Upon returning to Austin for the spring semester, Freddie and Linda tried to pursue normal lives. They went to class each day and studied each night with the hopes of graduating before summer. Freddie scored high on the LSAT and his chances of getting into law school were excellent.

Still, with each trip to MD Anderson, the news got worse. Freddie could barely stand the long needle being driven into his back. The chemotherapy treatments were coming once a month and the spots on his lungs were multiplying. Henderson witnessed his painful decline.

"He was getting violently ill every night," Henderson recalled. "It was hard to watch. He was so thin that he looked like a scarecrow. That type of cancer was terribly hard on him."

Gloria Steinmark sent herb remedies from Colorado with the hope that his strength would be renewed. The family bought exotic cancer medicines from Mexico, but none worked.

Freddie's face was ashen when he returned from a Houston trip in March. He walked into Henderson's room and laid out the facts.

"There's just not more they can do," he told his best friend. "The doctors aren't giving up. But they're running out of options."

Henderson had recently signed a four-week deal worth $1,500 with the Hamilton Tiger-Cats of the Canadian Football League. He would soon be moving northward and wondered how much he would see of Freddie in the coming months.

On the next trip to Houston in mid-April, doctors informed Freddie he would have to move back into MD Anderson. They were going to have to step up the chemotherapy even more.

Walking around campus one day, Bobby Mitchell began to wonder why he had not seen Linda or Freddie in a long time. Like most of the players on the Texas team, Mitchell thought that Freddie had already cleared the final hurdle with his cancer. After all, he had spent the summer playing golf and water skiing.

"We were all convinced that he was cured," Mitchell said. "Of course, we were so naive back then about cancer that we felt he would never die. No way. You amputate the leg and that should have been enough to save his life. We felt that from then on it would be the same ol' Freddie minus the leg."

As it turned out, only a few people knew of his condition.

When Freddie moved back into the hospital, the Steinmark family decided to circle the wagons. Most of the communication with friends, former teammates, and coaches was shut off. The doctors told the family that he could die in a matter of weeks, even days. Doctors and nurses came into his room and left with tears in their eyes.

Only a tight group of friends and family was allowed in. Linda sat in Freddie's room every day, along with Fred and Gloria Steinmark. The other three Steinmark children traveled back and forth from Colorado. The family's closest friends, Gladys and David Conway, were always there.

Trying to complete the book on Steinmark, Blackie Sherrod returned to the hospital for a third and final interview in early May. Sherrod looked down at the sleeping young man who weighed no more than a hundred pounds. Steinmark woke up and motioned for Sherrod to move closer so he could hear him.

"I leaned over him and Freddie said, 'I am actually getting better,'" Sherrod said.

Sherrod said he knew better. He hurried to finish the book. In the meantime, he received a phone call from a promotions person at Little, Brown.

"The book will be published very soon and we're ready to start planning Freddie's autograph tour," the man said.

"I'm not so sure that I would do that just yet," Sherrod said.

Hearing that Freddie's health was spiraling downward, Bomar made a quick trip to the hospital. Freddie woke up when he walked into the room.

"Father Bomar," Freddie said. "I'm surprised to see you. Do you have some business in Houston?"

"Nah, I'm just here for a visit," the priest said.

"Is there something you need to tell me?" Freddie said.

"I don't know anything more than you do," Bomar said.

Bomar had come to ask Steinmark about the dedication of the book. "Freddie, have you thought about who you would like to dedicate the book to?"

"Yes, I have thought about it, Father," he said. "I would like to dedicate it to our dear Lord, who has been so good to me."

When May rolled around, Linda had not been to class in over a month. Final exams were approaching and her chances of graduating on time were dwindling. Linda called her professors and told them about her predicament. They informed her that she would have to take the final exams on May 12.

"Freddie practically made me go back to Austin," Linda said. "The only reason that I graduated is because he made me do it. I really didn't care about it. But I went back. I still can't believe that I passed the finals and that I was going to graduate."

As Freddie's condition worsened, everyone realized that a wedding was out of the question. The May 23 event was cancelled. Thanks to kidney failure and water retention, Freddie's ankles and feet grew to twice their normal size. Because of the painful bed-sores, he was sleeping on egg crates.

"We took turns rubbing his legs and feet around the clock," Linda said. "I've never seen a case of edema like that. I would push my fingers into his legs and they would disappear into his skin."

In mid-May, Henderson was cut by the Tiger-Cats and decided to set his sights on a U.T. law degree. First, though, he wanted to see how his friend was doing at MD Anderson. He traveled to the hospital twice and left both times in a state of depression.

"Freddie was just not doing well," Henderson said. "Everyone at the hospital was praying."

On May 23, the day they were to be married, Freddie slipped into a coma. Still, no one in the Steinmark group was ready to give up. They prayed night and day.

Sitting on the couch in Freddie's room, Gladys Conway provided a reason for a miracle.

"If we can put a man on the moon then surely we can save Freddie," she said. Neil Armstrong had become the first man to walk on the moon less than two years earlier, on July 21, 1969.

"Everyone had to be upbeat about a miracle," Linda remembered. "Otherwise, Gloria was going to kick them out of the hospital."

Freddie slipped in and out of a coma for a week. On June 1, he lapsed back into a coma and the doctors thought he might not return.

Around ten o'clock in the morning on June 6, Freddie jerked awake and looked across the room at Linda. She was sitting on the couch next to his sister, Gigi. Freddie looked straight at her and yelled, "Linda, get my boots, I'm ready." A huge tear rolled down his left cheek as his eyes closed.

The glorious life of Freddie Joe Steinmark spanned twenty-two years, five months, and nine days. On the morning he died, he was a national symbol of courage. He had endured a horrible pain, but never gave up. He smiled his way through the struggle. No player was ever more loved by his coaches and teammates.

Forty years later, Linda still remembers the gorgeous spring day he came running toward her as she sat in the blue Jeep. She drinks the moment into her soul. She sees his big, sparkling eyes and the bright smile. She remembers their wonderful years together. No one lived their life any better than Freddie Steinmark. It was a tragedy he died so young. Yet the way he lived remains an inspiration for anyone who has ever heard the story.

Chapter 29

EVERLASTING

"Freddie was George Gipp without all of the hype."
—TOM CAMPBELL

Riding in the long, black limousine, Linda Wheeler looked into the blue sky and saw an image that left her breathless. The white puffy cloud just above her was shaped in the form of Saint Gabriel blowing his beloved trumpet. She pointed it out to Gigi Steinmark and together they watched it in awe as the limousine rolled down Colorado Boulevard in Denver toward the Church of the Risen Christ.

"Gigi and I watched the cloud for thirty minutes, all the way to the church, and it didn't change one bit," she recalled. "It was like Saint Gabriel was sending us a message that Freddie was safe."

In making plans for their wedding, Linda had designed a full-length strapless wedding dress with a long train. It was reported in a book that Linda wore the wedding dress to Freddie's funeral, but that was not the case.

"I would have looked pretty silly in my wedding dress at the funeral," she said. "The dress was very reminiscent of the style of the times and it had a lot of frills. It would not have been right for the funeral."

Instead, Linda sewed an off-white conservative dress.

Much to the surprise of many people, especially Linda, Bomar was chosen by Fred Steinmark to conduct the funeral mass. The day after Freddie died, Bomar was in Darrell Royal's office when he got the news.

"Darrell passed it along to me that they wanted me to do the funeral," Bomar said. "Believe me, I was really surprised. The family was pretty mad at me the last couple of weeks. They thought that I had spread a rumor that Freddie was dying. So I never thought they would ask me to do the funeral."

More than two thousand people flooded the church grounds and almost two-thirds had to wait outside the church. Officials estimated that it was the largest funeral gathering in the history of Colorado. Friends and family filed past the closed casket. To the side of the casket was a stand that held the obituary column written by Blackie Sherrod on Freddie. People read it and wept. The piece would be nominated for the Pulitzer Prize. Sherrod's column in the *Dallas Times Herald* read:

Six months after they took the left leg of Freddie Steinmark, he returned to the Houston tumor clinic for another of his nerve-wracking checkups. The little Texas safety had to do this every three months, as do all victims of osteogenic sarcoma. He underwent blood tests and X-rays to determine if the dread malignancy might appear in other parts of his strong young body.

For several nights preceding his trips to MD Anderson Hospital, Freddie would stare at the ceiling. He knew the odds. He prayed for a miracle.

"They told me not to worry, but that's easy for them to say," Freddie said. "They're the ones taking the X-rays, not the one getting them."

When Freddie would get a clean report, he would return joyously to the Texas campus and throw himself into another project with fierce energy. He took up golf, balancing himself on one leg while he swung. He learned to water ski. He went religiously to the Longhorn weight room to build up the rest of his body, as if muscle could hold off any return invasion of cancer cells. He worked his grades back to a B average. He made speeches and appearances. He wanted feverish activity to keep his mind occupied, so it wouldn't wander back to the calendar and the date of his next trip to Houston.

Last July a couple blurs showed up on X-rays of Freddie's lungs. It could be one of several things, the doctors told Freddie, we'll watch it close. A bit later, they told Freddie he would have to start a series of chemotherapy treatments. He didn't change expression. But he guarded the news as if it were the atomic secret. He wanted no one to know. It was almost as if Freddie thought the treatments were a sign of personal weakness. The news might bring pity from his teammates and friends and above all, he didn't want that.

The chemotherapy consisted of six days of shots that, hopefully, would kill or arrest any fast-growing cancer cells. They make the patient frightfully nauseous. But he masked the trips and treatments from all save a precious few. Scott Henderson, the linebacker and Freddie's apartment mate, knew but he respected the confidence.

One possible side effect of chemotherapy shots is the loss of hair. Freddie had a long thick black mane and he was proud of it. His teammates teasingly accused him of being a hippie. Okay, you guys, he said. I'm gonna help Coach with the freshmen defensive backs and just to show you how seriously I'm taking this job I'll get rid of the hippie image. I'll get rid of all this hair. As a matter of fact, I'll just shave it all off, just to show you I'm not kidding.

So the Texas squad had a little ceremony in the locker room and they all laughed and cheered as Bobby Wuensch shaved off the Steinmark hair. His teammates didn't realize he dreamed up the little act to hide the fact that he was taking treatments that made his hair fall out. He kept his head shaved. Rick Troberman took note of the bald head and missing leg and applied the nickname "Pirate." Freddie went along with the gag. He had his ear pierced and wore a gold ring in it for awhile.

He shared his worry and concern with no one. But sometimes when you were in a conversation with Freddie, he would be staring at you vacantly with those enormous black eyes and there would be a silence, and he would say, "Excuse me, I guess I wasn't listening. What did you say?"

To the last, Freddie refused to accept the idea that the cancer had caught up with him and finally dragged him down. When he was hospitalized this last time in MD Anderson, he believed—at least outwardly—that he was there to have some fluid removed from his body. When his priest from Austin, Father Fred Bomar, walked quietly into Room 514W and sat down, Freddie looked at him narrowly.

"Have you got some business in Houston, Father?" he said. The priest said no, he just came down for a visit.

"Do you know something I don't know?" asked Freddie. The priest said no.

His friends thought it was rather a miracle, Freddie having played regularly on a national championship team with the tumor already gnawing at his leg, and had survived the amputation. He returned to active life, had been able to move back into society, to tell people how he felt, to squeeze another 17 months out of precious life. Freddie didn't think it was a miracle; it was what an athlete was supposed to do and now that same fierce competition kept him hanging on for days, weeks, and after the average person would have let go. Doctors walked out of his room with tears in their eyes.

Two weeks ago, I visited the room. The shades were drawn. A television set suspended from the ceiling, with the volume off, flickered lifelessly with a soap opera. There was a skinny couch with bedpillows along one wall, where Freddie's mother, Gloria, and his girlfriend, Linda Wheeler, spent each day and his father spent each night. A vigil candle on a table burned 24 hours a day. Freddie was a gaunt shadow and his voice was about gone and I had to bend close to hear him whisper, "I'm getting better."

Freddie has written a book about his experiences. It will be published this fall. The editor noticed after Freddie was hospitalized, that he had not made a dedication of the book and he asked to whom Freddie wanted to dedicate his story. Freddie said to the Lord, who had been so good to him.

Several of Steinmark's teammates and coaches made the trip from Texas. Royal had requested the use of Corbin Robertson's Gulfstream jet that seated ten passengers. Robertson was the ultra-rich oilman father of Corby Robertson, the All-American linebacker who started three seasons from 1966–68. On the plane from Austin to Denver were Mike Campbell III, Fred Akers, Bill Ellington, Willie Zapalac, Bill Zapalac, Scott Henderson, Bill Ellington, and Spanky Stephens.

Most of Steinmark's teammates from the Wheat Ridge team were there. Stan Politano, Kent Cluck, and Dave Dirks openly wept, as did Coach "Red" Coats.

"I remember Kent Cluck and I embracing," Politano said. "We were both crying with nothing to say. It all seemed pretty unfair to us at the time. Death was not really part of our lives then. We, like most people, thought we would live forever."

Any time a young person with rock star celebrity status dies, the funeral carries a mystical feeling. The burial at Mount Olivet next to the church on a crystal-clear day was so emotional that it felt like a presidential funeral.

"Mr. and Mrs. Steinmark acted like they were okay, but it was clear that they were devastated," Scott Henderson said. "Freddie's younger brother, Sammy, was happy to see everyone. But he had no idea what his brother had been through."

Bobby Mitchell and Honor Franklin cried throughout the ceremony. Never had Freddie seemed so important to anyone.

Bomar's remembrances of Freddie were captivating:

"Nowhere at any time will we see anyone with such courage. Remember forever Freddie as the great young man with the great attitude. Tell your children and your grandchildren about him. Go forward with his memory."

After the funeral, the family and several friends went to the Steinmarks' home for dinner. Everyone on the flight from Austin was there. Nana Marchetti cooked spaghetti and the mood was upbeat for a post-funeral affair.

"The family was actually celebrating Freddie's life," Spanky Stephens remembered. "It was pretty cool. People were all over the place, out in the backyard, and everybody was talking about Freddie."

A thunderstorm struck late in the afternoon and everyone rushed into the house. Thunder followed a loud crackle of lightning. The lights went out in the house. Suddenly, several bricks were knocked from the fireplace and flew across the room. Everyone looked in wonder at each other.

"It was like Freddie was saying good-bye to us," Linda said.

EPILOGUE

"Freddie gave us a roadmap for life. When you are feeling lower than a snake's belly, think about how Freddie always rose up."
—SPANKY STEPHENS

In the grip of memory-loss issues at age eighty-six, a bright-eyed and smiling Darrell Royal sat next to a window and looked out at the rugged, rolling hills of Barton Creek. He remembered Freddie Steinmark like it was yesterday.

"Boy, he was a fighter, and he fought until the end," Royal said. "All that 1969 season, Freddie knew something was wrong with his leg, but he wouldn't tell anybody. He was afraid to go to the doctor because he knew that if the doctor found something in there, he might not get to play anymore. That leg was eaten up by cancer. The bone was just like a sliver. How in the world he didn't break that leg during the season, I will never know."

Asked if a cancer-free Steinmark would have made All-American, Royal said, "He would've been *my* All-American."

Everyone who ever knew Freddie Steinmark believed he would have become a success in any endeavor.

Scott Henderson said that Steinmark's score on the LSAT would have easily gotten him into law school.

"He would have been a heckuva lawyer," Henderson said. "He was a bright guy and he could have handled any phase of it."

Fred Akers believes that Steinmark would have gone into coaching.

"He was the most coachable player that I ever had," Akers said. "So I expect that he would have been very successful if he had tried it. In fact, Freddie would have succeeded at anything that he tried."

Scott Palmer said the sky would have been his limit. "If he had decided that he wanted to be the president of the United States, he could have done it. I'm not sure he would have liked that kind of attention, but he was a people magnet and everyone loved him. We would have all been better if we had lived our lives like him."

Like many people, Akers still regrets that Steinmark's cancer was not detected earlier.

"How did we miss it?" he said, shaking his head. "God, if I had just acted more quickly. I just wish we knew as much about cancer back then as we know today. We all just thought he had a bad bruise. It just didn't occur to me that he would have cancer."

Linda Wheeler married two months after Freddie died. The marriage lasted five years.

"I was just insane at the time," she said. "I guess I was looking for someone or something that would help me get over Freddie."

In the mid-1970s, she contacted Scott Henderson in Dallas with the hopes of finding Richard Meehan. She knew Henderson would know how to locate his former fraternity brother.

"I told Linda that he had finished medical school and was practicing in Portland, Oregon," Henderson said. "I knew that they had liked each other in college and that it might work out again."

Dr. Meehan had graduated from the University of Texas Medical School in Houston in 1974. Linda and Richard Meehan began to date again and were married for twenty years, living in Oregon and Iowa before moving to Boulder and then Denver. They have two children. For the past ten years, Linda Meehan has been a high school teacher in the Denver school district, instructing Spanish-speaking students in every course of the curriculum.

Dr. Bobby Mitchell runs one of the most prominent state-of-the-art dental offices in Dallas near the Galleria. His office walls are covered with photos and memorabilia from his All-Southwest Conference playing days at the University of Texas, along with plenty of photos of his dear friend, Freddie Steinmark. Mitchell's wife,

Dr. Honor Franklin, whom he met at U.T., works as a speech and language pathologist in the same building. They have two children.

Scott Henderson graduated from Texas Law School in 1974 and started practicing law in Dallas on January 2, 1975. He was a prominent civil lawyer for several years and is currently the staff counsel for Geico Insurance in Dallas.

James Street is one of the most successful structured settlement experts in America. His offices are located in Austin, about a "Hail Mary" (Right 53 Veer Option Pass) from the state capitol building. He flirted briefly with a pro baseball career, but suffered an arm injury in the college World Series and was talked out of it by Darrell Royal. In 2010, the *Houston Chronicle* picked the top fifty players in the history of Texas football. Street was chosen the thirty-second. He and his wife, Janie, have four sons. One of them, Huston Street, pitches for the Colorado Rockies and is one of the best closers in Major League baseball.

Bobby Wuensch was a two-time All-American. He played four exhibition games with the Baltimore Colts, broke his leg, and informed everyone that he was tired of football. He returned to his hometown and went to work for his family marine business on the Houston Ship Channel. For the last several years, he has operated Wuensch Sales Company, working with several family members. Wuensch was rated as the number-nineteen player on the *Houston Chronicle's* list of the top fifty players.

Bill Atessis and Wuensch went to Jones High School in Houston and remain close friends. Atessis and Wuensch were both named to the Texas Half Century Team. Like Wuensch, Atessis was drafted by the Baltimore Colts and suffered a knee injury in the exhibition season. He played for the New England Patriots in 1971 before leaving football. For the past thirty years, he has been an engineering and construction consultant and is currently the senior construction manager for Gunda Construction. Atessis was ranked number twenty-one on the all-time Texas list.

Tom Campbell lives in Austin and works for a cost-segregation firm. Out of college, he signed a free-agent contract with the

Oakland Raiders and was cut during training camp. He caught on with the Philadelphia Eagles late in the preseason and might have made the team if not for the shenanigans of his twin brother, Mike. On the afternoon of an Eagles' preseason game in Houston, Mike showed up at the team hotel inebriated and started challenging the Eagles players to footraces down the hallway. Unfortunately, Mike so closely resembled his brother that the coaches thought it was Tom showing off. Tom was cut the next week. In 2006, Tom Campbell was inducted into the Texas Hall of Honor.

Mike Campbell has spent most of his life in oilfields all over the world. He worked for three years in Singapore and Indonesia and was brought back to Houston and went into sales for Baker Hughes Oilfield Services.

Bob McKay enjoyed the longest pro career of all the players involved in the Big Shootout. He played six seasons for the Cleveland Browns and three more with New England before he retired. He went to work for GCR Trucking and has been selling tires ever since. During player reunions, he still regales his ex-teammates with some of the funniest stories ever told. McKay was ranked forty-seventh by the *Houston Chronicle.*

Bill Bradley enjoyed the longest pro career of the players from the 1968 team. He played with the Philadelphia Eagles for eight seasons and was selected All-Pro three times, leading the league in interceptions twice. In the NFL, he coached the defensive secondaries in Buffalo, San Diego, and with the New York Jets. He was the defensive coordinator at Baylor from 2004–2006, and became the secondary coach of the Florida Tuskers of the United Football League in 2010.

Forrest Wiegand suffered a torn knee ligament against Notre Dame when he was hit from behind by fellow Longhorn Bob McKay. "I told McKay that I was going to have to buy him some glasses," Wiegand said. He has spent most of his life as a high school coach. He joined the LaPorte High School staff in 1974 and became head coach in 1988.

Steve Worster finished fourth in the Heisman Trophy balloting in 1970 and seemed primed to launch a successful pro career when he was drafted in the fourth round by the Los Angeles Rams. He could not come to contract terms, though, and took off for the Canadian Football League, where he played one season with the Hamilton Tiger-Cats. He still lives in Bridge City, where his home was destroyed by Hurricane Rita. When he was inducted into the Texas Sports Hall of Fame in 2008, Worster spoke for only three minutes. The high point of the talk was his thanks to his former teammates. "When I lost my house in the hurricane, my teammates came out of nowhere after forty-some-odd years. I never could have made it without them." After Rita, Worster said he lived in the back of his car, in a trailer home, and with his son, Scotty, before he could get back on his feet six months later. Occasionally he still opens his mailbox to find a copy of *Sports Illustrated* that featured him on the cover in 1970. It usually contains a note from a Texas fan asking him to sign the magazine. Worster was ranked twenty-third on the all-time Texas list.

Ted Koy was drafted by the Oakland Raiders and played one season for John Madden before going to the Buffalo Bills for four years. He graduated with a journalism degree, but went to Texas A&M veterinary school. For thirty years, he has owned his own veterinary clinic in Georgetown, just north of Austin.

Randy Peschel is still approached by total strangers in Austin who say, "Randy, dammit, that was the greatest catch I ever saw." Of the game-saving reception he made in the Big Shootout, he says, "My life would have never been the same if I had dropped it." He has worked most of his life in the Austin banking industry. He is a senior vice president with Capital Bank.

Scott Palmer was moved to defense in 1969 and replaced the injured Carl White for the Big Shootout. He received high praise from Darrell Royal for his performance against Arkansas and Notre Dame in the Cotton Bowl, and started every game in 1970.

Bill Zapalac played three seasons for the New York Jets and went into the construction business in Austin in 1974. He is the co-owner of Zapalac-Reid Construction.

What are the odds that the starting guards in 1969–70 would both go into dentistry? Mike Dean was initially accepted into law school, but decided on dental school and went to Baylor-Dallas, like Mitchell. He has worked as a dentist ever since and owns a practice in Marble Falls.

One of the most interesting players from the 1968 team was Corby Robertson. Born into wealth, his grandfather, the legendary Hugh Roy Cullen, discovered the huge Tom O'Conner Field in South Texas in 1932. Corby grew up in the richest area of Houston, River Oaks, but chose to go to public school at Lamar High so he could play a tough brand of football. Recruited by Texas, he considered quitting as a freshman because there were so many players on the roster that he figured he would not make the team. Instead, he became an All-American in 1967, and as the captain of the '68 team, helped turn around a season of chaos. The Longhorns finished 9-2 with a victory over Tennessee in the Cotton Bowl. Robertson is the most successful ex-Longhorn football player of all time. He runs a billion-dollar company started by his father called Quintana Petroleum in Houston, and operates three companies that yield twenty billion tons of coal, more than any other entity besides the United States government. An entire book could be filled with the number of boards he serves on, the amount of civic duty he has done, and the awards he has won.

Michael "Spanky" Stephens took over as the head trainer in 1978 when Frank Medina suffered a stroke. He worked with five head football coaches, five head basketball coaches, and nine teams that won national championships before he retired in 2000. Four years later, he was inducted into the Longhorns Hall of Honor. He currently serves as the executive director of the Texas State Athletic Trainers Association.

Mike Campbell III left coaching in 1976 when he was passed over for the head coaching position at Texas. Royal recommended Campbell for his job, but the school's administration decided to bring Fred Akers back from Wyoming, where he had gained two years of head coaching experience. Campbell became the head of the athletic department's scholarship fund-raising wing and was inducted into the Texas Hall of Honor in 1984. He died of lymphoma in 1998.

Akers was fired from Texas after the 1986 season in spite of an impressive record of 86-31-2. He then coached the Purdue Boiler-makers to a 12-31-1 record from 1987 through '90. He and his wife, Diane, live on the lake at Horseshoe Bay, outside Marble Falls. Fred and his son, Danny, run Akers Performance Group, a motivational firm.

Blackie Sherrod, who co-wrote *I Play to Win* with Freddie Stein-mark in 1971, celebrated his ninety-second birthday in 2011. He lives with his wife, Joyce, in Dallas, along with "a crippled dog and a blind cat." He no longer writes or paints, but remains an avid reader. Asked when he was going to write his autobiography, he said, "It wouldn't be much of a book, but it would be long. I would make up for quality with length."

Freddie Steinmark has not been forgotten in Wheat Ridge or the Denver area. In 2011, the Fred Steinmark Award will be presented to a Colorado male and female athlete for the fortieth time. To be nom-inated, a student-athlete must have participated in at least two sports, making all-state in one. The student must have maintained a 3.0 grade average. Citizenship and community involvement are all factored into the award. The Steinmark Award was renamed after his death in June 1971. It was formerly known as the Golden Helmet Award, which he won as a senior at Wheat Ridge High in 1967.

In a period of three months in the summer of 2010, Texas Long-horns football lost two of its biggest names with the deaths of coach Willie Zapalac and Monsignor Fred Bomar. Zapalac, who died of cancer at age eighty-nine, coached for twelve years under Darrell Royal. He played at Texas A&M in the 1940s and coached there under Paul "Bear" Bryant in the 1950s, and was named to the uni-versity's Hall of Fame.

On August 16, 2010, close to a thousand mourners jammed the church in southeast Austin for Bomar's public funeral mass. In attendance were about eighty ex-Longhorns, along with athletic director Deloss Dodds. Darrell Royal and his wife, Edith, attended the reception afterward in the Centennial Room at the stadium.

The hour-long service for Bomar included several mentions of his lengthy affiliation with Texas football. During his homily, Bishop John McCarthy said, "You could be sure that Father Bomar would have never been caught dead or alive in College Station." Bomar was the pastor of the church for forty-one years.

At the reception following the ceremony, former quarterback James Street said, "Father Bomar was a unique individual. He was a guy who was always your friend and would always be your friend for life. He was a big part of our lives during that period of time in learning how to live life."

Remembering the parties that Bomar threw at the rectory, Street said, "What was interesting is that Father Bomar wasn't that much older than us. So he was growing up as we were growing up, too. Believe me, he was a wild-man priest at first."

One of Bomar's closest friends was David Ballew, a letterman on the 1970 Longhorns national championship team. It was Ballew whom he called after falling and hitting his head at the rectory on Wednesday, August 11. Ballew rushed to the rectory and found Bomar reluctant about going to the hospital. He dialed 911 anyway.

"Who is going to walk these dogs?" Bomar said of his enormous sheepdogs.

"Don't worry, I'll walk them," Ballew said.

Bomar was still conscious when he got to the hospital, but the bleeding in his brain became fatal in a matter of hours. He was seventy-five at his death. Bomar was buried on August 12 at the Texas State Cemetery.

"I loved Father Bomar," Ballew said. "He would give you a good, hard lecture and he didn't care if he bruised your feelings. One of his greatest sayings was 'the harder the truth, the truer the friend.' And what a true friend we had in Father Bomar."

Upon hearing of Bomar's passing, Bill Atessis said, "God bless his soul. I'm sure that St. Peter had to let him in wearing burnt orange."

After his death, a group of ex-players and friends of Bomar donated $50,000 to start a University of Texas scholarship in his honor.

Yet another Texas icon died on February 10, 2011. Emory Bellard had much to be proud of. On the back of his wishbone offense, the Texas Longhorns won two national championships. He became the head coach at Texas A&M in 1972, and during his final four seasons (74–77) his teams compiled a record of 36–11 with three bowl appearances. On the day before he died at the age of eighty-three from ALS, he whispered into the ear of former A&M coach R.C. Slocum, "I've had a great life. I got to do exactly what I wanted to do."

AUTHOR'S NOTES

One of the best books I've ever read on college football was *Horns, Hogs, & Nixon Coming* written by Denver-based author Terry Frei. It was about the 1969 "Big Shootout" between Arkansas and Texas.

Frei's book contained several anecdotes about the life of Freddie Steinmark. It motivated me to write *Courage Beyond the Game*. Ironically, Frei told me he had been inspired to write his book after reading *The Junction Boys*, which I authored in 1999.

Another reason that I decided to write *Courage Beyond the Game* was all of the interest stirred up in recent years by head football coach Mack Brown. One of Brown's first projects upon becoming head coach at the University of Texas in 1998 was to add a second picture of Steinmark and a plaque dedicated to Steinmark leading to the playing field at Royal Memorial Stadium. During the Darrell Royal years, the players had tapped the picture with the palms of their hands. Under Brown, they rap it with the Hook-em-Horns sign. During the 2005 season, Brown decided to take a picture of Steinmark to the road games and hang it in the locker room. All of the players "horned" it as they headed to the field. It was on the wall that night in January 2006 when the Longhorns defeated USC to win the university's fourth national championship.

I would also like to thank Blackie Sherrod and Freddie Steinmark for cowriting *I Play to Win*, the autobiography that provided some great information.

I would be nowhere in the book business without Peter J. Wolverton, the Associate Publisher of Thomas Dunne Books, and the editor on my last seven books. Together, we started the successful run with *The Junction Boys* and I firmly believe that *Courage Beyond the Game* will enjoy the same kind of success. My agent, David Larabell of the David Black Agency, moved swiftly in negotiating the contract with St. Martin's Press.

All of the players, coaches, and trainers mentioned in the epilogue were interviewed by me for the book. Those I hit up more than a few times were Bobby Mitchell, Tom Campbell, Mike Campbell, Scott Henderson, Bill Atessis, and Bobby Wuensch. Special thanks to Stan Politano, Kent Cluck, and Roger Behler from Colorado. They were with Freddie during fourteen years of organized sports. Along with June Coats, they provided wonderful remembrances of a brave young man. I spent a weekend with Linda Wheeler Meehan in Denver during the spring of 2009, and these interviews were some of the best and most productive of my career. She opened her heart and soul on Freddie Steinmark.

Much thanks to Bill Little, my good friend for the last forty years and the heart and soul of the Texas Sports Information Directors' office since 1968.

Kathryn Shrum provided emotional support and kept me going through the tough times with the book. She is also a fantastic proofreader.

The players from the 1968–69 Texas teams remind me in many ways of the Junction Boys. They have similarities to the players of other books I've written, including the 1964 Notre Dame team (*Resurrection*), and the gang from *Twelve Mighty Orphans*. In the late 1960s, those great teams at Texas spawned some well-grounded, funny-as-hell, successful and interesting men, who remain bonded to this day. The 1969 reunions produce the biggest turn-outs at Texas. Everyone I interviewed went out of their way to bring the story of Freddie Steinmark to life.

When I began the project, I was told that I would not be able to interview Darrell Royal because of his memory loss. In truth, I spent more than two hours with Darrell and his wife, Edith, at their beautiful condo at Barton Creek. The coach was in great spirits and had forgotten nothing about Steinmark, or the national championship season of 1969. As I walked out of the condo, Royal winked and said, "How could I ever forget you, Jim Dent?" Then he pointed to a grease board next to the door with my name and the time of the appointment.

I am often asked what touched me the most about the book I just finished. This is going to sound like another author bragging about his stuff, but I happen to think this is the best sports story ever. Where else can you find a road map to life in a sports book? I agree with former Texas trainer Spanky Stephens who said that Freddie Steinmark showed us all how to live. I never knew Freddie personally, but upon finishing the book, I don't think I could have known him any better.

My lasting impression of Freddie is that he did not cry even at the depths of despair. He almost never complained. As Mike Dean said, "He never gave you the impression, 'Why is God doing this to me?'" Freddie never cried because he did not want others to feel sorry for him. Freddie lived his life more selflessly than anyone I've known.

After losing his leg, Freddie decided to go out and have a good time. He drank, danced, laughed, and traveled all over the country. He went to the Playboy Club in New Orleans. He dated a lot of girls because he wanted to know people better. If he had only one year to live, he was going for it.

Along the way, though, Freddie never lost his core values. He realized how much he loved and missed Linda Wheeler. In the end, he pulled his life together and left the earth with everything in order. His great friend Bill Atessis said, "Freddie was the kind of guy you'd want your sister to marry."

Spanky Stephens said to me one day, "You've done all of this research. You've talked to all of these people. Did anyone ever say anything bad about Freddie?"

Without even blinking, I said, "Not a single solitary soul."

I say without equivocation, that Freddie Steinmark was the most courageous person to ever play sports. I also say that he was the most beloved.

Readers over the years have become familiar with my famous cat, Rolly Dent, from reading about him in the pages of my books. He always sat on my desk and slept while I wrote, then plopped down in my chair to keep it warm during the coffee breaks. I know that everyone believes their pet is special. Rolly, however, was really *human*.

As my friend Woody Berry said, "Sylvester was the only cat that came close to Rolly in literary recognition. Sylvester was fiction. Rolly was the real thing."

When we were living in an apartment in Las Colinas near Dallas in the mid-1990s, Rolly liked to jump off the second-floor balcony so he could chase a stupid rabbit around the swimming pool. He knew he would never catch the rabbit, but still loved the chase. My neighbors would cheer him from their balconies. After one lap around the pool, the varmint would duck into his hole, leaving Rolly angry and baffled.

Having grown up on a Dust Bowl farm in the depths of the Depression, my father had little use for cats—that is, until he got sick and spent an entire night sitting in his living room chair. Rolly stayed by his side all night, as concerned as anyone in the family. That is when Jimmy Dent Sr. fell in love with "his cat."

In his later years, when he suffered from congestive heart failure, my dad slowed down considerably. Rolly would see him hobbling toward his chair and take off across the room, trying to beat him. He would dive into the chair and turn his back. Patiently, my dad would gently pick him up and place him on the floor. Then Rolly would dash into my dad's bedroom and jump onto his bed. Because cats do not belong on the bed, my dad would spend the next five minutes trudging across the room to remove him. Then Rolly would gleefully run back to the living room and grab his spot in the chair. These games went on and on.

Rolly was born in my closet in "beautiful downtown, crime-free, Flower Mound, Texas" on April 5, 1992. He lived his last seven years with his beloved grandmother. Between my sister, Janice, and my mother, Leanna, no cat was ever more loved or cared for.

After eighteen glorious years, he went to heaven on July 29, 2010, and is now with his grandfather, playing chase.

RESOURCES

BOOKS

Frei, Terry: *Horns, Hogs & Nixon Coming*, Simon & Shuster

Steinmark, Freddie (with Blackie Sherrod): *I Play to Win*, Little, Brown

Hawthorne, Bobby: *Longhorn Football: An Illustrated History*, University of Texas Press

Jones, Mike: *Darrell Royal: Dance With Who Brung Ya*, Masters Press

Morris, Jeannie: *Brian Piccolo: A Short Season*, Rand McNally

Royal, Darrell (with John Wheat): *Coach Royal: Conversations with a Texas Football Legend*, University of Texas Press

Banks, Jimmy: *The Darrell Royal Story*, Shoal Creek Publishers

Little, Bill and Jenna McEachern: *What It Means to Be a Longhorn*, Triumph Books

Henry, Orville and Jim Bailey: *The Razorbacks: The Story of Arkansas Football*, The Strode Publishers

Freeman, Denne: *Hook 'Em Horns: A Story of Texas Football*, University of Texas Press

Newspapers, Magazines, Internet

Texas Football, 1969

Time Magazine, 40th Anniversary Special, 1969

Austin American-Statesman

New York Times

Houston Chronicle

Dallas Morning News
Denver Post
Fort Worth Star-Telegram
Sports Illustrated Vault
Orangebloods.com

INDEX